Blessing the Curse?

Blessing the Curse?

One of the most attractive aspects of this outstanding book is how Ksenija Magda very thoroughly examines Scripture and lays out the foundations carefully. From these foundations she challenges our views on male-female relationships throughout history and up to today. She convincingly points out how these views have had severe defects and have hindered the spread of the kingdom of God through his church. She goes on to explain how in fact the church is responsible for many of the negative effects and reactions in society.

I appreciate how she shines light on hierarchy and how this affects all areas of life and society including male-female relationships. I wish this book would have been published forty years ago. It certainly would have helped to straighten out my warped understanding of the role of women. It would have sped up what I have had to learn through much pain.

This book deserves wide distribution.

Thomas Bucher
General Secretary, European Evangelical Alliance

Blessing the Curse? is a fascinating journey through a deep and wise theology of God's perfect will in our contemporary scene. Redemption and restoration are its goals. In fact, recovering the original purpose for both women and men is the main purpose of the book and to read it is to enjoy an amazing journey. I am thankful to the Lord for the day he let Ksenija Magda come up with this wonderful literary work – the timing is perfect! Please open your spiritual eyes and listen to the sweet voice of God who says, "I will bless you . . . and you will be a blessing."

Liliana Fernández
Psychologist and Writer
President, UFBAL (Union of Baptist Women in Latin America)

Dr. Ksenija Magda has decades of academic insight and personal experience about the roles and gifting of men and women in the church. Her underlying point – that the church has accepted and even fostered inequality, rather than the partnership seen in Genesis 1 and 2 – is a really helpful way to understand the whole Bible narrative of men and women. It is dangerously easy to take individual verses about women out of context and Dr. Magda's explanations of those passages (with much academic firepower) reminds readers that God's design is for women and men to be a blessing to each other and to our needy world.

Amanda Jackson
Executive Director,
Women's Commission, World Evangelical Alliance

This book is based on sound biblical scholarship, wide-ranging experience and deep spiritual reflection. Ksenija Magda engages with the issue of male-female relationships at a profound level, exposing the damaging "hierarchies of sin" that destroy life-giving human relationships, churches, society and the environment. Those who promote these "hierarchies of sin" deny God, seek to make themselves "gods," are materialistic and use power in an abusive way. This is a thought-provoking book that can change the way women and men think and live. The application of its prophetic insights can infuse the everyday realities of our lives with God's life-giving salvation and bring hope to our troubled world. I consider this book to be well worth reading – and living.

Louise Kretzschmar
Professor of Theological Ethics,
University of South Africa, Pretoria, South Africa

This wonderful book speaks to the little girl I once was, who desperately wanted to love Jesus with my whole heart, yet couldn't quell my urge to rebel against the church's constraints on me as a female. I wanted to speak, preach and lead, but instead I was encouraged to clean, cook and care for children. This same girl grew to a woman who desired to honour God in her marriage but was repelled by teachings on submission; at worst I feared abuse, at best I feared my liberty would be limited. I have spent years trying to make peace with this tension without losing my freedom in Christ. Dr. Magda's intelligent and thoughtful book is a godly and gracious guide through this ongoing process. She has demonstrated that challenging the church notions of hierarchy is integral to this process. By reading this insightful text, I have undergone a paradigm shift regarding assumptive power structures within church. I have been challenged to question these structures and to analyze if they reflect the curse or the cross. For if they reflect the curse, women will remain in bondage to inequality and vulnerable to abuse; if however they reflect the restorative power of the cross, as Dr. Magda suggests, gender inequality and indeed perhaps other forms of injustice will be dismantled.

Elissa Macpherson
President,
Baptist Women of the Pacific, Baptist World Alliance

We have good reasons to believe that as the 1900s have been the century of ecclesiology, the current period may well be the century of anthropology. And probably no other area of this theological discipline needs more prophetic renewal than that of gender relations. Ksenija Magda's daring book tackles head on the responsibility of the church, in all its traditions, for supporting and promoting the oppressive hierarchical patriarchy that still dominates our world, hurting not just people, but everything else. She calls this ecclesial blindness "blessing the curse," the foolish attempt to redress the consequences of the fall into expressions of normality, even presenting it as "God's eternal plan," and thus, literally ignoring the work of the cross in this area of the plan of salvation. The harm that this has done to the world and to the gospel of Christ was enormous. Yet, even if this may have been, as Fiorenza suggested, a coping mechanism that the church has adopted in order to survive in a misogynistic world, Magda believes there is a better way. Nevertheless, in order to find it, we all, men and women alike, need to willingly take our crosses and follow Christ on it.

Danut Manastireanu
Director of Faith and Development,
Eastern Europe and Middle East Region, World Vision International
PhD Coordinator,
International Baptist Theological Seminary Centre, Amsterdam, The Netherlands

In an ever-winding narrative of Scripture and cultural application, Ksenija Magda expounds the challenge of gender equity with robust frankness. In pages punctuated with personal stories and anecdotes from years of visiting other nations, Magda unpacks Scripture in a way that dignifies both men and women, but not without warnings. She has something powerful to say to both genders and it needs hearing. This book is not for the faint-hearted and needs to be embarked upon with openness of mind and humility of spirit.

Acknowledging the many obstacles ahead, the leadership path for women may still be one of suffering, Magda points out, but hopefully there is a better future: a future where we are willing to learn from one another; a future where men and women flourish together; and a future where we step into mutual strength and celebration of one another.

Karen Wilson
Chairperson and CEO, Global Leadership Network Australia
Director, Strategic Relations, Transform Aid International
President Elect, Baptist World Alliance Women

Blessing the Curse?

A Biblical Approach for Restoring Relationships in the Church

Ksenija Magda

GLOBAL LIBRARY

© 2020 Ksenija Magda

Published 2020 by Langham Global Library
An imprint of Langham Publishing
www.langhampublishing.org

Langham Publishing and its imprints are a ministry of Langham Partnership

Langham Partnership
PO Box 296, Carlisle, Cumbria, CA3 9WZ, UK
www.langham.org

ISBNs:
978-1-78368-792-3 Print
978-1-83973-080-1 ePub
978-1-83973-081-8 Mobi
978-1-83973-082-5 PDF

Ksenija Magda has asserted her right under the Copyright, Designs and Patents Act, 1988 to be identified as the Author of this work.

All rights reserved. No part of this publication may be reproduced, stored in a retrieval system or transmitted, in any form or by any means, electronic, mechanical, photocopying, recording or otherwise, without the prior written permission of the publisher or the Copyright Licensing Agency.

Requests to reuse content from Langham Publishing are processed through PLSclear. Please visit www.plsclear.com to complete your request.

Unless otherwise stated, Scripture quotations are from the New Revised Standard Version Bible, copyright © 1989 National Council of the Churches of Christ in the United States of America. Used by permission. All rights reserved.

British Library Cataloguing-in-Publication Data
A catalogue record for this book is available from the British Library.

ISBN: 978-1-78368-792-3

Cover & Book Design: projectluz.com

Langham Partnership actively supports theological dialogue and an author's right to publish but does not necessarily endorse the views and opinions set forth here or in works referenced within this publication, nor can we guarantee technical and grammatical correctness. Langham Partnership does not accept any responsibility or liability to persons or property as a consequence of the reading, use or interpretation of its published content.

To Baptist women of the world:
May they always find a church that will accept and nurture them.

Contents

Introduction: How the Church Makes the Gospel Bad News
for the World 1

1   Blessing the Curse 9
      Genesis 3: A Curse or a Blessing? 9
      The Contemporary World from the Perspective of the Curse 12

2   Church Structures as Structures of Sin 37
      Hierarchies as Sanctifying the Curse 40
      Church Hierarchies as Systems of Abuse 46
      Hierarchies as Systems of Ecological and Economic Abuse 55

3   The Solution to the Problem of Sin 59
      Looking at the Curse with Paul's Eyes 64
      Christ Takes the Curse of the Body upon Himself 91
      Bearing Fruit: The *Sarks* and *Soma* Dichotomy in Paul 104

4   The Church as New Creation 153
      A Biblical Word to Men 154
      A Biblical Word to Women 188

Epilogue: Next Steps 209
      Combatting Slavery and Human Trafficking 209
      Women's Ministries in the Church 217

Bibliography 227

Index of Names 247

Index of Scriptures 251

Introduction

How the Church Makes the Gospel Bad News for the World

Strictly speaking, this book is not about women, nor is it written exclusively for women. It is about the church and its mission to the world, with particular attention given to male-female relationships because I believe these relationships need to be mended in order to advance the gospel in the world today.

By "blessing the curse," I am suggesting that the church needs to live within the framework of Christ's redemptive work, which has overcome the curse, rather than interpreting the parameters of Genesis 3 (at least when women are concerned) as God's commandment for the church.

This book was born out of my global work with women for the past twenty years, and so the examples of women reflect my own female world experience. The female perspective needs to be the starting point for this kind of investigation, since the problem of "the blessed" curse, so to speak, is not evident if we do not recognize the deep, ongoing pain of women and the ripples this pain creates for everyone else. Pain rarely goes away if it is not first diagnosed, a process that involves listening in order to identify symptoms and triggers. Only then can its root causes be addressed and mended.

Because this book has been triggered by my ministry to the global Baptist family, both the readership and scholarship is partial, though I hope it can be read and discussed more broadly. As this book has developed, I have come to see it as a map through a vast amount of learning, themes, and discussions that either have been put forward – or need to be – so that the place of women in church, family, and society can be aligned with God's biblical vision of shalom. This book has been in the making for so long that the books and conversations that have shaped it have become so embedded within me that it is difficult to distinguish what is from me and what I have taken from them. Also, thoughts and conversations have a way of cross-pollinating, and their importance is rarely evident until later in life, when you reflect on them in relation to some new thoughts or authors. Moreover, while it may have followed proper form to reconstruct all these discussions and their various derivations, I felt it would have burdened the text. Whenever possible, I give these sources credit and note where they can be found.

Though this book has been growing with me for a long time, for many years I found it hard to write down anything about this subject, and I kept quiet because I doubted anyone would listen to me. I have come to realize that many women keep quiet, especially those who do not easily fit within society's set roles. It took me many years to discover my voice in my own circumstances, living as a theologian in a small country with a shyly emerging community of theologians. Looking back, I can see that I have been an extremely slow learner, but small, tangible pieces of this book have been emerging for many years through papers and diary entries. Today, I know that I can be noisy, determined, and unbearable, and sometimes I over-communicate, but I have decided to accept these things as part of who I am on the way to God's perfection.

I grew up as a Croatian in southern Germany in the 1970s, a mighty place and time for learning about liberation and feminism. I was raised in an ex-pat Baptist church that miraculously did not discriminate against women due to a godly pastor, Drago Šestak.

Growing up, I thought that women's ministries were unnecessary in church. My mother piously dragged me to such meetings, and I could not relate to the constant whining about the hard life of women. While I had a strong urge for ministry, I never imagined nor wished to end up in women's ministries. I have now been working as a professor for over thirty years, and I have rarely seen students who target working with women, as I think there is a stigma on women's ministries among young women students. Working with lepers might have more appeal and be more appreciated! I still remember the looks of confusion and pity from some of my friends when I became the president of Baptist World Alliance (BWA) Women in 2015. Some were brave enough to comment, "Really, you accepted this? What for?" The undertone of the question was, "How desperate you must be!?"

My interest in the role of women in the church became a hot topic during my undergraduate years at the Evangelical Theological Seminary in Osijek, Croatia. Despite the institution's lip service to the equality of men and women in ministry, none of the women in my class preached in church for their homiletics class, even though it was required, whereas all the male students preached. At first, this seemed incidental, since the church could only accommodate a limited number of student preachers in one semester. However, as I continued to express what some might call "male gifts" in many Christian communities, I became aware that – consciously or unconsciously – gender selective forces were at work.

At first, I tried to combat these forces with more learning, assuming that I was not chosen because I was not good enough for the structures to recognize me. I know now this experience is typical for women in so-called "male" professions, for the structures continued to ignore me, and my increasing learning only deepened the abyss. If the structures were threatened by me when I was completing my bachelor's degree, they were petrified after I completed my doctorate in biblical studies. This path of revelation was difficult and painful.

My master's thesis, which was a reflection on the work of Antoinette Wire's *Corinthian Women Prophets*,[1] catapulted me into the challenges women face in the church and society, as I tried to make sense of Scripture, interpretation, and church practice, searching for my place in the church. Since that time, Elisabeth Schüssler Fiorenza's *In Memory of Her*[2] has been a constant and valuable companion in the way it opened my eyes to the role of concealed biblical women in the church. In my many years of Bible reading, I had never even noticed some of these female characters. I am glad that Fiorenza's book is now published in my Croatia, where I hope it is being read.

In 1994, I was elected to the Croatian Baptist Women's executive board, and four years later, I became its president. This ministry's connections and relations to global communities through the European Baptist Women's Union, the Commission on Women's Concerns of the Protestant Evangelical Council of Croatia, and the World Evangelical Fellowship (WEF) helped me to see the depth of the problem faced by women in church and society.

My primary lens during this time was the violence against women in family contexts. *No Place for Abuse* by the sociologist Nancy Nason-Clark[3] was prominent, and I continue to revisit her evaluations of abusive family structures and how they work. I have also profited greatly from a personal friendship with her and also Catherine Kroeger.

My work within World Evangelical Alliance (WEA) was also blessed by the amazing book *Gender or Giftedness* by Lynn Smith, a Canadian Baptist, which has now been translated into many languages. In 1997, the Commission on Women's Concerns of the Women's Evangelical Fellowship (WEF, which later

---

1. Antoinette Wire, *Corinthian Women Prophets: A Reconstruction through Paul's Rhetoric* (Minneapolis: Fortress, 1990).

2. Elisabeth Schüssler Fiorenza, *In Memory of Her: A Feminist Theological Reconstruction of Christian Origins* (London: SCM, 1996).

3. Catherine Clark Kroeger and Nancy Nason-Clark, *No Place for Abuse* (Downers Grove: InterVarsity Press, 2001).

became the WEA) distributed the first printing of this booklet in Abbotsford, Canada, to help identify the place of women in the church. Lynn helped me to see that the church views women from the perspective of the structures of sin – what she calls the "paradigm of the Fall"[4] as opposed to the "paradigm of Redemption in Christ." This booklet is a forgotten milestone in WEA's dealings with women, but its undercurrents can be seen in more recent documents (e.g. the 2010 Cape Town Commitment). Unfortunately, these documents have been gravely challenged (though not referenced directly) by some prominent conservative American evangelicals, who consistently shame and defame Christian women and their ministry across the globe.

I devoted the first decade of the twenty-first century to a serious study of Pauline theology at the London School of Theology. I tried hard to keep away from the subject of women, having been warned, "As a scholar, you will be considered less serious if you deal with women's issues." Instead, I dealt with Paul's global mission strategy in Romans, because I was more interested in the Great Commandment than the issue of women, but I was still drawn to try to understand the undercurrents of Paul's thinking about women.

This period of study was characterized by many authors who helped to shape Paul in my mind, particularly N. T. Wright, who helped me navigate the immense and diverse understandings of Paul in a paradigm-changing environment. As I learned what Jesus meant for Paul, I began to identify and expose legalistic readings behind every women's issue in Paul's writing. For instance, it is impossible to reconcile Paul's theology of grace with the thought there is a separate way of salvation for women (e.g. through childbearing) or that women have a different head than Christ alone. Texts that seem to suggest otherwise must be understood within the context of the occasion and concrete social setting of Paul's writing. For Paul, the question is always about how to live out the freedom of the gospel in patriarchal settings and circumstances – that is, how to live in the suffering of the present day (Rom 8:18) in order to influence and change it towards the biblical ideal. I am still learning what Paul's being "in Christ" means for everyday living in the church and in the world.

During that time, I also learned about the difference between *soma* (body) and *sarks* (flesh) in Paul's theology. Knowing the relationship between these words solved for me the larger theological grid in Pauline theology. For instance, the idea of coming together in Christ in the Eucharist (1 Cor 11) is

---

4. Lynn (M. B.) Smith, *Gender or Giftedness: A Challenge to Rethink the Basis for Leadership within the Christian Community* (Manila: World Evangelical Fellowship, 2000), 6. This booklet was first distributed as photocopied material at the WEF meeting in Vancouver in 1997.

central to his theology, for in Christ we understand who we are, and we can live out our unity in diversity as the church and also as women and men, different but equal parts who are fuelled by the Spirit of God. This is God's will for the salvation of the whole world. The body is incomplete and nonfunctional if its parts only function as each one according to its own capacity, instead of functioning together. This concept has been misrepresented and described as "complementarian," which is misleading and has come to be used for a perspective that blesses hierarchical structures of men ruling over women as God-given. God's gifting far transcends the biological and hierarchical agenda of such a short-sighted worldview, which will hopefully become evident in this book.

Because I live in a small country that has been torn apart by big interests, I have also been swirled into the problems of global sustainability and have come to believe that our problems are not external (in the systems of the world), but rather internal. Systems rarely matter if there are people with a caring heart inside of them. The opposite is also true: the best system counts for nothing if the people within it are consumed by evil. Any good thing will immediately become corrupt when it is touched by selfish human interest or driven by insignificant goals. All this points to both the hopefulness and tragedy of the equation.

My theoretical learning on this matter finally came together through a course called "How to Change the World" by Michael Roth of the Wesleyan University, which I took in preparation for my global leadership role as the president of the BWA Women. This course revealed research that located women at the core of global change and connected many puzzle pieces, forming a picture of the kingdom of God as lived out in the church as part of the good news for the world. Change is possible – and if you want to change the world, you have to get women involved in more than motherhood! My sporadic interests in global change, missions, biblical research, and women in leadership all came together, disclosing a most amazing course of thought and action. All this made God unthinkably great and exciting – and also made God's mercy an overwhelmingly beautiful future vision for the glory of the children of God. This vision came as an incredibly sweet word of hope in a dark place.

My recent study focuses on Romans 8, a chapter that conveys an optimism and hope that keeps me going. For the past couple years, I have followed the work of the Consultation on the Status of Women of the UN. My own work as the president of BWA Women globally has underlined what I have learned from professor Duchrow of Heidelberg: the Bible is a script for living a free life in places where the structures of sin enslave, buy, sell, and kill people for profit. From that perspective, there is nothing "free" in a "complementarian" perspective about men and women. Any perspective that functions on the premise, "I am born as your leader, and you are born as my follower," does not reflect the "freedom of God's children" that all creation yearns to see. Rather, such a view is strictly opposed to Jesus's teaching about power, which is that it must grow from below through service, and nobody is entitled to it because of colour or genitalia.

Finally, the greatest contributors to this book are the women and men with whom I worked in the context of my global family of Baptists. Their stories and insights into the Bible have made the theories come alive, sometimes providing a decisive piece of information that helped complete the picture. In Lusaka, for instance, a brother (whose name I did not hear and could not track down), said (roughly quoted), "I am encouraged when I see women come together like this. I see Genesis saying, 'You, sisters, are the first line of defence against the devil and I am glad you are standing firm in the battle!'" This statement prompted further questions about why women are the ones who have to start the change.

It has been a massive undertaking to pull together so many years of learning into a single book that will be read by a diverse and global audience. My hope is that this book will be scholarly enough for theologians, but also readable for the broader public, especially millennials and the generation Y. While I am not at all sure that I have succeeded, I am encouraged by the positive feedback that I have received when I have shyly mentioned this book in the course of my travels to diverse continents.

Reservations

First, this book is about the male-female relationship regardless of our other identity markers. In my years as BWA Women's president, I have glimpsed our racial blindspots and the excruciating pain and hardship experienced by those who are not Caucasian. Taking the racial component into consideration would further benefit the discussion and make this book even more valuable. But for my whole life, I have lived in an almost exclusively white environment, and so I feel I have no right to write that segment of the book. While writing this book, I have tried to see all people of various colours and shapes, but entitlement blinds people, and so I ask for forgiveness for any places where these issues should have been mentioned and have not been. I would appreciate feedback from anyone who would be willing to share with me, and I do hope that someone will pick up where I have left off and write this missing segment.

Second, this book is intentionally systemic, as I believe that an overarching approach to the problem of male-female relationships in both theology and the church is long overdue. I am aware that systemic solutions cannot be presented in all the pragmatic detail that gives readers small pieces of information that they can swallow and put straight to practice. While such an approach may be appealing, some of the deeper teachings of the Bible have been watered down into simple stanzas of a cheap and shallow feel-good faith that leave many asleep in churches. Moreover, this book may not satisfy activists who are looking for simple, practical solutions. Though I have fought for women's rights and am dedicated to stopping violence against women, I have come to see life as a complicated network of intertwined and reciprocal interdependencies, and so it is sometimes impossible to see the causality of origins and outcomes. Sometimes, these intricacies make direct activism simplistic and, on occasion, counter-productive.

Third, according to the Myers-Briggs personality assessment, I have a judging personality that always sees faults first. I have fought hard with this tendency in my soul, but I have not yet arrived. This will become apparent when I point to examples that do not reflect our greatest behaviour as the church in the first two sections of the book, "Blessing the Curse" and "Church Structures as Structures of Sin." Although I begin with a lot of criticisms as I trace my biblically informed evaluation of our failures as Baptists (in particular) and Christians (in general), I love the church and am a Baptist – with conviction. Moreover, I have found that the Baptist approach offers the best contextualization of the Bible's servant leadership and the effort to partake in the church as equals. Please bear this in mind as you read some of the self-critical notes about this tradition.

Though Baptists have a long history of fighting for the rights of the oppressed and are active and dependable leaders and doers in any interdenominational effort or ecumenical project, we fail women miserably from a global perspective, and so we are also losing them to mainline denominations and the world. On many occasions, I have cried because I felt disrespected and ignored, sometimes even ridiculed and rejected, simply for being a woman. I know now that my own path has been easy compared to the experience of women in the global context. I still cry, but now I cry for my sisters who are being denied life, education, or the freedom to make even small decisions about their own lives or ways to use their gifts. I cry for all the abused and trafficked women, because in more places than not, this is the way for women – including church women (and Baptist women).

Although I have encountered godly leaders in all cultures around the world – regardless of the level of "development" – who promote a theology that regards women as equal partners in the church, there are also vast numbers of people who simply accept the way things are and continue to perpetuate them. To change this, we must begin by examining the gloomy circumstance of the curse (Gen 3) and its global implications. We cannot change anything if we do not first acknowledge the pain and look the evil in the eye.

I hope to make up for the initial pain in the second half of the book, where I chart the way forward through Bible readings and examples of best practice. In my global work, I have encountered strong and godly women everywhere who cannot be stopped from using their gifts for the glory of God – as well as men who have a servant's heart. We are still alive and kicking because of them!

Fourth, when I challenge men, I am not doing so as a hurt and angry female. In male/female relationships in the church, there continues to be much self-worship and a glorification of men that keeps us from revealing God's glory, and this reality is not just the men's fault. My learning has brought me to a point where I can clearly see that if men and women are not partners in God's glory, they are partners in the devil's crimes. I hate to call women partners in this evil when I see the physical, economic, social, and political pain that is inflicted on women daily by men. Though women have been bashed and estranged from themselves and others, taught to bend quietly to fit into the structures of sin, and to survive instead of living life to the fullest, they also need to be confronted with the truth in order to be able to change the structures that keep them enslaved.

More than anything, I have written this book to help all of us reflect the glory of God that the world is eagerly awaiting to see in the children of God. I am not talking about eschatology, for God wants us to reflect this change sooner than later. We have been entrusted with the job of tending and caring for the world by the one who saved us, because it is God's world! Supported by the Spirit and everything else that has been bestowed on us for life and holiness, we are to offer our bodies as living sacrifices that will glorify God.

May we all have the courage to challenge the death-dealing structures of the world wherever we are with the good news of God. God has not created us as men and women to live under the curse of Genesis 3; rather, he has sent Jesus to take the curse of our bodies upon his own body so that we can partner together for the renewal of the world and bear witness to the already here and now of the glory that is to come.

1

Blessing the Curse

Genesis 3: A Curse or a Blessing?

If we observe a problem long enough, we usually discover that we have only scratched its surface. For when we dive into the problem and begin to probe its depths, we discover a complex web of reciprocal relationships and complications. For instance, in Africa, on the surface, we see the problem of teenage mothers who are unable to cope with their children. We want to help them cope, and so we set up institutions, teach them parenting, maybe also how to sew. Then there is another child out of wedlock, another hardship or inability to move forward, and we begin to feel overwhelmed about how to help, or we feel unable to care.

Recently, a church group from the US complained that as an organization, the BWA Women's Department has become too liberal and concerned with the social gospel, and that if the poor nations only accepted the preaching of the gospel, they would become as affluent "as we are in the US." Regardless of where we are in the world, we all inherit shortcuts to doing away with the pain of the world. Some believe that life is simply difficult, and we need to endure it rather than change it; others believe that we have somehow earned the right to be better off than others. We inherit these traditions matter-of-factly and often unconsciously.

But rather than bowing to the imbalance and suffering of the world, activists and advocates stick out their necks for what does not make sense, believing that every person counts. Pure activism, however, is often counterproductive because it either grows out of the trauma and suffering of the activist, or it does not see the bigger picture. In this way, activism can be naïve and even abusive. For instance, as much as every single life matters in the atrocious business of human trafficking, the fact is that for every one person you save, two other people will likely get trafficked in their place. Thus activism can actually enhance suffering: the first victim may never return to "normal" life, and the two others have now been drawn into the same abyss. The more productive such an activist is in the business of saving *one*, the more successful the business of trafficking becomes. Thus the activist is up against intricate structures of evil that operate according to their own principles, and the only real cure is to stop the demand. But for that, something deeper must happen in the lives of the those who buy people for pleasure – and that cannot be solved by activism. We need a shift in paradigm: where there is no demand, there is no trafficking. This simple, complicated truth applies to all the suffering and oppression in the world.

To return to the African story of unwed mothers, the girls and their hormones do not drive teen pregnancies. Rather, a set of cultural and traditional structures of evil feed on the hormonal drive and are sustained and enforced by traditions, which are backed by cultural understandings of the divine. From an early age, girls learn that their sole purpose in life is to be wives and mothers. Many parents support this because they believe that this traditional role prepares their daughters for their futures both properly (in our case, biblically!) and practically. They do not stop to think about their daughter's need for an education or independence, or the fact that her life and the lives of her offspring will depend on her ability to provide for them. Early on, while she is unable to think for herself, her culture makes that choice for her. School is expensive, and since girls will marry anyway, it is considered a financial loss.

So when the hormones hit, and tradition confirms that a girl is old enough to make her dreams and purpose come true, she will try and find herself a man. He, too, was trained by tradition – not to become a husband and a father, but to go places. His success is often determined by counting how many women he has had – even in the church, because when men are blessed, God gives them many women (like Abraham, Jacob, David, or even Solomon). I have been told all this by a girl from South Africa! Such narratives enforce the structures of evil, taking a good thing (such as a narrative approach to the Bible) within a vulnerable place (an illiterate environment) and abusing it.

In this recipe for disaster, a girl looks for a husband to marry and father her children, and a boy looks to have as many women as possible. She has not been taught about her sexuality, but when she becomes pregnant out of wedlock, everyone is surprised and angry. Tradition did not cover this part, except through strict prohibition, but she never expected to have her baby out of wedlock. From the girl's perspective, she did what she was supposed to do to fulfil her purpose as soon as possible – and nobody told the boy about the children, or the cost and inconvenience of supporting them in a rundown economy where there is no work. So when his girl becomes demanding and wants a home and sacrifice, he moves on to a new woman. Without work or training, the girl is shamed and possibly abandoned by her family, and so her only chance to get food on the table comes from the pimps and traffickers – and the hope that she might find another man who will accept her. This girl is easy prey, and her scenario is just the tip of the iceberg, for it not only affects her life in the present, but also the lives of her children in the future – many of whom will be abandoned and end up roaming around the streets, trying to find a way to live.

This is but one story that depicts the mighty, seductive, and fatal structures around us. Such stories happen everywhere, luring people in, promising life, only to drag them down into deepening pain. The children come from the streets, broken families affected by AIDS and other illness, the trauma of war, physical abuse, constant poverty, and so on. Their lives have been so broken that it is difficult to know where to start the healing, and so the activist's life becomes impossible.

Though these structures of sin are everywhere and work against everyone, Jesus came to break their power to enslave and to lead people to freedom. Jesus confronted evil in all its forms: he healed the sick physically, emotionally, spiritually, and socially. For when we are sick, our whole person suffers. If the body did not matter, Jesus would not have bothered to resurrect Lazarus. If the spirit was all that mattered, perhaps Lazarus would have been better off dead. But Jesus resurrected his body, because God's creation matters to God.

As Christians, we are called to treat people in their entirety, just as Jesus did. This is what it means to proclaim the good news! Yet more often than not, the church fails to follow its master. In its teaching, it catapults faith into the spiritual realm, where it has nothing to do with real life. At the same time, the reading of Scripture has become influenced by the culture of the world rather than Christ. Instead of exposing and dealing with the sinful practices that the Bible clearly and systematically rejects, the church feels compelled to reflect and uphold the structures of sin because doing so makes its life in the world much easier.

When I teach a course on Revelation, I wonder what it was like for prophets such as John or Ezekiel, who were called to "swallow" the book of prophecy that God gave to them, which was both sweet and upsetting. God's word brings liberation, but it does so within the structures of evil. We have to take the bad with the good to find the path towards freedom.

The UN claims that there are more slaves today than there have been at any time in history in spite of the fact that most countries have an antislavery act in their constitution. Having been banned to the dark side, slavery has assumed more subtle ways of existing, even within countries that are proud of their democratic heritage. The treacherous and concealing powers of enslavement encourage people to be content with things as they are – especially when the bad happens elsewhere – because, "I could be so much worse off." The fact is, those of us who are living in "freedom" are just living on the upper levels of a hierarchical ladder, which is being upheld by hosts of exploited slaves elsewhere.

One of the upsides of globalization is that these intricate relationships become more openly visible when we try to live together and establish complex economical connections. Thus globalization has revealed that the systems from the past are defective, which, of course, is old news. Nevertheless, the nationalistic shift towards the right – what is known and traditional – attempts to split up the more unifying canopy of these global relationships and conceal these connections.

And yet revolutions are not the answer, as each revolution attacks problems partially, on the surface, without plumbing the depths in order to make thorough and lasting changes. We throw things up in the air only to realise that when they come tumbling down, they are assembled in exactly the same way. We all feel the curse, as if we are in a never-ending horror movie, and just as the credits come up, we begin to relax because we think the evil has finally been conquered, and then it pops up and glares at us from the trunk of the car as it drives into the sunset. Why do we always end up in the same enslaving structures? I believe that the path of liberation can only be recovered by reading Genesis 3 through the lens of Christ's incarnation and redemption for the whole world.

The Contemporary World from the Perspective of the Curse

In the Bible, the problem of Genesis 3 is often described as "the curse." The uncomfortable (and unpopular) message is that we are evil, sinful, and, as the Apostle Paul says, "dead," like living corpses (Rom 5:12; 7:5; 7:14–25). As "dead" to God, we continue to bring death rather than life into the world. Nobody wants to hear the notion that we are intrinsically bad. Contemporaries who are shaped by an individualistic worldview are particularly upset by the notion of sin, because they see themselves as good people.

Thus there have been long discussions throughout Christian history about complete or partial defilement by sin in the Christian church. These discussions have been documented back to the fifth century, when Augustine won a debate with Pelagius through his claim of total human corruption.[1] As good as people sometimes appear, the true motivation of their hearts is often concealed – sometimes even to themselves. Depending on the circumstances, even the best people become corrupt by opportunity. The driving force behind Augustine's reasoning derived from his philosophical explanation of Adam's sin as "original sin" in Romans 5.[2] Since then, Christianity has blamed the state of intrinsic corruptness on Adam through the doctrine of original sin. Had Adam not sinned, the doors to evil and death would have stayed closed. Humans would still live the blissful lives of innocents in paradise. Yet such thinking is a shortcut, for people in any time will inevitably do what people do best – blame others. For this thinking suggests that the unfortunate affair of sin is that it isn't really anyone's fault; if anything, God should be blamed. What is sin after all?

This oversimplifies a long philosophical discussion, but in our time, the concept of original sin is not self-evident. The book of Romans communicates a concept that can be more easily understood than "sin" by disclosing Paul's preoccupation with the *death* that sin brings. Paul's driving mission is to reveal how Jesus cures the problem of the death caused by sin. He points out that "death" reigned from Adam to Moses, even over those whose "sinning was not like the transgression of Adam" (Rom 5:14). Theoretically, like our contemporaries, Paul can envision people who did not sin like Adam, although they are already all condemned (Rom 3:9). But even if there were some sinless people, they would not be spared, for those who live without God will still suffer the deadly consequences of other people's sins in this world. If we read Romans less doctrinally and more literally, we see that Paul's problem is with

---

1. The discussion in the fifth century was between Pelagius, a Brit and teacher in Rome, and Augustine of Hippo about human cooperation in God's salvation of the world. Pelagius opposed Augustine's idea about the absolute human inadequacy to do the will of God while Augustine insisted that evil was an absence of the real, "a deficiency, a privation of what is good." Quoted from Joseph Fitzpatrick, "Original Sin or Original Sinfulness," *New Blackfriars* 90 (July 2009): 460. See also the discussion in Alister MacGrath, *Christian Theology: An Introduction* (Chichester: Wiley-Blackwell, 1997; repr. 2011), 351–354.

2. Alexander J. M. Wedderburn, *Adam and Christ: An Investigation into the Background of 1 Corinthians XV and Romans V, 12–21*. PhD thesis (Cambridge: University of Cambridge, 1971), 215, was the first to criticize this understanding and he brings a comprehensive discussion on previous scholarship on the matter. Meanwhile, a discussion developed from it but there are still serious scholars who hold on to the old interpretation (see Joseph A. Fitzmayer, *Romans* [New York: Doubleday, 1997], 407; or C. B. E. Cranfield, *The Epistle to the Romans I* [Edinburgh: T & T Clark, 1970], 269). I have noted elsewhere that the discussion about "original" (i.e. "hereditary") sin as it is frequently understood, does not fit well with the literary context of the letter to the Romans (Ksenija Magda, *Paul's Territoriality and Mission Strategy* [Tübingen: Mohr/Siebeck, 2009], 139–142).

the *death* sin brings to everyone and everything – not just the sinner! Sin sets up structures and networks that catch and harm innocents. Sin does not ask whether or not people deserve it, or whether there is a law against killing. Sin likes to kill.

Often and easily, evangelicals who believe in *sola gratia* still explain sin as "bad acts" for which a grumpy white-bearded God punishes people on the spot. The definition of sin as acts of misbehaviour is entrenched in our heads even after five centuries of reformation and the thought, "I am not a sinner because I sin, but I sin, because I am a sinner."[3] Yet the problem is far bigger than a person's sporadic malfunction. The problem is a systemic defect, which needs a systemic answer.

It has been shown recently that Paul does not argue from Adam to Christ – that Adam's sin was so great that only Christ could overcome it – but the other way around: because the Son of God had to descend from heaven, die, and rise again in order to deal with human sin, we can now understand the extent of Adam's one-time transgression. Once introduced, sin produces a state and structure of decay, which brings death to the world one sinful deed at a time. Sin permeates all areas of life and impregnates it with seeds of death. Under its domain, people remain entrapped in sinful structures. On our own, we remain blind to these sinful structures. We realize that death is the result of sin when it hits us personally. Yet when tragedy hits others, we tend to see death as the natural course of things, a normal part of life.

And some object, "Surely we cannot all be that bad." But let us look at Genesis 1–3 with a different set of eyes and try to keep our defences down so that we can immerse ourselves in what the Bible has to say about the depth and extent of sin. This is a first step, Paul would argue, to dealing with the problem. Without God's law (the Old Testament or the Hebrew Bible), we would die unconscious deaths, for God's law gives us a feeling for what sin is and shows us its dreadful and hopeless depths. Only after we have seen and understood our own inadequacy to deal with it can we accept and appreciate God's solution.

The story from Genesis 3 is known in most parts of the world. People learn it early in life. It is important to dwell on what God tells Adam and Eve on the day they decided to eat from the one and only forbidden tree in Paradise. As in any story, motives are more important than the deed itself, and the Bible is

---

3. "Actual sins essentially consist in this that they come from out of us, as the Lord says in Matthew 15:19: 'Out of the heart proceed evil thoughts, murders, adulteries, fornications, thefts, false witness, blasphemies.' But original sin enters into us. We do not commit it, but we suffer it." M. Luther, *Commentary on Romans,* trans. J. T. Mueller (Grand Rapids: Kregel, 2003), 95. Luther still thinks within the prevalent paradigm, but opens it up to an important new insight.

clear that turning away from God is the underlying sin. Adam and Eve turned away from God to become as gods and to know good and evil. The Tree of the Knowledge of Good and Evil (Gen 2:9) was called that for a reason. We are not told if Adam and Eve knew this name. If they did, we can call them childishly naïve (as some commentators interpret the story) for eating from it. But we do know that God told them that they would die if they disobeyed God and ate from it.

In the story, it is important to note that the readers are painfully aware that there is nothing "good" to be acquired from this fruit as the snake makes its way to tempt Eve. The readers have already read the opening chapters of Genesis, where it has been hammered into their minds that everything that God made up to that point was "very good" (1:31). What else could be experienced by eating from the Tree of the Knowledge of Good and Evil but evil and, as God puts it, death?

Yet the first humans were unaware that they were living a perfect dream under God's complete provision. When temptation hit, it hit hard. They wanted to have everything. They wanted to be like God. They were already walking in God's presence every day. We may find all sorts of reasons that wanting to be like God was a legitimate wish for Adam and Eve. Yet when humans want to be like God, they are acting upon a death wish. The phrase, "You will surely die," is not a threat so much as a statement of a fact. If you are a creation, which is a vital presupposition of the biblical story, then the decision to detach yourself from the Creator means you stop being. A created being who is made "in God's likeness" is not God. Humans are not fit to be the Almighty, all-sustaining, eternal Being, who, as Jürgen Moltmann put it, is great enough to make space in himself for the other, possibly even a hostile other.[4]

After the disobedience, the emancipated and detached creation does not really feel divine at all, but rather exposed and threatened by the death that is approaching from everywhere. The detached creation feels it must take things into its own hands to protect itself and fight for itself against everything and everybody, especially God. Thus the detached creation learns to feel fear, jealousy, and contempt for others, especially those who threaten its existence, and so it conceals itself, becomes defensive, and acts out against its enemies. The creation is left to protect its own life, but it is unsure about how to do this in light of all its limitations and its lack of the life elixir. It feels it can never gather enough to provide for the skinny years it anticipates in its dark hours of isolation.

---

4. Jürgen Moltmann, *God in Creation* (Minneapolis: Fortress, 1993), 87–91.

Wanting to be God has many other implications as well. First, everyone fights for their own territories in whatever ways they can. The inner motivation is to make it for ourselves. The hierarchies we so often identify as divine are actually a temporary status quo that support our instinctual self-preservation. We agree to give a hierarchical precedence to someone we cannot beat ourselves – just yet. No wonder hierarchies form early on in life – and are established everywhere!

Because we only accept hierarchies when it is obvious that it would be counterproductive to fight opponents, we are always waiting for a new opportunity to regroup and attack. Thus systems establish myriad mechanisms to keep people in place so that they will believe they cannot change the order of things. Those who are at the top of the hierarchy want the status quo to hold on for as long as possible, and yet those at the top also tend to ignore the temporality of hierarchies. They feel they've finally made it to the God position, where they can make all the rules and own the mechanisms of change, thereby enforcing eternal obedience. But the history of hierarchies tells a different story: every single one falls because of the unquenchable human urge to get to the top, to be God. When Nicolae Ceaușescu, the dictator of Romania, died in front of a firing squad on Christmas Day of 1989, the world was amazed. Friends who had visited us at the end of November that year to smuggle a contingent of illegal Bibles into Romania had commented, "His power is as firm as ever!" And yet, not even a month later, Ceaușescu was no more.

Hierarchies are so basic to our experience of life that most people believe there is no way to live outside them. However, recent research in the business world has found that hierarchies are truly inefficient. For various intricate reasons, most organizations that rely on hierarchical structures lag behind because they tend to inhibit human potential. Though they may speak of progress, hierarchies only support the interests and needs of whoever is at the top rather than those of the business.

More often than not, the Christian church is smitten by hierarchies, which makes delusions about being God particularly interesting. Church hierarchies are often more important than God, the Bible, faith, or justice. Any challenge to those at the top of a church hierarchy will immediately reveal how minimally God is actually in the system. Even at the lower end of a local church hierarchy, church members will walk on eggshells to avoid waking up the human god who is in charge. Many human gods in such churches – and one finds them in *all* denominations – go so far as to micromanage the lives of their followers and to set up structures to enforce this power. They believe – and have taught others to believe – that they alone have the divine right to intervene, forbid, or allow any action, including whom church members will see or greet, whom they will avoid, or whom they will marry!

Hierarchies are so prevalent in the church and society that it may be difficult to find any alternatives. Undoubtedly, hierarchies seem to be an inevitable expression of our life on earth. Moreover, many Christians will say that the Bible affirms, if not orders, hierarchies. In several places, the Bible mentions a house code, which depends on a hierarchical structure and forces women to obey their husbands, children to obey parents, and slaves to obey masters. In 1 Corinthians, the Apostle Paul argues from the creation order for a hierarchical family system. This system was maintained and affirmed by church writers even before the Cappadocian Fathers (c. 330–395), who described women as ontologically inferior to men and therefore unfit to rule over them.[5]

Thus it is generally believed that hierarchies reflect the nature of things. Much of our hierarchical church order and other related concepts derive from the patristic church. These theologians from the first five centuries are valued primarily because of their proximity to the New Testament writers, a line of reasoning that always puzzled me, since reading the Church Fathers and reading the writers of the New Testament is such a different experience. Can we really claim that our contemporary theology should in some way be proximate to the Reformation theology of the sixteenth century? Rather, the experience of reading early church materials should teach us that proximity can get lost – and probably in less than a century. The church itself did not feel the historical proximity that we ascribe to these writings, for it only allowed those writings that (among other things) had a proven connection to the apostles in the first century into the Canon of Scripture.

In addition, we must ask whether the hierarchies in the Bible actually reflect the complete picture that the Bible paints about the will of God for creation. For instance, shouldn't the way Jesus treated women and turned hierarchies upside down have a more serious theological emphasis, since

---

5. The idea of who women are was disputed. Origen, for instance, debated that women are created ontologically inferior to men because they were supposed to be a "help" to men – and there is no other area in which men need help but in bearing children, because they could not do this alone (*Homilies on Genesis 1:14*). In *On the Paradise*, Ambrose argues for the ontological inferiority of women (chs. 4 and 6). In comparison with John Chrysostom, who believed that female inferiority developed after the Fall (*Homilies on Genesis 15* and other places), Ambrose taught that because woman was created from Adam's body and not his soul, she was meant to be ontologically inferior from the very beginning of creation. It is no wonder that a later council in Lyon in 584 CE discussed whether women had souls at all. Comp. Dave Butler, "Church Decision Whether Women Have Souls. Results," online at: https://groups.google.com/forum/#!topic/net.women/PtEmp8kJC4A.

Jesus is our main authority? Yet his teaching gets lost in the theologies (and hierarchies) of the later church. And shouldn't we consider the theological framework that Jesus employed when he approached the hierarchy-obsessed Sons of Thunder in Mark 10, telling them that hierarchies are an expression of the rulers in the world, but it should not be so "among you" (v. 43)?

I have come to believe that Jesus challenged and reversed hierarchies because he wanted to redefine the world from the perspective of a new creation rather than the curse. While the creation is obstructed by the structures of sin, and hierarchies are the dominant experience of the world and the ambitious disciples, Jesus says, "this is not how it should be among you" (Mark 10:42–43). Hierarchies insist that someone needs to be in charge, and someone has to have the last word, and someone generally needs to rule over others with force. Yet such hierarchical structures do not reflect God's intent or will for the creation, nor any ethical approach to life.

For example, when God first created the world, what was "good" was for people to "care" for the world, which was "very good" (Gen 1:31; 2:15). They were not created to lord over it. Moreover, the equal status of the man and the woman was also "good" (2:18). She was from the man's side (as some rabbis tended to teach – Gen Rab 17.2), which meant she was a helper who was equal to him, not a slave to obey him (2:20 comp. Yeb 63a). While Jesus affirms hierarchies as the prevalent structures of the world, he specifically claims that they do not reflect the true nature of the kingdom of God. For in the kingdom of God, greatness is expressed by serving others and washing their feet, regardless of their gender or social status (see Mark 10:44–45; John 13:12–16).

So as Christians, how did we come to establish hierarchies and mandate them to people we claim to love, just so we could reach the top and rule over them? Why is having power over others so appealing in the church?

Returning to the Genesis narrative, I think the answer lies in the structures of sin and the primary human sin of wanting to be God. For once people emancipate themselves from God, hierarchies give them a sense of structure in a world that they have made God-less, which is a dead and disintegrating world. To understand the outcome of this God-less agenda, we will need to read Genesis 3 from a new perspective – not as God's order and punishment, but as a statement about how the now God-less will constellate themselves.

It is as if God is saying, "Now, because you have disobeyed, this is what your life will look like. The women and her offspring will be constantly challenged by the snake, but will crush its head eventually – luckily! (This is a promise and a way out.) The man will try to rule over the creation, but the creation will grow increasingly unresponsive to his authority and will neither bring forth what he wants nor how much he wants. Additionally, the woman will try to build a relationship with her husband, but the man's focus and urge to rule over everything and everybody (including her) will make their bonding an impossible agenda. His rule and her lack of relationship with him will bring her constant, great pain. After all, she is the one who will bring new life into the world, only so that it may be destroyed by pain and agony."

The Curse as a Male Problem

For the time being, we will skip God's curse for the snake (Gen 3:14–15) and resume this discussion near the end of this book as we examine the future of our world from the perspective of Romans 8. We will also look at Adam's curse (vv. 17–19) before we turn to Eve's (v. 16).

After dealing with the roots of evil and the first perpetrator (vv. 1–10), the story in Genesis 3 continues with God's word to the male (v. 11). From the storyline, God first addresses Adam, and so then he blames Eve for what happened (v. 12). While Adam turns on Eve, she accuses the snake (v. 13). The first curse begins where this last accusation finishes (v. 14). In some ways, God's word to Adam is the peak of the curse (v. 17), and so that culmination needs to be our starting point in order to understand the outcomes of sin for all. Men somehow set the tone for what becomes a downward spiral of the human experience of death after sin.

In traditional environments that enforce hierarchies, some maintain that the fall happened because Adam failed to enforce his hierarchical position over Eve. In other words, he was a wimp. Had he shown Eve her place, what a difference this could have made! Instead, he let the subordinate take charge, which is not a good idea in any hierarchy. So the story of the man's sin is interpreted as if the evil begins when hierarchies are disregarded. Yet there is a problem with this reading, because Genesis 1 and 2 do not reflect hierarchies and, most interestingly, God places the curse against Eve (v. 16) in between the curse against the snake (vv. 14–15) and Adam (vv. 17–19).

This myth that locates the core of evil in Adam's disregard for hierarchies is a strong rope in the net of our human experience of deadly structures. We see it in basic male-female relationships, marriages and families, and businesses and societies in general. Some may argue that in more recent history, we have idealized the diminishment of social stratification and promoted mobility between the hierarchical strata – but this is changing. Globally, there has been a steady return to stable hierarchies with immovable structures and strong, tyrannical leaders, Big Brothers who will watch us and keep us "safe." We are even giving up our personal freedom to such autocrats because we are afraid of terrorist threats and dissolving families.

Some claim that liberalism brought us here, creating an unstable global society with a postmodern view of individualistic approaches to life and too much emphasis on freedom. The solution being offered is that we need to return to traditional hierarchical structures. *Someone has to take charge. Someone has to rule and keep us safe to preserve our freedom.* And so the world is scrambling to restructure its hierarchies and elect strong leaders to head them. When we feel weak, we tend to put all our hope in those who seem strong and wealthy enough to solve our problems. Yet these people became strong by ruling over us, and they did not become rich by caring for others. When we hand our freedom over to these leaders on a silver platter, they become even more powerful. They are not using their strength in order to nurture us, but to conquer even more powerful hierarchical positions for themselves in an ongoing competition for the exclusive god position in the world. The best we can hope for is to be given concessions that will benefit us. But the purpose of these concessions is to keep us quiet under their feet while they establish their higher positions.

Thus the god-wars are on, and they have been raging forever – though sometimes they change outward appearance and become more sophisticated technologically. Darwin noticed this in the biological world and called it "survival of the fittest," but in human societies, it is the survival of the most ruthless – those who accumulate power and manipulate people and then rationalize any concerns of conscience.

So far, I have focused on those who are at the top of these hierarchies, and some may think that only the men at the top are to blame. There are certainly plenty of incorrigible men up there, initiating this sort of evil, taking away freedom and resources from others in order to secure their own positions. It is common rhetoric in shops and cafes, on street corners, and at family reunions to blame the men on top. We want to believe that things would be better if only we had better politicians. From a feminist perspective, we might think that everything would change if only we got rid of the patriarchy. But we have already established that sin is at the core of each human heart – not just the male heart.

Moreover, hierarchies do not exist without the vast number of victimized people's submission. For becoming a god in the world requires power, people, and means, and gods cannot be expected to care for their children, vassals, servants, and slaves, for they need to fight other contenders for the god-position in the hierarchy arena – and if possible, they do it via proxy. To give just one example, how often do the warlords die in a war? Thus those who reach the top of hierarchies could never be there if they had not been helped by grassroots supporters and champions, who either live in the illusion that they will profit from hierarchies, or else the delusion that one day they will be on the top!

For instance, most people think hierarchies bring order to a society. The argument is that some measure of peace is better than chaos – and in a God-less society, this has some truth to it. Humanism, for example, is a God-less system in which the human is the highest good and the measure of all things. This sounds like exceptional altruism and even lines up with some traditional Christian doctrines, such as the sanctity of human life.[6] However, the main question behind such a system may not be neglected: exactly *which* human is the measure of all things? This question reveals humanism as egotism in a more sophisticated disguise. Even humanism that places the other before the self feeds into the *Übermensch* ideology (the concept of, "Oh, he serves me, so I must be God"). From early on, we are fed these traditions and myths so that we are ready to offer our freedom and potential to such human gods. Nationalism is one myth that easily convinces people to give up everything and stop thinking altogether, but there are numerous others. Myths can be driven by basic human needs for food, shelter, and medicine, but also by the desire for extended luxuries, such as travel and the privileges of an easy life.

As much as we may want to believe that these gods are keeping us safe, our language (that marvellous vehicle of social experience) betrays our ordeal, for in a hierarchical system, creation and people become commodities ("Every man has his price"), and commodities are there to be sold ("He would sell his [grand]mother for this"), and commodities are often "sacrificed" for some greater good ("It is better for one man to die for the nation"). Of course, the god at the top of the hierarchy determines what this "greater good" should be and then seeks to indoctrinate and manipulate the people below.

Thus from top to bottom, hierarchies are the pragmatic result of negotiations between those who are contending for the god position, each serving its own little interests. During a war-free period, the status quo accumulates new resources and envisions new strategies to launch a new attack and attempt a new hierarchical structure.

---

6. Recently, this old doctrine had to be reviewed because of the demands of ecology. A resource book on the issue of the old and new paradigms is David P. Gushee, *The Sacredness of Human Life: Why an Ancient Biblical Vision Is Key to the World's Future* (Grand Rapids: Eerdmans, 2013), esp. ch. 11 on the sacredness of God's creation.

In the Balkans, for example, there is a war approximately every fifty years. The real surprise is that whatever "peace" is negotiated holds for fifty years! But it takes time to build a new generation of indoctrinated innocents who will act upon the myths of the holy sacrifices that were made in the past to preserve their happy youth.

An old woman who used to live with us after the Croatian war told us stories about her life between the two World Wars amidst a family of nineteen children in what was then First Yugoslavia. She started working as a servant in a well-off family when she was ten, as did her other siblings. When one of the kids became sick (and some did in fact die at a young age), her father would just say, "Oh wouldn't I be so lucky . . .," meaning, if the kid dies, he could get drunk for free! Some human gods do not have high standards for satisfaction and are happy with a small entourage and resources to support their own little pleasures – such as alcoholism. In those times, having children meant having more work power to manage more land and get more crops. To work more land meant to have more influence, or in the case above, to be able to get drunk when one of those children died.

In our own day, there has been a shift away from big families. In the new circumstances of today's life, people are expensive, both in families and in industry. In former times, you needed thousands and thousands of people to run a production line, but today, at least in the Western world, workers have become expensive, and robots can easily and more economically take their place. Human power is still appreciated in the Majority World, where children are still employed – as Ben Skinner found out when he was only four and began producing silica sand for practically no pay.[7] In some places, humans are still very cheap to buy.

In the Bible, God's plan for humans to "care for creation" became a command to "lord over" creation within the hierarchical structures of sin. Those at the top of this structure continue to exploit the earth as long as it is profitable, without giving any thought to the consequences. The gods at the top need to accumulate stuff to prove their position, and so they seek to lord over as many resources as possible and to keep as many people under their control, working for their purposes, as they possibly can.

It is easy to see how such structures have brought our generation into our current global sustainability crisis. The creation has been abused and torn apart by the gods of corporations, banks, and global enterprises with a complete

---

7. E. B. Skinner, *A Crime so Monstrous* (New York: Free Press, 2008), 206–251; silica or quartz sand is widely used in various industries; its dust is extremely hazardous to health.

disregard for sustainability. But one cannot think about sustainability while waging a war to secure the top position in the hierarchy. Thus creation has become a commodity to be bought and sold at will between the big players. Not even sophisticated negotiations, such as those set up by the UN through their research and advocacy, help the situation, since the negotiators and advocates have their own agendas and are vying for someone's interest. The big players do not sign agreements about a more sustainable use of resources, because they would suffer big losses in their global hierarchical positions. A world run by the profit wars waging amongst hierarchical contenders will never be good news for creation – neither humans, nor nature, which has no direct way to fight back. As we are seeing, however, the creation is responding in the form of natural disasters.

The Bible predicted death for any God-less system that establishes hierarchical structures to be ruled by the gods on top. God did not ordain a curse over the world, but stated the facts: a God-less system cannot sustain a creation that finds its beginning and end in the Creator. Detached from God, the creation is on its way to ruin, a process that is accelerated by those who contend for the god-position and abuse the creation for their own gain. God gave the creation the freedom to detach itself from the life-giving sustenance of its Creator. By following that path, death has become imminent.

When the Bible speaks of sin, it is not only referring to human's sinful deeds, but to the reality that all of creation has been turned over to the mechanisms of God-less world structures that sell everything for profit, including humans. These structures of sin cause the innocent to suffer alongside the perpetrators, leading the whole world towards a slow but certain death. Though this may sound pessimistic, the world is running towards its painful end simply because humans have sought to become gods in God's stead.

The Curse as a Female Problem

This leads to an inevitable question about the role of women in bringing about these death-dealing structures of the world. Having come through some male-inflicted pain in my own life, and having spent the better part of my life working with women who have had to cope with immense male-inflicted pain, it is difficult to talk about the curse as a female problem. I would much rather skip this section. But if we want to find freedom, we need to have a thorough look at the sins of Eve.

In contemporary society, women are often portrayed as victims of patriarchal systems. The establishment of a *pater familias* has developed into an array of male-dominated structures that domineer women. Though women might not be formally excluded in some cultures today, they experience what is commonly described as a "glass ceiling" experience. Women are invited to contribute to projects, but they are excluded from positions of decision-making or power. Yet rather than describing women as victims of patriarchal processes, the UN suggests that we call them *survivors*. I think this paradigm shift lines up with the biblical story. If women and men are created as equals, then they are equals made in the image of God, and they are also equals in sin.

Although the Bible ascribes the initial sin to Adam, we grew up being told that it was the woman's fault. Women lead men astray. Women trick men into their own ruin. It is women's fault when men abuse them. That woman was dressed inappropriately – that is why she was raped. That woman was abandoned by her spouse and left alone with the children because he could not listen to her complaining. Women are mass murderers because they choose to abort babies. The list is long.

Historically, men have either described women as feeble and ontologically inferior, on the one hand, or sneaky, strong, evil, seductive, and manipulative, on the other. Women have been called many names. Not long ago, a Croatian bishop blamed women for the way boys had become feminine because they had to grow up in single-parent homes. He never mentioned abuse in the home or the fact that men abandon their families![8] Often, these examples are underlined by Bible verses, and women grow up with these Scriptures hanging above their heads, waiting for them to come tumbling down with the wrath of God. From early on, a girl learns that something is wrong with her and her body. While boys may sit as they want, a girl has to learn to keep her knees together. In my own country, I have seen mothers prefer sons to daughters, and I have heard women and men in the Balkan region call their daughters *sine* (son).

I met a woman who was hardly five when her mother stripped off her panties because she repeatedly forgot to keep her knees together while playing

---

8. Plausible research on the reasons for divorce is rare in my country, so my conclusion is based on my counselling experience. A recent doctoral research by Petra Međimurec confirms that after a divorce, women remarry much less often than men, even though their financial situation worsens. Staying unmarried with children is a difficult task, especially since women in Croatia are paid 15% less than men for the same job. Kristina Turčin, "Razvodi u Hrvatskoj: Prva analiza takve vrste ikad napravljena u Hrvtaskoj," *Jutarnji Life* (18 Nov 2017), online: https://www.jutarnji.hr/life/obitelj-i-djeca/prva-analiza-takve-vrste-ikad-napravljena-u-hrvatskoj-evo-zasto-kako-i-kada-krahiraju-brakovi-gradana/6757746/. The mainline church in Croatia is concerned with this fact because they fear that boys are "feminized" by mothers as single parents. For instance: "Nadbiskup Barišić: Otac je postao sporedan, nije dobro da se generacija bez oca feminizira," *IndexHR* (26 Dec 2016), online: https://www.index.hr/vijesti/clanak/nadbiskup-barisic-otac-je-postao-sporedan-nije-dobro-da-se-generacija-bez-oca-feminizira/940101.aspx.

alone in the house. She was made to sit for hours in the corner like this until her father came home, when her mother lifted her dress to expose her nakedness to her father. This grown woman sat crying like a baby in my office, unable to decide what had hurt her more – her mother's action, or her father's silent acceptance of the abuse. "I was hoping my father would take me and clothe me and make it right again," she sobbed. But this never happened. She was left alone, ashamed, angry, and confused about this great "sin" for years to come. In this story, we see a woman and man abusing a little girl just for being a little girl.

Recently, I did some internet research on Female Genital Mutilation (FGM) in Africa and came across a Kenyan woman who is a passionate proponent of this gruesome practice that is inflicted on young girls simply because it is a tradition. Many mothers send their girls through the painful ordeal of FGM and pay for it, which from my Western perspective seems utterly incomprehensible, but should not be.[9] On a trip to the US, I sat down with a woman in a high governmental position, who could not understand my desire for women's equality – particularly women in leadership. She gave me an angry cannonade of insults about women who she knew who had made it to the top: "They are the worst! They are worse than men, a hundred times! If I had the say, I would never allow a woman to sit high up on the ladder!"

These examples all suggest that, as the saying goes, women might be their own worst enemies. As mentioned in the introduction, I have hardly ever come across any student who thought that working with women in the church was important or who wanted to prepare for work with women. As a student myself, I remember praying to God about my ministry and asking God to place me anywhere – *just not with women*. Evidently, God has a great sense of humour!

My resistance to women's work bothered me, but eventually it dawned on me that the problem isn't so much that men don't like women, but that women don't like themselves. The more I investigated this phenomenon, the more I saw how much of the pain and ugliness of the world has been unloaded on women.

---

9. For instance, Siegfried Modola, "In Rural Kenya, Traditions Run Deeper Than Law on Cutting Girls," *Reuters* (12 Nov 2014), online: https://www.reuters.com/article/us-kenya-circumcision-widerimage/in-rural-kenya-traditions-run-deeper-than-law-on-cutting-girls-idUSKCN0IW1BK20141112. However, Kenya is not the only place where this is happening. See report on West Africa, "Female Genital Cutting," *VoA* (28 March 2013), online: https://www.youtube.com/watch?v=tEyaxw4bR2k. Yet the practice is not confined to Africa, as demonstrated by a recent case from the US that made headlines in Europe, where a white woman spoke up against her strict Christian parents, who let her be cut for chastity. E. Batha, "US Woman Says, Strict Christian Parents Subjected Her to FGM," *Thomson Reuters Foundation News* (1 April 2019), online: https://news.trust.org/item/20190401142012-hf8eu/. According to the World Health Organisation, FGM is practiced regardless of religion: *Female Genital Mutilation: A Student's Manual* (Geneva: WHO, 2001), esp. 23.

In considering the problem of women as both victims and perpetrators of female suffering, it is important to look at the initial sin of wanting to be like God and the structures and hierarchies that have been created by this sin. Though women have also wanted to be like God, they have encountered objective obstacles to engaging that war head-on.

One primary obstacle is biological. Though this may sound discriminatory, women are biologically different from men. Their sexual relationships happen within them, and they conceive life and bear children into the world. Though this is a privilege, it is also a huge disadvantage in a world that is structured by sin.[10] I am not suggesting that this biological difference assumes any traditional gender roles. It is not possible to determine what is biologically determined and what is socially constructed, so I will not engage in this discussion. Yet because women bear and tend children, they are often more dependent on other people's nurture and help. They also have a relational bond and feel responsible for the children that were part of them. Men are not as intrinsically dependent on women, and their children have never lived within them, which changes the nature of their relational bond. Giving birth is an amazing experience for women, but it is also a position that makes women more vulnerable than men. Put like this, God's curse to Eve makes a lot of sense: "I will greatly increase your pangs in childbearing; in pain you shall bring forth children, yet your desire shall be for your husband, and he shall rule over you" (Gen 3:16).

This "curse" of the biological challenge for women extends beyond giving birth. Women handle enormous changes within their bodies on a regular basis as they live with varying hormonal levels and experience menstrual pain. Moreover, women can never enter a sexual relationship freely or thoughtlessly, since the "What If?" question is always on their minds: *What if I get pregnant? Do I want children with this man? Do I want children in this stage of life? How will this child change my life? Will I be able to handle the change? Is this man reliable as a father? Can I rely on him to help care for our child?* Contraception

---

10. Research on this is manifold (see for instance, Sascha O. Becker, Anna Fernandez, Doris Weichselbaumer, "Discrimination in Hiring Based on Potential and Realized Fertility: Evidence from a Large-Scale Field Experiment," in *Labour Economics* 19 [2019], 139–152) and it resulted in Europe ratifying the so-called *Istanbul Convention* which brought together all "gender-based violence" and attempted to give legislation some teeth in processing all forms of violence, including structural, social and economic; online: https://rm.coe.int/168046031c. Interestingly, the ratification of this convention has been fought fervently, which is no wonder as it exposes the depth of discrimination against women. Trying to set this right necessarily requires means that governments are not prepared to invest, but more importantly, it upsets large systems based on the exploitation of women and/or their discrimination.

makes sexual relationships easier for women, but they introduce another set of questions about risks, health issues, and moral and religious concerns.

In responding to these challenges, women have become strong, resourceful, and responsible. And yet the ability to bear life has also made women more vulnerable, especially in hierarchical systems that run on material possessions and exploitation, which are driven by power rather than oriented toward life.

While caring for children does not lead one up the ladder, it does have some benefits. Though children are a burden when they are little, they are an asset when they grow up. There is only so much one man can do, but having others do the work for him frees him for climbing up the hierarchies. Acquiring grown slaves is the one way to generate a fast profit, but raising your own children is a less expensive way to acquire a loyal work force, especially in rural societies that are supported by land and food production. Children are still the best and surest retirement investment, as they can continue to work when the parents grow old and feeble. Thus in hierarchical systems, women and children become commodities that enable men to climb up hierarchical ladders. Though this generalization has become more nuanced in our technical, urban age, the rhetoric of culture around the world suggests that is not far off the grid.

All hierarchies depend on myths to uphold them. Though these differ from place to place, they carry the same essential message. The recent Twitter hashtag, "What Women Hear In Church," reveals the role of the church in perpetuating these myths that uphold the structures of sin.

There is a wide perception that Croatian women in rural regions consider it acceptable for a man to beat them "if they deserved it."[11] Though rural women in Croatia tend to be Catholic, I have seen enough evangelical cases to know that denomination is not the defining role. Usually, in Christian counselling, these women are advised to "keep quiet and carry their crosses as God intended it," because this is their calling to benefit their families. This myth of the adult woman who deserves to be punished physically by her husband reveals deep-seated convictions about women's place in the Slavonian hierarchy, as the women are taught that it is acceptable for men to beat women when it is for their own good. This myth gives men the right to determine when women have behaved out of line and when they need to be punished. The myth also reveals

---

11. I remember reading a newspaper article about this in *Glas Slavonije* some years back, which suggested that roughly 64% of women believe that it is all right for a man to hit his wife if she deserves it. My own work with women confirms this high percentage. In counselling, abused women tend to be surprised by the question, "Who determines that you have earned punishment?"

that women accept the conviction that men can determine these things, even if they may occasionally disagree with their judgment.

This myth has several other implications that the church has failed to consider. The church teaches these women to put up with abuse because marriage is God-ordained, and so it must be maintained by any means. The church also teaches these women that men own them and can do what they want with them ("A man is king in his own castle!"). Thus their relationship is not the partnership described in Genesis, but that of a master and a slave, where women are commodities rather than a people.

Historically, at the Council of Mâcon in 585, the church discussed whether women had souls, and only one voice weighed in their favour. Some argue against this council, since only Protestants refer to it, and it has disappeared from official books, but I am encouraged that at least there was a majority (although tight) in the church who looked at this teaching and saw where it was going.[12] All these myths suggest that women are to blame for the violence that is inflicted on them when they have done something to make men angry. In this way, man's sins are blamed on the "woman who you gave to me" (Gen 3:12).

As natural victims in the structures of sin, women and their children often suffer trauma, with varying levels of severity depending on the level and type of abuse (physical, psychological, or both). But victimization often leads to lashing out, finding ways to retaliate against the perpetrator, or to let off steam against those who are weaker. Children who grow up in abusive homes become collateral damage, believing that violence is the only reaction to the excessive anger they feel.

But in all this, women are not innocent. They are also guilty of vicarious violence, particularly the violence of passive aggression. From a biblical perspective, women also succumb to the desire to be God. I have recognized at least three ways that women struggle for a deified position.

---

12. See also fn 5 on pg 17 on the Council of Lyon; the names are used exchangeably and sometimes the years differ. This can be attributed to the fact that these councils went on for years, and the bishop of Lyon seemed to preside. Adriana Valerio affirms the council in "Women in Church History" in *Women: Invisible in Church and Theology*, ed. E. Schüssler Fiorenza and Mary Collins (Edinburgh: T & T Clark, 1985), 63. Criticizing this information as "liberal demonology given to historical events that never happened," see Michael Nolan, "Do Women Have Souls?" online at: *ChurchHistory Information Centre* http://www.churchinhistory.org/pages/booklets/women-souls-1.htm. It seems to me that given the climate of the medieval church and other writings of church leaders in that period, the likelihood of such discussion is both embarrassing and probable.

The Goddess

Men who are situated at the top of a hierarchy often try to acquire a goddess, a woman that has climbed to the top of a beauty hierarchy through pageants and beauty contests. Having a beautiful goddess at one's side is an additional proof of a man's success, for every god needs a goddess. There is a whole industry that supports goddesses, and a constant war about who is more beautiful, which is supported by ever-changing fashion trends, expensive salons, pedicures, manicures. Being a goddess takes a lot of work and money, but if the right man comes along, it will all pay off, for a man of stature will pamper his goddesses because her beauty adds to his status in the world.

Yet goddesses pay a huge price for this status, as they have to surrender their other gifts to the pursuit of beauty. Nevertheless, a whole culture of mothers teaches their daughters (sometimes as early as two or three years old) that if they want a good life, they need to win beauty contests. In most cultures, women are taught that getting a man as soon as possible and as high up the hierarchy as possible will ensure her a good life. Unfortunately, when sex and money are no longer satisfying, goddesses often realize that they want a life for themselves apart from their successful husbands. Moreover, when they lose their looks (and beauty is temporary, as we all know), they are usually exchanged for a younger goddess. Other women often look at goddesses as witches and fear that they will lure away their husbands, jeopardizing their own positions.

The Matron (Holy Mother)

The status of motherhood is much more stable for women, because the mother bears useful subjects and a large work force of dependents, who add prestige to the father's hierarchical status. These dependents are also emotionally tied to the mother, which gives her power. Though the power of matrons may be not as immediately visible in modern society as it was in the past, it is apparent to a young wife when her husband cannot help but run home to mom, or to a young husband when his wife spends hours on the phone with her mother.

In the contemporary Western world, there is a sociological subcategory of "yummy mommies," who are well-educated, stay-at-home moms with a couple of children. They engage the internet for endless advice on child rearing, nutrition, medical care, beauty, and fitness. They work hard to maintain their youthful looks and engage with other "yummy mommies" at prominent cafes. Their husbands tend to be highly paid IT specialists and other CEOs on their way to conquer the world, while their wives hold up their fort at home.

There are many advantages to being a matron or "yummy mommy." This status gives them some authority over the household matters and the children, which are areas that men tend to despise. If a woman can stay happy within these boundaries (and many women seemingly can), then this might seem to be a perfect match. Nevertheless, many matrons feel unfulfilled, at least when their nest becomes empty. They often try to continue living through their husbands and children, but they want to live their own lives without the constant interference of their mother or wife. As a self-sacrificial victim, the matron may think she has earned the right to live through them, as she has given her life, potential, and sleepless nights to them. Her manipulative demands on others strangle relationships. No wonder Freud described them as "hysteric."

The Dragon Woman

Some women, who are often more qualified and determined than their male counterparts, seek to face male structures head-on and to climb those hierarchical ladders just as ruthlessly as men. These women are often described as "emotionless," "masculine," or "dragon women." As they fight for their rights, they become tough and aggressive, determined to prove that they are capable of any position – even if they need to rely on deceit, self-deceit, self-denial, violence, or destruction.

When these women reach the top of male-dominated hierarchies, they can become as brutal as men in their everyday management of their subordinates. They can be especially hard on quiet or submissive women who do not fight directly for positions, but assume them via the achievements of their men. Given the opposition, injustices, and violence that "dragon" women have had to face on their way up the hierarchical ladder, they can become ruthless executives. But these women have had to make huge sacrifices to get to the top, often giving up dreams and deep relationships with family and friends. Goddesses and matrons tend to hate the female dragon, because she rocks their safe place and points to the confines of their existence. She is a reminder that they have potential that could not be developed.

Moreover, women also get abused by the male structures. For instance, modern Western institutions that want to show an egalitarian face might appoint women to sit on their boards, but they often choose a beautiful and silent woman, often referred to as an *ikebana* (a "flower arrangement").[13] This

---

13. This was a common expression by frustrated feminists in the times of Yugoslavian communism. It is claimed that Yugoslavian feminists won a huge victory at the end of World War II. The constitution of Yugoslavia and its diverse documents and laws proscribed equality of

practice is not only humiliating and useless, it is also tragic and contrary to gender equality, as the women who are chosen often become objects for moral licensing – that is, they are the reason that boards, companies, and also churches feel morally entitled not to consider other capable women for such positions anymore. They have done their share of inclusion.

Women of all three types are victims of an oppressive hierarchical system that they sustain by playing along with its rules. Though the system does not satisfy anyone, everyone plays along. When men identify women as commodities, they are deprived of authentic partnerships and become objectified as providers of their livelihood and security.

The Curse as a Problem of the Earth

This brings us to the effects of the curse on the earth, which is also affected by human structures of sin. Even though the earth had nothing to do with human sin, the earth's curse is intrinsically bound to the curse of humans (Gen 3:17b). We see the effects of the curse when humans try to impose themselves over a creation that is not easily subdued. We also see it in our current global sustainability crisis and the effects of climate change and the diminishing quality of food, water, and air.

Yet the environment is fighting back with natural disasters, such as floods, tsunamis, drought, heavy winds, and hail. The excess plastic in the ocean is

---

women as an "outright result of the struggle of the women themselves through their feminist and anti-fascistic female organizations before and during the War" in 1945. But already in 1959, the Anti-Fascist Women's Front supposedly suspended itself as obsolete. That is the official version. Behind the scenes, these women's groups were becoming too annoying to the Party, pointing out its repeated shortcomings of putting the laws into practice! For the Party, that was it: the laws were put in place and will eventually sort themselves out when all the comrades have been properly educated. Later, Yugoslavian feminists came to disagree with this optimism. When their "militant" organization was terminated, they claim, the women were practically again at square one: they were either *ikebanas* on the diverse boards to prove the ideology of equality right (with no real voice); or they had the fake choice between staying at home and getting a "female" low-paying job. Comp. N. Ler Sofronič, "Fragmenti ženskih sjećanja, 1978. i danas," ed. u Dugandžić Živanović D. ProFemina 2. Online: http://pro-femina.eu/ProFeminasadrzaj_specijalni_broj_2_leto-jesen_2011.html; N. Božinović, "Istorija ženskog pokreta' Beograd: Autonomni ženski centar," available at www.womenngo.org.rs/content/blogcategory/28/61/; also H. Markuse's deliberations on "repressive tolerance" in R. P. Wolff, B. Moore Jr. and H. Markuse, *A Critique of Pure Tolerance* (Boston: Beacon, 1969), 84–85. See also Tanja Topić I dr. *Akademija političkog osnaživanja žena: Učešće žena u politici*, Canada Fund for Local Initiative and Transparency International Bosnia and Hercegovina (Banja Luka: Grafix, 2017), 53.

coming back as "food" to human tables.¹⁴ Hormones and antibiotics used in raising of animals for food comes back to haunt humans through various illnesses and resistance to drugs.¹⁵ Instead of obedience, creation produces what its self-made lord thinks he did not sow: fruit that is not food, for it does not sustain life, but harms him.

In the nineteenth and twentieth centuries, the vast majority of the earth's population was thrilled with the achievements of science. Science seemed like the amazing cure to the inability of humans to govern and impose their will on nature. Science identified the principles that made creation tick. As atomic power was invented, people raved about the excess energy that could be used to light up the whole world. Modern technology was expanding food production at a rate that would eliminate hunger from the earth. Modern medicine would do away with sickness and death. Everyone would have access to information, and so people could no longer be manipulated by a lack of information.

Many people still believe in this fairy tale and cite statistics that suggest the world is improving.¹⁶ However, one must read statistics with caution, since they tend to consult the advanced economies in the world that still show a steady growth in GDP. For instance, the marker, "more people living in democracies," does not mean that all people are living in freedom, for liberal democracies (where all people are granted freedom), are different from majority-rule democracies (where minorities are often persecuted). Though life expectancy has increased and fewer people are living in extreme poverty, disaster and hardship remain everywhere. Though wars aren't being waged in the affluent world, the "great powers" have been involved in numerous local conflicts, leaving the rest of the world with the constant expectation of a major war. Statistics don't do much to help the world. We have now been catapulted into the IT era, and yet for all the mind-blowing breakthroughs in science, things have not changed much. The A-bombs that hit Hiroshima and Nagasaki in 1945 serve as a symbol of science's twin faces for all times. Any invention can either be used to benefit or harm people. If it is intended to benefit people, it will probably be sold for a profit, and the rich will get richer, and the poor will

---

14. See C. Smith, "Here's How Much Plastic You Eat Every Year," *Huffpost* (7 June 2019). Online: https://www.huffpost.com/entry/microplastic-food-bottled-water_n_5cf93154e4b0e3e3df16ab9d.

15. See W. Witte, "Medical Consequences of Antibiotic Use in Agriculture," *Science* (1998): 996–997.

16. J. Probst, "Seven Reasons Why the World Is Improving," *BBC Future* (11 Jan 2019). Online: https://www.bbc.com/future/article/20190111-seven-reasons-why-the-world-is-improving.

become poorer much more easily and swiftly (something even Probst admits in his optimistic article).[17] The 2008 global financial crisis was caused by people who abused technology and knowledge for their own benefit, leaving families who trusted the banking system homeless practically overnight. Things have certainly not changed for the Majority World, as an abyss remains between the third that is comparably well off and the two-thirds who struggle immensely. It is a matter of time before the two-thirds will rebel against the system, which relies on the myth of constant growth and prosperity for those who are wealthy. This rebellion, it seems to me, is already seen in economic migrations from the East to the West and from the South to the North.

Worldwide, enough food was produced in 2012 for ten or twelve billion people – an amount that far exceeds what is needed for our current world population of just over seven billion. Yet a large proportion of the population remain hungry and cannot afford to buy food. On the other hand, the surplus food is so cheap that it is being thrown out. "Hunger is caused by poverty and inequality, not scarcity," concludes Eric Holt-Gimenez, the director of Food First. To resolve the inequality, he says that poor farmers need to receive enough land and means to run small organic farms. In view of climate change, he suggests that if this doesn't happen, it will be an "unsustainable no."[18] Most people in the world still live in inhumane circumstances, unable to produce enough to live and blocked from access to technology and medicine. The one-third who have enough money have easy and cheap access to the resources of the poor. The few human gods at the top of the world's hierarchies rule over the food as well. When we read about the 90 billion dollars owned by some merchant, we don't consider the fact that those dollars really belong to the people who produced whatever is being sold. Eradicating extreme poverty is one of the goals on the UN agenda, but the progress is slow. We should not be surprised. In human divinity, privilege is never abandoned voluntarily, but lost in combat.

Technological progress has been achieved on the backs of the poor, who are kept poor through exploitation. Those who sit at the top of the hierarchy say that people are poor because they "just don't want to work," or because "they

---

17. J. Probst, "Seven Reasons."

18. E. Holt-Gimenez, "We Already Grow Enough Food for 10 Billion People – And Still Can't End Hunger," *HuffPost* (5 Feb 2012). Online: https://www.huffpost.com/entry/world-hunger_b_1463429?guccounter=1&guce_referrer=aHR0cHM6Ly93d3cuZ29vZ2xlLmNvbS8&guce_referrer_sig=AQAAAKC4XP2emPOO0UfeQxjz9KCTO0cpAU_0y-cU_J2etLe8H9fM2Qhrk6B6fukok-Hc1qzbjeVr7xoYgGXtqbhqtlE-Jhpiswelf2ONSIwbiJJ_ZdjizrGA3C2neuLi4-ijKlEhUCMaLsnNjK8e2BRV9ZLNQ9sniNjGJUW5qq9uUcQA.

do not believe in God, and if they did, things would miraculously change for them." Such myths are rationalizations to soothe the affluent mind. Christians should strive to see those living in the Majority World as brothers and sisters. We need to take responsibility for how our affluent lifestyles oppress and rob them. Requesting justice for the poor does not diminish the gospel of Christ. Chris Caldwell observes that "when we stand opposed to any remedy that takes into account that descendants of slaves did not, and still do not, begin the economic, educational and social race at the same starting line, our children catch the concept: 'Oh, I see, if blacks are behind and no accommodation needs to be made in the race, then there's something wrong with them, and something right about us, since we're ahead.'"[19] Though Caldwell is writing about the race issue in the US, his words are true for poverty and inequality around the globe. People buy into privilege easily, and it is extremely hard for them to let go of its benefits or to stop believing that they did not earn the privilege. There is no sustainability without a just distribution of resources and knowledge for all. Yet it is difficult to control advanced technologies, which can be used to exploit those who have no access or have limited knowledge. At the beginning of the last century, the promise that everyone would have equal access to the information and benefits of science sounded promising, but it has been pragmatically relegated to those with money at the top of the hierarchical systems.

The richest people in the world are involved in trade, selling energy, luxury, and advanced technology, but it would be unfair to blame everything on them, especially since there are far more poor people. The truth is, the poor also try to climb up the ladder to live in the vicinity of human gods.

A British Jamaican historian once complained to me that after the end of colonialism, nothing much changed. "For some unclear reason, the roles of the whites have been taken up by some local people, who started behaving like the former slave owners towards their own people." This is hard to understand, but privilege and rationalization go hand in hand.

The world seems to be under a curse, and most people have accepted this system – just as long as they can continue with their small lives. Those who rule people settle for their own small privileges, making politicians the most unpopular people in the world. Although we call them civil servants, Jeremy

---

19. C. Caldwell, "Ten Bogus Ideas My White Culture Taught Me Growing Up," *Baptist News Global* (20 Jan 2019), online: https://baptistnews.com/article/10-bogus-ideas-my-white-culture-taught-me-growing-up/#.XbkOBuhKhPY.

Paxman concludes, "You cannot trust politicians!"[20] I would add that we cannot trust ourselves, either! A Lutheran humanitarian friend who worked with us during the war in Croatia and has travelled through many war-torn areas throughout the world concluded, "I have no idea what I would be like given the ordeal of the victims, or the power of the perpetrators." All Christians should ponder this confession.

The Apostle Paul associates the cure for the hopelessly ruined creation with the Spirit of God, who indwells Christians and therefore the church. In Paul's words, the creation eagerly awaits the "glorious revelation of the children of God" because that will also mean the healing of the entire creation as it participates in this glorious freedom with the children of God (Rom 8:19–22). We will return to this thought in "Bearing Fruit – The *Sarks* and *Soma* Dichotomy in Paul" as we examine Romans 8, 1 Corinthians 11, and Galatians 5 in more detail.

Thus the curse can be easily observed in people's lives and relationships and also how the world functions politically, sociologically, socially, ecologically, and scientifically. Though occasional expressions of mercy may bring about some benefits or partial improvements, everything good is destroyed by human selfishness. As Christians, we expect the church to demonstrate a hope for salvation to the world.

But in the aftermath of #ChurchToo, we must admit that churches are contributing to the pain of the world rather than offering hope, healing, or salvation. Does this mean the church is just another earthly institution?

---

20. J. Paxman, "Why We Can't Trust Politicians," online: https://www.youtube.com/watch?v=uUlv6r8c_hI.

2

Church Structures as Structures of Sin

Though the church has been around for two millennia, and it has conquered most of the world's nations, we have not seen this glorious revelation of God's children and its vision of salvation for the whole creation. Rather, the church is being accused of having played a major role in cursing the world – not blessing it. In the name of Christ's church, many parts of Africa and Asia have been exploited, and Christian mission endeavours throughout the nineteenth century have generally been refuted as imperial cultural conquests.[1] As victims speak up, sex scandals by church leaders are uncovered. A huge pile of sin seems to linger over the church. Was Paul wrong about his projections for the glory of the children of God? As a Christian writing for Christians, this is not an easy chapter to examine. And yet, only sincere self-critical evaluation and repentance can show us the way forward. Though Christians are generally sincere about the importance of personal repentance, they can be blind to systemic sin. We have established doctrines that separate sin into superficial categories, making it difficult to confront sin, particularly regarding the taboo subjects of money, sex, and power. From a global perspective, the church is misrepresenting both Scripture and God when it blesses the curse by adopting

---

1. For instance, R. Dunch, "Beyond Cultural Imperialism: Cultural Theory, Christian Missions, and Global Modernity," *History and Theory* 41, no. 3 (2002): 301–325, attempts to define cultural imperialism and how it impinges on Christian mission. He suggests that if there is "a single group most commonly held to exemplify the operation of cultural imperialism in modem history, it would have to be Christian missionaries. The assertion that missionaries were implicated in imperialist expansion precedes the more recent theoretical discussions of cultural imperialism by several decades, extending back to attacks on the missionary enterprise by nationalist critics in China and elsewhere in the 1920s. Missionaries are routinely portrayed in both literature and scholarship as narrow-minded chauvinists whose presence and preaching destroyed indigenous cultures and opened the way for the extension of colonial rule" (307).

worldly criteria about subjects that are so central to the way things work in the world.

One such superficial belief is that the curse in Genesis 3 is a prescription for Christians and God's will for the world. In this view, God established a hierarchical structure, where men must rule over women because women are not fit to live without men.[2] Moreover, if men are ordained by God to rule, then they must have dominion over all of creation, and they must exploit the world and its resources because the world was created for that purpose. These premises have been widely attacked theologically, but they have proven stubbornly resistant to change in the Christian church.

Another superficial belief that diminishes the "glory of the children of God" in the world is escapist eschatology, which claims that the world is destined to go up in flames.[3] Such interpretations read Genesis 3 over Genesis 1 and ignore the overarching theme of God's salvation for the world in Christ, who abolishes the curse. We need to read both Genesis 1 and 3 through the Christ story of a redeemed creation, as the Apostle Paul does in Romans 1–8. The Bible is not so much a set of doctrines, nor a divine philosophy that we accept without question, but a story about God's love for the world and a vision about God's people as co-labourers for a renewed creation. People who stand humbly before God can participate in God's original plan by becoming a blessing to others and the world.

My reading has been largely shaped by a single line in Miroslav Volf's systematic theology class: "The church is a charismatically structured, eschatological community." The church is *charismatically* structured, because the Spirit gives believers the gift of life and all other gifts. Because the Spirit gives these gifts, they are meant to be expressed in the church by the people who have received them. We are not meant to ask the usual questions about

---

2. See W. Grudem, *Systematic Theology* (Downers Grove: InterVarsity Press, 1994), 439–453. Grudem begins his anthropology by insisting that "the practice of using the same term to refer (1) to male human beings and (2) to the human race generally is a practice that originated with God himself" (440) and therefore we should not find it "objectionable or insensitive." For me, this is a major problem of method, because it does not take into account the history of tradition, especially oral tradition and the *Sitz im Leben* (that is, the primary context) in which the traditional material was first delivered, especially for material concerning primeval history. This interpretation is the basis for Grudem's "complementarity" of male and female, deducing, I suppose, that if man is sometimes equal in meaning to the male, then female must *a priori* be an appendix to humanity. Men could live without women, but not vice versa.

3. An example of this can be observed in the recent article by the Australian, Ken Ham, "Is There Hope for This Planet." Online at *Answers in Genesis:* https://answersingenesis.org/racism/is-there-hope-for-this-planet/.

social exclusion. The structure of the church is compared to a body – it is not meant to be chaos. Though there is a God-given ministerial structure in the Bible, there is no hierarchy, where some rule over others. The church is *eschatological* in the way it models the circumstances of God's future in the world. In the now of humanity and its structures of sin, it is a community that lives by a different law. There are no solo Christians that demonstrate God's purpose for the world on their own. In the many years of my ministry to the local and global church, I have observed Volf's little sentence to be true.

The church is meant to be led and structured by the Spirit so that all its members contribute to one another's growth and minister to each other. As the church grows, its members are transformed to the likeness of Christ. As they are thus transformed, they will go out and meet the needs of the world and seek to change its circumstances. Such a community does not talk, but shows to the world what God's eternity could look like if people embraced and lived out God's will.

This does not suggest that the church can or will bring about God's kingdom to the earth. As we shall see a little later, Paul emphasizes both aspects: first, the final revelation of the children of God is a promised event that will be fulfilled in the future; second, God has already started to fulfil this promise for those who are his. Paul insists that only God can fully transform the structures of sin. But he also insists that the resurrecting Spirit of God lives in the believers and resurrects them to new life within the structures of sin (Rom 8:11). Paul expects the church to be led by God's Spirit of resurrection to break the structures of sin in their environments. The Spirit of God that was upon Jesus and his ministry has not changed. When Jesus says that the prophetic word from Isaiah 61:1–4 is fulfilled in him (Luke 4:18) by the Spirit of God, it is also fulfilled in those who have his Spirit, for "Anyone who does not have the Spirit of Christ does not belong to him" (Luke 8:9). Unfortunately, churches often express the culture of the structures of sin rather than God's eschatology. Even more troubling, many church members actually believe that these structures of sin are God-ordained, and so they see themselves as keepers of certain kinds of human culture – as if the culture were eternal rather than God's vision of salvation for the world. Such Christians feed on rigid legalism and harsh boundaries around leadership roles, yet their rules are often only enforced for others but rationalized in their own lives.

In our internet age, every scandal in the church can be blown up out of proportion and exposed for everyone to see. Whenever people who should be caring for others abuse or hurt them, hope for the future is diminished.

No wonder the youth of this generation feel a general state of confusion and apathy.[4] When the church fails to live up to its mission to reflect God's eternity, the world neither hears nor believes its messages of hope. When Christians behave like the rest of the world, there is no good news. To respond to this dilemma, we need to look at the Christian church critically, particularly at how it promotes and even ordains structures of sin as divine. This will not be an easy chapter to read, but in order to change, we have to reckon with our failures.

Hierarchies as Sanctifying the Curse

In the groundbreaking book *Die Soziologie der Jesusbewegung: Ein Beitrag zur Entstehungsgeschichte des Urchristentums*, Gerd Theißen describes the unavoidable destiny of any movement – becoming an organization with fixed leadership positions and hierarchies.[5] E. Schüssler Fiorenza adds to Theißen's thesis by recognizing that women typically leave leadership positions after a movement becomes an organization.[6] In a movement, leaders work hard, endure strife on a daily basis, and receive little gratuity for their toil. In an organizational structure, leaders secure power and often receive economic gratification. This is an important finding that can be easily observed on many levels and in many situations in churches. Although churches and Christian organizations should pay their workers fairly, churches often approach this issue in an inequitable way that resembles secular organizations. In fact, churches can be even worse. In most places I visited, there were only rare examples of equal employment or equal pay for men and women who were ministering full-time in the church.

Research has shown that such hierarchical structures cripple an organization's development[7] by seeking to accommodate leaders and ensure

---

4. Kate Lyons gives an overview of the issues troubling them in "Generation Y, Curling or Maybe: What the World Calls Millenials," *The Guardian* (8 March 2016). Online: https://www.theguardian.com/world/2016/mar/08/generation-y-curling-or-maybe-what-the-world-calls-millennials. "It is perhaps these troubles [e.g. in Spain: '*ni trabaja, ni estudia*', or terrorism, or a plethora of options with no idea how to choose, or loneliness] and their concern about the future that lead millennials to be, by and large, a serious generation, less prone to either the wild optimism or hedonism of their forebears, leading Norwegian millennials to be christened *Generasjon Alvor*, or Generation Serious, in 2011."

5. Gerd Theißen, *Die Soziologie der Jesusbewegung: Ein Beitrag zur Entstehungsgeschichte des Urchristentums* (Tübingen: Mohr/Siebeck, 1989), 79–105, 268.

6. E. Schüssler Fiorenza, *Zu ihrem Gedächnis* (München: Kaiser, 1988), 123–124.

7. See a short, but revealing, sketch by Jens Rinnelt, "Bottom-up Approach," *Human Business* (8 December 2016). Online: http://www.humanbusiness.eu/bottom-up-approach/.

their longevity in the organization rather than focusing on the cause for which the organization exists. Hierarchies also become battlefields, where the struggle for influence and power is the leading motive for existence. In some cases, hierarchies despise and belittle the people at the bottom – or, for a church, those in the pews – and those who are at the bottom don't realize the strength being wielded by the leaders at the top, who so closely represent the cause. The Baptist tradition insists, unlike some other traditions, on the priesthood of all believers.[8] One reason I remain Baptist is their commitment to involving all church members in the daily decision-making process of the church (and anyone who has decided to be a member is included). Yet in spite of this biblical determination to involve all, hierarchies of men often degrade the importance of the "other priests" in local churches (women in particular, though it could be anyone whom the gods have relegated to lower positions). They, too, often believe that someone has to have the last word in a dispute. But this belief is part of the hierarchies of sin and develops from the idea that some have the power to rule over others. An institution that takes the route of equality under Christ and servant leadership will find ways to include, rather than exclude, and to work in everyone's interest.

To give contextual examples of how the sanctification of the curse by the church is impacting the global stage, I would like to examine some issues that are at the forefront of the UN's sustainable development agenda.[9] Projections for sustainability are gloomy, although there have been attempts to downplay the gloom.

Sustainability & Migration

Sustainability refers to efforts to respond to the ecological devastation of the earth and the real shortages of food and water that will impact many places on the planet – though there is enough food for all at the moment. Many anticipate that this devastation will cause wars in the future, particularly since

---

8. See, for instance, *The Second London Confession*, Chapter XXVI.2: "Of the Church" which refers to believers as "all persons" regardless of the otherwise common generic "man": "All persons throughout the world, professing the faith of the Gospel, and obedience unto God by Christ, according unto it; . . . may be called visible Saints and of all such ought all particular Congregations to be constituted," according to W. L. Lumpkin, *Baptist Confessions of Faith* (Valley Forge: Judson Press, 1969), 285.

9. For a number of years now, the UN advertises Sustainable Development goals. Among them are several that push sustainability. Goal #5 on Gender Equality is considered basic to sustainability. See, for instance, online: https://www.un.org/sustainabledevelopment/sustainable-development-goals/.

the war industry has never been as advanced and innovative as it is now. If the entertainment industry can be seen as prophetic – and they have been in the past – the scenario for sustainability is bleak.

Through the anti-terrorism acts in the West, people are giving up privacy for security. Even the mandatory "cookies" that automatically spy on our internet preferences can be used against us, as the system can be used to prohibit our individual decision making. One diabolical human mind who thinks he is God can do great evil when given access to so much information and power. Though this is not a new concern, it has become more threatening because of the power of the technology to reach out globally.

This scenario has already been described in the Bible. Revelation describes the "universal" circumstances of the Roman Empire and how its "divine" ruler and "lord" could use those circumstances against Christians who wanted to remain loyal to God. In *Homo Geographicus*, Robert Sack refers to humans in a global society as Leviathans – the monstrously dangerous biblical beast[10] – precisely because of how their impact on the earth is being multiplied.[11] In antiquity, the Roman Empire was not really universal, and it lacked technologies for perfect surveillance, but in our global era that is supported by so many technologies, those who are considered to be outcasts struggle to live outside of the system. This tragedy is already visible in the migrant crises and the way that the world is handling "migrants." According to the UN, almost 300 million people roamed the world as migrants in 2019, and few found shelter.[12] Once on the move, people risk becoming permanently homeless. For instance, refugee camps were established in 1985 in the northwest of Thailand for the Karen people from Burma (today Myanmar), and they are still being run as refugee camps today. Even worse, the Rohingya people, a Muslim group, has been hosted by Bangladesh in a refugee camp since 1975, with no developments. People live as permanent outcasts with little prospect of a future. Those who are by definition "earthlings" and are bound to their places have become displaced and declared placeless by others. Though this story is hard and disturbing, it is even more disturbing that so many "good" Christians are driven by fear and

---

10. Job 40:25–41:26.

11. Robert D. Sack, *Homo Geographicus* (Baltimore: Johns Hopkins University Press, 1997), 7–26.

12. According to one article, less than 564 people (out of the 600,000 migrants that crossed through Croatia in 2015–2016) were granted asylum since 2006 in Croatia. See M. Pauček Šljivak, "Bojite se migranata?," Index.hr (1 November 2018). Online: https://www.index.hr/vijesti/clanak/bojite-se-migranata-evo-koliko-ih-je-u-zadnjih-12-godina-ostalo-u-hrvatskoj/2036314.aspx.

despise refugees. These Christians have never contemplated the implications of Psalm 24: "The earth is the LORD's and all that is in it, the world, and those who live in it" (v. 1). God, the giver of life, calls everyone into being on this earth. While life may be easier when we live among those who have been socialized in a similar way, we will inevitably undergo the experience of meeting others who are very different. When migrants come to live near us, or when we have to migrate, we are forced into this situation.

Yet migration happens for a reason, and a commitment to basic human rights must allow space for it. Our fear of migrants stems from our fear of the other, but it is nurtured by our medieval tradition of land ownership. Those who rule a nation make the laws, and religious laws are particularly important for uniformity – *cuius regio, eius religio* (whose realm, his religion). Yet in this belief, the structures of sin victimize others and deny them the right to existence. Christians cannot bless this curse by blaming the victims for the "crime" of looking to find a place to live.

Sustainability & Gender Equality

Another area where Christians all too readily support a structure of sin is through gender inequality. The UN's emphasis on the equal inclusion of women in leadership positions and finances goes against many traditions that relegate women to the lowest stratum. In UN jargon, there are two ways for women to be agents for sustainability. First, they make up roughly 50 percent of the world's population. If half of the world is silenced and their potential and gifts are quenched, then the world is only functioning on one half of its potential. Second, children depend on their mothers, and so if there is a lack of care and options for women, this will negatively impact the well-being of future generations, of nations in general, and the global population – including men.

Moreover, those who are negligent and abusive of women are also – because of the functioning of the structures of sin – often abusive of God's creation, which further impinges on the future. Thus the UN promotes the inclusion of women in all ruling structures and advocates legislation to ensure sustainability. Yet even though women need to be at the core of common global interests, the Consultations on the Status of Women (CSW) forums suggest that even the most cataclysmic predictions for the earth are not averting the irrational interests of the predominantly male hierarchical structures around the globe. Breakthroughs in equal participation take a long time and often seem insignificant. In addition, as one layer of discrimination is removed, new enslaving traditions emerge.

Sustainability, Equality & Legislation

From earlier reflections on the curse and the structures of sin, the main obstacle to the earth's prosperity seems ontological and therefore dependent on the nature of humans. People need to change from within, letting go of their preoccupations with themselves and their own profits. This is not a new question: how can we accomplish, order, legislate, and implement this intrinsic change? Can we legislate people's being?

This question was already raised by the Apostle Paul in his letter to the Romans. Naturally, he raises it in the context of the usefulness of the Mosaic law for his people. He concludes that any people will be dreadfully misled if they believe that laws can save them. Even at their best, laws sanction a deed that has already been done. They cannot force or motivate people to obedience. In my own region, people seem more motivated to avoid, find holes, and skip over laws or interpret away the critical matter at hand. Laws are there to be broken!

Laws are also abused and used to hurt people who should benefit from them. In our region at least, when a politician swears that "everything has been done by the law," the public can assume that some grave injustice has been done. The bureaucratic state establishment constantly adjusts laws instead of furthering their implementation for the least. Even the adjustments to the European legislation, which is often perceived as superior to our own, prevent justice by constantly changing the law.

I recall a high-positioned officer who was fighting human trafficking proudly explaining, "We constantly adjust legislation to that of the European Union. We have the best and most up-to-date legislation!" Her enthusiasm was gone when asked about the results of their work. She admitted, finally, that they did not bring many cases to justice. Her pursuit of legislation made her equally blind for options outside her job in legislation. She maintained that churches could not do anything regarding human trafficking, and so they should leave the job to people (like herself) who knew the laws. When stopping demand was mentioned as an area where churches could help immensely, she laughed out loud and said, "Yes, out there, that's the new buzz word. I can only say that in my experience, boys will always be boys!"

Legislation is not only unhelpful, but it is often blind to justice and how to achieve it. At best, legislation punishes evil after the fact, which hardly helps the victims. Stabbed or shot victims find no satisfaction in the perpetrator's prison time. Lame laws are often guarded by equally lame bureaucrats – not only in places like Eastern Europe, but also in highly developed democracies. I have listened to testimony in a CSW breakout session by women from Iceland who tried to persuade their chief of police to prosecute those who were buying sex rather than the prostitutes. He laughed in the face of legislation: "I have no intention or manpower to prosecute the 'Johns.' It is impossible," he allegedly told them. But these women organized an event promising exotic dancing and demanded registration. Subsequently, they escorted a whole hall of men to the chief's offices, showing that it could be done. When the registrations were processed, it became evident that many were already in police records for various crimes.

Legislation does not really change anything. Rather than motivating people towards the good, it lets them find more intricate ways to commit crimes. UN research has shown that between 2015 and 2020, twenty-eight trillion dollars could have been gained for the world economy if women had been given equal opportunities to men in higher leadership positions and equal access to resources. However, the study also claimed that it might take 138 years for the same outcome at the current rate of female involvement. With the turn to the right around the globe, even these 138 years seem to be an optimistic projection. When all laws and logic speak for those who are benefited by systems of sin, the world remains stubborn and set in its ways. The rulers often only see their own immediate profit.

So where does one start the change, if not with the laws? Social media recently carried outcries by individuals who were demanding an intrinsic change of human beings to help sustainability. To me, this is a confirmation of what the Christian faith offers, which has always featured changed hearts and insisted on selflessly sharing with others and putting others first. When we trust that God loves and cares for all his creation and for all who believe in him in particular, we have the strength to do what is illogical from the perspective of the structures of sin and stand up for others. Christians have faith that God cares for them while they work for the benefit of others.

In addition, in its earliest creeds, the church defined herself as "catholic" (from gr. *catholicos*, or "general"). Thus people of any race, social status, nation, or gender are welcome – and equally so. Christianity is also the oldest universal institution, with branches throughout the world, and hardly any geographical areas where it is not represented. Logically, the 2.2 billion adherents to the Christian faith (as of 2010) should be able to accomplish the change towards just and sustainable living on earth if they truly believed God and worked for the common good. Malcom Gladwell showed that very few people (sometimes even less than 5 percent) could bring about the tipping point of social change.[13]

---

13. M. Gladwell, *The Tipping Point: How Little Things Can Make a Big Difference* (Lebanon: Back Bay Books, 2002), 19.

So why is this holy third of the world unable to bring about change? Sadly, and for many reasons, the church betrays its faith. It adapts itself to living according to the curse. It gives up on the paradigm of salvation in Christ in its everyday living, sometimes for pious reasons, but often because it is easier. Many church doctrines have been shaped by the culture of death that reflects the structures of sin and the curse rather than Jesus's countercultural life and salvation.

In the following section, we will trace how the paradigm of the fall permeates the life of the church, making it one of the main obstacles to life. Then we will search for theological reasons that may explain the phenomenon and suggest what can be done.

Church Hierarchies as Systems of Abuse

We have already discussed how hierarchies of power are a logical outcome of a world that is defined by the fall. Because we have turned away from God and sought to be like God in the godless realms we have created, our state is defined by loneliness, feelings of detachment and threat, along with an urge to amass more and climb higher than others. If there is only room at the top of the hierarchy for one leader (as secular motivational speakers often suggest), then all hierarchies are temporary structures, even though those at the top act as if they are permanent.

Hierarchies often appear useful to people, as they seem to bring peace when leaders take a break from battling for the top position. Because of this desire for ongoing order and peace, churches especially love hierarchies, forgetting that Jesus confronted hierarchical systems as ungodly (see Mark 10:34–43 "It should not be so among you"). The way of the kingdom is to serve others, even unto death. This concept of ministering to others rather than attempting to rule over them is modelled by Jesus and repeated often in the New Testament (e.g. Phil 2:5–11). Thus it could be described as the paradigmatic behavioural pattern for Christians.

Yet the service model of placing ourselves at the bottom of church structures was abandoned by the church very early on, probably already in the second century. Through the centuries, Christians have continued to abandon the Way as they have given into the ways of the world.[14] Hierarchies became

---

14. E. Schüssler Fiorenza, *Zu ihrem Gedächtnis* (München: Kaiser, 1988), 114–116. Though millennial movements are normally not long-lived, Christianity did maintain its movement character well into the second century. The consolidation of ministry and the establishment of hierarchical structures started in the second part of the first century and even then was opposed by many.

so holy that wars for primacy in church leadership did not stop even in view of the large-scale divide between East and West, a divide that still generates wars in my region.[15] In some instances, the hierarchy of priests became the church, while the general Christian public – in particular schismatics – were not accepted as the church.[16] In these traditions, the Christian public could be accepted into God's kingdom if they adhered to all the proscriptions of the church, but even then, they had to count on purgatory at best. How did the Reformation movement, which was both countercultural and biblical, fail to rid itself of hierarchical power structures? Even worse, most right-wing evangelicals, who insist on a literal application of Scripture and would be anti-Catholic, insist on hierarchies and argue that the church cannot (and should not) live without them. From both the pulpits and pews, these Christians insist that hierarchies are God-ordained. In the beginning, Baptists (along with other minority groups) challenged hierarchies in their doctrines and adopted congregationalism.[17] Yet I have lived as a Baptist my whole life, and I still hear this mantra about the divine ordination of hierarchies in Baptist congregations. Those of us who know our history resist hierarchies as a necessary structure for church leadership, and this continues to be a doctrinal beacon of light that helps me hold on to my heritage and hope for the best.

The argument generally goes like this: if God is a God of peace, then hierarchies must be God-ordained, because without hierarchies, there would be constant strife for positions. But it is the world that has convinced us of this shortcut thinking, for it is more likely that churches copy the hierarchical environments of the world because power feels good to humans. Patriarchal societies tend to create patriarchal church patterns that strictly adhere to

---

15. V. Perica, "Religion in the Balkan Wars," in *Oxford Handbooks Online* (October 2014). Perica states that "religious differences between, say, Eastern Orthodox Christian peoples (i.e. Serbs, Macedonians, and Montenegrins) or between Serbs and Croats as Eastern-Orthodox and Western-Catholic Christians did not suffice to mobilize people for a war until ethnic nationalist myths and ideologies had been incorporated in church liturgies and religious organizations' social activity." Online: https://www.oxfordhandbooks.com/view/10.1093/oxfordhb/9780199935420.001.0001/oxfordhb-9780199935420-e-37.

16. *Dogmatic Constitution on the Church: Lumen Gentium,* in particular Chapter III–IV. During the Second Vatican Council, this dogmatic constitution on the church has played with the thought of terminating the word "sect" for non-Catholics, especially the Protestant groups, calling them instead "separated brethren" (e.g. IV, 69).

17. This is evident from disputes with the hierarchical churches, particularly in the seventeenth century. W. L. Lumpkin, *Baptist Confessions*; I. M. Randall, *Baptist Beginnings in Europe* (Schwarzenfeld: Neufeld Verlag, 2009).

hierarchical chains of authority.[18] However, by blaming patriarchy, we may be barking up the wrong tree. The problem of hierarchies runs deeper than patriarchy, for matriarchy will not solve the problem any better, as we will see. Biblically, the problem of hierarchies is a problem of the heart. As Paul describes it, if Christians do not "live by the Spirit of God" and obtain their freedom, they will live "by the flesh" and be driven by the curse to scramble towards the god position in the hierarchical strata, a position of power that they will describe as God-ordained. The majority of Christians relegate their freedom in Christ to these hierarchical gods, believing that the hierarchy represents a God-ordained order. Thus without realizing it, Christians idolize these gods, thereby abandoning their faith, freedom, and responsibility.

Because of these strong hierarchical structures in the church, it is not surprising that women have no immediate access to leadership or ministry. For when we define leadership and ministry as those who have authority over others, all who help those at the top function as servants. Their role is to support the hierarchical gods and demiurges and help them maintain their positions of power. Later, we will turn to some crucial New Testament passages that reflect this dynamic.

First, I will take you on a tour of the world, revealing how Christian men rule over hierarchies of leadership and ministry with the help and support of women. My purpose is not to blame, but to recognize the intricate connections and chains of reactions and reciprocal counter-reactions that exist in male-dominated hierarchical systems. Nor am I writing to plead for women's human rights or women's authority and freedom, although I do believe that such advocacy is needed. Our voices must be raised against the ongoing suffering, injustice, and violence that women have experienced through hierarchical systems.

Rather, my main motivation is to show that hierarchies cannot be upheld in a world governed by God. In hierarchical systems, all people – not just women – are reduced to commodities to be sold and bought in order to benefit the system (though women, in particular, have been trained to offer themselves to these human gods). From the perspective of biblical theology, it is unthinkable for churches to adopt hierarchies and proclaim them as holy and God-ordained, since they oppose the very centre of Christ's good news, which is to set the captives free (Luke 4:14–21). Rather than setting himself at

---

18. Fiorenza (*Gedächnis*, 118–119) summarizes the arguments brought forth by a number of sociologists and theologians, which is that the Christian church would not have survived without giving into patriarchy as a "social and historical necessity for survival."

the top of a hierarchical system, Christ *gave up* his position of authority and became a slave for this purpose.

Confronting Spiritual Abuses within Church Hierarchies

After the undisputed veil of sanctity was lifted from the church in the nineteenth century[19] – and even more through the twentieth and twenty-first centuries – many background injustices that were committed by the Christian system against the "little ones" in the church have come to light. Long concealed by church structures, the unveiling of these sins calls Christians to mourn and repent, but also to rejoice. For when we address structural sin, healing and freedom become possible. The church must be confronted by the horrors it has committed "in the name of the Lord" and confess these acts as spiritual abuse, for any human abuse of power conceals the glory of a good God. This confrontation has often felt like a cataclysmic earthquake (e.g. H. S. Reimarus or Ludwig Feuerbach),[20] and more recently, through the #MeToo and #ChurchToo movements, many Christians have had to rethink their faith or wonder how the church will survive. Tragically, many people knew about the atrocities, including victims and their loved ones, and yet they still kept silent. Though hierarchies of power invent traditions to enslave people and use violence to intimidate them, this reality does not take away our responsibility. A mother may say, "I was too weak to protect my children from their violent father," but by failing to protect them, she abandoned her children.

Tucked away in the spare room for centuries, these sins were rarely challenged, and no boundaries were established. Perpetrators were silently moved from one place to another, where they continued their sinful business, reassured that this time, they would get away with it. It is impossible to give an extensive report about all that has gone foul in the church, but everyone knows of the sex scandals, power abuses, and money embezzlements. Elaine Storkey's book *Scars of Humanity* depicts the suffering and pain of the "little

---

19. Some, like a Croatian bishop, have evaluated historical research into the New Testament during the nineteenth and twentieth centuries as a "bad experiment." V. Košić, "Recepcija Koncila u Hrvatskoj – uloga Kršćanske sadašnjosti u tome," u *Kršćanska Sadašnjost u misli svojih utemeljitelja* (Zagreb: KS, 2008), 23. However, he may be joined by many evangelicals in this assessment.

20. L. A. Feuerbach, *The Essence of Christianity* (1841), online: https://www.marxists.org/reference/archive/feuerbach/works/essence/.

ones" throughout society.[21] This all suggests that the church is not a safe place for women, children, or anyone who is not part of the power structures. No hierarchy is a safe place.

Confronting Abusive Hierarchical Family Structures

In family structures around the world, more rural cultures tend to be more hierarchical, and Christian women, who are driven by their desire to do what is good, often enforce these unhealthy hierarchical structures. In Africa, I have witnessed older women become outraged when they see younger women getting a profession and becoming economically self-sufficient. The older women describe the younger women as selfish and unchristian for insisting on their freedom.

In Eastern Europe, I have witnessed something of a cult of motherhood. In conferences, women who have many children are brought forward as examples of real Christian character. While many of these women are professionals in their everyday life, they are defined by their motherhood, which is the only area where they can prove their Christian worth. But defining women by motherhood keeps them out of the realms that "belong" to men, where they are expected to submit to men in all things. For as soon as women venture out of this proscribed territory, they are challenged and described as unholy.

In Asia, I have talked with women who were involved in ministry by helping their husbands, who were pastors and church planters. I asked them about their dreams and the vision God had given them for their lives. They stared at me, unable to understand what I was asking. We were talking through a translator, and eventually the translator asked, "What do you mean by vision?" At first, they seemed unable to understand the notion that God could speak into their lives as women, but as I explained, a lively discussion developed. The translator was drawn in, and I could only read their faces until a question surfaced: "Why must women work so much harder than the men?"

I later learned that during the lively conversation, they had been discussing the ministry they did along with their husbands – how they accompanied them to villages, talked with the women, and worked with the children, setting up and doing whatever else was needed. After they came home, the husbands would rest, because they deserved it after a long day of ministry, but the

---

21. E. Storkey, *Scars Across Humanity: Understanding and Overcoming Violence against Women* (London: SPCK, 2015). While Storkey features the violence against women, the brutality of the world in which this happens is painfully visible.

wife would continue working, preparing dinner, getting the children to bed, whatever else needed to be done.

Whether in Eastern Europe, Asia, or Africa, I have found that women are "allowed" to do a lot of things – such as support their husbands and the ministry vision – as long as they stay in the role of a submissive mother. In most cases, they carry this imbalance in work without question, transferring these behavioural patterns to the next generation by modelling the role of a do-it-all mother and teaching their children that women are defined by how they give up their lives to their husbands and children.

No Place for Abuse,[22] a study on violence against women in churches by Catherine Kroeger and Nancy Nason-Clark, describes how hierarchical relationships in marriage destroy partnerships and open up space for violence and abuse, including incest, which carries the trauma into the future. It has been painful for me to listen to wedding sermons that propagate this inequality agenda as a foolproof recipe for a godly marriage, as it runs against all the principles of a Spirit-filled life. A healthy relationship in marriage allows for parents to "rule over" their minor children together in love so that they do not come to harm. Though children need to be loved and guided into maturity and equality, the principle of "ruling over" does not apply to women. First, marriage partners are both adults, and they do not need permission or instruction from other adults – only council and discussion. Decision making depends on various capacities, such as learning, intellect, intuition, experience, and gifting – none of which are gender-specific. Only a hierarchical "order" judges a man's view and judgment as *a priori* more important than a woman's.

Second, inequality is impossible in a Christian marriage, where both partners have the Spirit of God, who leads them both into "all truth." And as Paul says, whoever does not have the Spirit of God is not Christ's. There is not one passage in the Bible that says that women receive the Spirit in a different measure than men.

Finally, parents must work as equal partners in the family because an equal standing enables them to share with one another and to fulfil their needs for intimacy in all areas of life. By working as partners in the work of parenting, parents expose their children to different parenting and personality styles. This exposure contributes to a balanced education and teaches children unity in diversity. Such a partnership model is necessary for healthy relationships in

---

22. C. Clark Kroeger and N. Nason-Clark, *No Place for Abuse* (Downers Grove: InterVarsity Press, 2001), 100–112.

the family, for hierarchies that separate a mother and father as unequals open up the following treacherous dangers.

Male Hierarchy with Limited Transfer of Power
The first classic version, which is endorsed in many churches as biblical, places the father at the top of the family hierarchy as the ruler over his wife and children. The mother is subordinate to him, but she can rule the children in his absence. This arrangement alienates the parents from one another and eliminates space for intimacy in their home, leaving both feeling lonely. Intimacy should be not only sexual, but a deep feeling of concern and connection with another, which all humans need. Without intimacy, sexual relations become duties or rights, with the sole purpose being procreation, a display of power, or an expression of lust rather than love. Rather than creating mutual satisfaction, this leaves the wife feeling that she has been sexually abused. Mutual sexual satisfaction only develops when we have the freedom to give ourselves to one another and to share intimacy, a sense of belonging or partnership.

This hierarchical description of a "Christian marriage" is bound to alienate a father from his children. Because of his power and distance, he has no direct connection with his children. In fact, his hierarchical distance deems it a lack of respect if he expresses care for his children's immediate needs, for their care has been transferred to the mother alone. A mother can further abuse and alienate an absentee father by treating him like a "grey eminency," who comes home occasionally to deliver punishment to those who misbehave.

Women in such relationships are often overwhelmed by raising children, as they have been taught that they have no authority apart from their husbands, and so they cannot imagine how to discipline their children alone. With her husband remote and absent – and therefore unable to give her the intimacy she needs – she may take one of her children into her confidence. Confused about her loyalty, she burdens this child, forcing him or her into an adult role prematurely, where s/he has to become a mother or father to his or her own mother. Or she may find intimacy outside of her marriage and family, which contributes to the disintegration of the family.

Contrary to the popular myth, no man only needs sex and power. All humans need intimacy and true love, a place where they can be vulnerable and open, where they can share their deepest selves. A man who is seen as the sole provider and authority in a hierarchical family system is remote, alone, isolated. Forced to keep his distance, he cannot obtain intimacy in his family. When a man uses power over his wife and children, he experiences further exclusion from the love and affection in his home, which they share among themselves. Love cannot be ordered, and so he seeks intimacy outside his home. This pattern is enforced by a culture that defines a man's worth by the number of women he can force into a relationship with him, a process that disintegrates his own family.

These are the inevitable outcomes of the hierarchical model that is presented in churches as biblical and God-ordained. Though globalization and migration have loosened this hierarchical system and revealed so-called "Christian marriages" as whitewashed tombs, the system has been held in place by strong traditions, taboos, and social norms. Now, global developments and fear are bringing this instant recipe for a strong traditional family back to haunt us. This is short-sighted, for if the system had worked in the past, women would not have needed liberation – let alone a sexual revolution. We would all be growing up in happy hierarchical homes! Obviously, hierarchical family structures did not work in the past either! The only difference today is that couples (women mostly) will not endure the endless disappointment of a philandering, emotionally detached, abusive god.

If we are serious about our Bible reading, we must understand that a hierarchical model reflects the curse – not God's intention for marriage. In the past, societies could force people to stay together formally, but these traditional families have been anything but strong and nurturing. They may have kept up appearances, but there was a lot of stinking decay underneath, which is readily shown in the testimonies of literature or film. From a Christian perspective, hierarchical marriage is certainly not a model to replicate.

New movements for men and women, such as "Promise Keepers" or "Daughters of the King," will not bring us forward, as they are just enforcing unhealthy stereotypes. Propagators of these hierarchies need to realise that a painted grave still stinks, and if family garbage is stored in a locked spare room, the neighbours will still choke on the stench of decay even if they cannot see it. In light of this, many people are running for their lives! Rather than enforcing stereotypes about manly or womanly behaviours, we need to be modelling true exchanges and partnerships, where women and men can become who they are at heart.

Male Hierarchy with No Transfer of Power

The second hierarchical family model places the man on top of the hierarchy, without transferring any of the power to his wife for raising the children or overseeing the home. In this sanctified curse model, the man insists that he has the God-given authority to control everything. A woman can't have authority over the children, because that would be a threat to the man's divine authority.

Stripped of all power, even over her children, the woman practically becomes as one of them. This model opens space for incestuous relationships. Since the man has placed his wife and children under his authority as equals, if sex with his wife is unfulfilling (and it cannot be fulfilling, because love cannot be ordered), or if sex is not unavailable (because she is pregnant), he can easily replace his wife with one (or more) of his daughters (or sons).

Biblical texts such as Ephesians 5, Colossians 3, 1 Corinthians 11, and 1 Timothy 2 have been recited to newlyweds to instruct them about the holy hierarchical constitution of Christian marriage. Unfortunately, they have been taken out of context and have never been examined against the central doctrines of the Christian faith, which are encompassed by the biblical messages of salvation, freedom, mutuality, and service. Rather than nurturing a love that seeks to care for the other and give him/her freedom, young people are led to believe that if they force themselves into this God-ordained hierarchy, a mysterious blessing from God will descend upon them. But as the demands of a growing family increase, and they face the challenges of the world, their need for intimacy becomes greater, along with their increasing sense of alienation and isolation. Yet they have been handed over to a sinful hierarchical structure, which will eventually tear them apart.

In the Western world, we see this in the ever-growing divorce rates and the casualties of psychically dismembered kids who have been stripped of their primal trust. If you cannot trust your parents, who can you trust? One-parent families have become an ordeal for many. Regardless of superb social care in places such as Sweden, raising children alone is a difficult task that was never meant for one. Our world is full of isolated individuals who are longing for intimacy and friendship, but unable to form meaningful relationships because they never experienced them in their life.

In parts of the world where there is no social provision for disintegrating families, the pain is even greater, along with its negative impacts on the future. Abandoned women and children roam the streets of cities, trying to find a basic living, a meal a day. They sell their bodies as a last resort, or others exploit them by selling their bodies (and body parts) to violent and sick men across the "developed" West.

Hierarchical marriages that are hailed as biblical need to be identified as a curse that has been sanctified by those who do not know the heart of God. Those who claim to have unchallenged authority from God over others act on sinful urges and bring death into the world. Jesus has so much to offer when it comes to relationships, but it is miles away from this so-called "biblical" model. Before we turn to the wonderful, difficult relational message that Jesus models, we need to look even more deeply at the ways a Christian "blessing" of the curse contributes to the suffering of the world.

Hierarchies as Systems of Ecological and Economic Abuse

Hierarchies are just as hazardous for the environment and economics as they are for churches and families. When Christians buy into the structure of the power of human gods, they fail to become new creations who can reflect Christ's redemptive counterculture and testify to the power of the transforming Holy Spirit.

Ecological Abuse: Blessing the Exploitation of the Earth

Though many influential men of the world may deny it, the world is on the brink of extinction. Even more worrying is the fact that many Christians believe that the Bible predicts the destruction of the world as necessary. Consequently, they bless the curse by claiming that the Bible allows them to continue to exploit the earth's resources and people in order to bring about this final end.

I have met people who believe this on my travels in all parts of the world. They insist that their privileged place in the global hierarchy of power and entitlement is a compensation from God for their "right" Christian beliefs. They argue that those who are poor and underprivileged do not believe in the "right" God in the "right" way. Moreover, they believe that the troubles of the poor prove that they were either created inferior, or they were disobedient to the will of God.

Yet the global picture reveals a different truth. The Christian doctrine of the sanctity of *human* life has brought humanity to the point of near self-extinction. In the name of human supremacy, creation has been abused and polluted to such an extent that it has become hazardous and threatening for all life, including humans.[23] Those at the top of global hierarchies who have assumed godlike power and authority have jeopardized the entire world through their decisions and actions. Many of these semi-gods think that they are unsusceptible to mere human suffering and will be exempt from the general destruction of the world. But as we have seen in family hierarchies, nature has

---

23. Called "the most comprehensive examination ever of the sacredness of human life," D. Gushee's opus magnum, *The Sacredness of Human Life: Why an Ancient Biblical Vision Is Key to the World's Future* (Grand Rapids: Eerdmans, 2013), is a worthy read on the issues of how "sacred human life" is connected to the requirements to honour God's earth. With this, it is also a game changer. See in particular 388–408.

the power to strike back against humans who want to be gods. Like any other humans, these semi-gods are reaping what they have sown (Gal 6:7).

Nature works according to the principles and rules ordained by the Creator, and these rules are countercultural to the reigning principals of exploitation in the world. Though god-deluded humans may delay some of the consequences of pollution in their own yard for a while by abusing nature on the other side of the world, they cannot dodge them endlessly. As the old saying goes, "What goes around, comes around!" Yet those at the higher end of the hierarchy continue to deceive themselves, assuming that they are exempt from the destruction that they have created for others.

Human autocrats often superficially assume that they can supervise nature by knowing how it functions. And yet, we know more about nature now than ever before, but any serious scientist will admit that this has only increased our awareness of what we *don't* know. New discoveries lead us to new depths of knowledge and more things to explore. Even with the help of computers, the intricacies of interrelationships are incomprehensible because of the sheer number of combinations. To give a simple example, though LED lights consume less energy than traditional incandescent lights, the production and recycling costs dim the initial optimism of this scientific "breakthrough."[24] Decisions cannot be based solely on the immediate benefit for the final producer. We have to take into account the whole process and its impact on the earth.

Economic Abuse: the Privatisation of the Common Good

The economy, which is closely connected with ecology, is concerned with the management of what is intended for the common good and therefore belongs to all people. When we talk about the common good, people often believe that there are goods – resources and our access to them – that are not common, but private. Yet nothing that we possess is intrinsically ours. Hierarchies have deluded us into thinking that those who are higher up on the system are entitled to a bigger portion of the common resources – bigger living spaces, more water per day, more food, more oil. This thinking is directly linked with the delusion that we are somehow better than other people because of our race, gender, nationality, or a birth right passed down from a wealthy or even Christian family. Feminist ecology draws attention to this irrational line of

---

24. J. Caferkey has investigated this for the Green Tech Media in 2017. Online: https://www.greentechmedia.com/articles/read/sustainable-led-reusable-materials.

reasoning.[25] However, much feminist political ecology is partial and dogmatic, offering vague, one-sided solutions for women to act more like men in order to compete on equal terms or to engage in contextual, "spiritual" approaches based on female goddesses.

Structures must change if women are to prosper as women, and this is not a question of women and feminism alone. We also need to see the injustices endured by those who are at the very bottom of the hierarchy and how their rights and needs are being trampled upon, for human economic injustice targets everyone who is inferior on the hierarchical system – children as well as men can be excluded by the human gods at the top through anti-Semitism, nationalism, racism, and so on. Exploitation does not recognize gender or political standing in terms of left (social) or right (capitalism). It just likes to find determinants which easily carry the myth of exclusion.

By definition, hierarchies are structures of exploitation. Those who are higher up the ladder create dubious systems that rely on myths and traditions to exploit others for generations in order to keep the common "goods" in their hands. How can selling money be a legitimate source of income? How can true success in business be measured only by financial profit? These are absurd notions, because there is obviously no real value in such transactions. Bank "products" were invented to shift information about accumulated common good from one end of the world for huge profit, but without real cost. Whoever outsmarts the other by intricate unclear schemes wins – and the outsmarting is linked with direct immoral action, as the economic crisis of 2008 displays. Yet the big players somehow disappear, while the "little people" are left with unjust laws to make up for their mistakes. This has become an easy game. Banks invented it, but this system of selling nothing is used by many economic sectors that deal with what would otherwise be seen as a common good – for instance, energy. These exploitive economic systems function with the overall blessing of the ruling structures, because they share in the income from this rip-off.

For instance, in my country, it has become impossible to track what a family really spends on electricity due to newly invented "products" in the energy industry. The formulas have become too complicated for people with basic maths skills. Water, too, is becoming a commodity, and companies are buying the water sources from the state and bottling it. There are already places on earth where water is scarce and is becoming more inaccessible by the day. In

---

25. See the overview to feminist political ecology by B. P. Resurrección, "Gender and Environment from 'Women, Environment and Development,'" in *Routledge Handbook of Gender and Environment*, ed. S. MacGregor (Oxon: Routledge, 2017), 71–85.

many places, people no longer own the land on which their house stands, which means they do not have rights to drill for oil or water – or to keep business and government interests from doing so for their own profit. In some places, even the air above one's house does not belong to them anymore. The absurdity of these examples reveals the absurdity of an economy based on hierarchies of power, whose only goal is increased profit. Meanwhile, hierarchies in the economy and politics walk hand-in-hand. Hierarchies work to accumulate the common good for a small number of people who are sucking life from the masses.

These stories are so simple, and yet people willingly work within such structures of sin, motivated by the hope that one day they will find their way closer to the top. If we just try hard enough and comply with the injustices long enough, we will be able to trick the system, and it will somehow catapult us among the fortunate ones on the top. The sinful systems of the world work because so many people feed into them by hoping for their little bit. When we live according to the curse, we bless the curse. But the system of the curse must be starved in order to give way to new life, which we find in the biblical principle of *being in Christ*.

3

The Solution to the Problem of Sin

Being in Christ

The broad strokes of the biblical narrative are still widely known in most of the world. Many people have heard some form of the story about humanity's problem with the sin of disobedience to God's commandments and their unwillingness to comply with God's plan of salvation. Yet Christian doctrines have stopped making sense to most people. At best, church traditions are accepted as old truths without giving the matter much thought. Once people dare to test these truths, they often discover that they can no longer believe them.

A man I met on a flight from Fiji told me that he had to travel for work, but he was afraid of flying. When he realized that I also travelled for work on long flights, he asked how I could stand the anxiety. He told me he had been brought up as a Christian, but had left his faith, and then returned a couple of years before in the hope of finding salvation. "I have to admit," he told me. "I am not sure I understand what is going on in the church – it does not seem to work for me!" He was working as a scientist in the field of global warming, and our discussion turned to evolution and the story of creation.

I asked him to imagine God making a space within himself to free it up for humanity,[1] an image that reveals how God would do anything to save us and not to harm us. The man was taken away as he imagined the love of God

---

1. Comp. J. Moltmann, *God in Creation*, 86–91.

that would make this possible. He suddenly understood that the space God freed within himself for humanity created a challenge, because we might turn away from him. And yet the emptiness we experience without God can also become a place of learning, where we turn toward God because we willingly want to be part of him. The love we both felt as we talked about the salvation of God seemed to heal his fear, and he managed to sleep on that long flight. God wants to speak, and there is such a need for us to hear him, and he also speaks to and through people who do not know him yet.

Theologically, doctrines seek to maintain the face of the church at all costs, even when bad things happen. The old traditions carry the authority of Scripture and experience, but they no longer communicate what they used to for the past generations, and this has brought the church into a scary place. Ever since Gotthold Lessing dropped Hermann Reimarus's A-bomb of doubt about the historicity of the Christian faith on an unsuspecting Christian public at the end of the eighteenth century,[2] there has been strife between those who want to prove that Christianity is wrong, those who want to prove that Christianity is unique, and those who argue that Scripture is the literal truth. Theology, however, requires us to walk into that scary place to determine how doctrines can be evaluated and adapted so that they will make sense to new generations. This is always a painful process, but Christians must be able to take a leap of faith, believing that God will meet them on the other side, stronger than ever, and that they will be able to recognize the Lord as they live through times of evaluation and adaptation. This journey has become particularly challenging in our current age, since an end-of-the-world scenario is not merely an apocalyptic vision, but a very real threat for the immediate future.

I embarked on the topic of re-evaluating doctrines only by chance – or, more properly, by the mercy of God. I was looking for a research topic for my doctoral thesis at the end of the last century, and I thought that Paul, in his

---

2. H. S. Reimarus, *Apologie für die Vernünftigen Verehrer Gottes* (Leipzig: Brockhaus, 1986). On account of historical research and a lack of data on Jesus in non-biblical sources, Reimarus thought that serious adherents to Christianity needed to draw consequences from this fact: Jesus never existed, and so it was all fraud. Reimarus never published the material himself, but it was published posthumously by his friend, the German philosopher and writer G. E. Lessing. Meanwhile, the method of historical research has been refined, and as G. Theißen and A. Mertz show in *The Historical Jesus: A Comprehensive Guide* (Minneapolis: Augsburg, 1998), there is a vast sum of plausible facts that can be extracted from the Gospels and extra-biblical material following the life of Jesus. An interesting discussion on this work and the dilemma it brought can be found in C. Voysey, *Fragments from Reimarus* (London and Edinburgh: Williams and Norgate, 1879), online: https://archive.org/details/fragmentsfromrei00reim/page/n3.

time, had done what we needed to do in ours: he had sought to find a way to communicate the Scriptures so that they would speak to his own generation.

I realized that Paul's time had many parallels to our own. First, his was a "global" community. Though our partial experience of the world often makes us believe that we think universally, my son challenges our current globe-centredness: "There are planets out there which are very similar to earth. What if there are also people like us on them?" We need to think through this, because the global village is becoming too narrow, and research into the universe has become a priority. What does our theology have to offer this new generation? Second, the Roman Empire had a clear centre of power and a common language and culture that easily overrode local languages in rural parts, such as Galilee and the fishing regions on the shores of Lake Gennesaret. The Roman Empire even mirrored our contemporary obsession with worldwide travel for tourism – even medical tourism!

But why was Paul's mission so successful? What made him go out and evangelize to other regions while the other apostles ignored the direct order by their Lord and stayed put in Jerusalem? From a social perspective, Christianity could never have been considered *the* option among the plethora of religious options that Rome had to offer. Christianity was a tiny sect within the old, despised religion of the Jews.[3] It did not fit well with the politicians and had a strange attachment to a man who had been crucified as Rome's opponent.[4] And yet, it became a world religion in a few short centuries, and it still holds its ground after two millennia. There are certainly many more ways to approach this topic, but the fascinating draw for me was the old Jewish phrase, "Word of God," which suddenly resonated in the hearts of pagans, who had never heard it before. How was this possible? I think the key was Paul's take on "the Scriptures," as he continues to be the best-preserved author from among the Christians of the first century. In retrospect, he managed both to hear and understand "the Word" and to hear and understand "the world" at the same time. Paul's training in the Scriptures (Gal 1:14; comp. Acts 22:3; 26:5) is evident in all his writing, but particularly his letter to the Romans, which is an exposition on the biblical theology of salvation.

---

3. Tacitus describes the Jews' "perverse and disgusting" religion in his *Histories*, Book V. Online: http://classics.mit.edu/Tacitus/histories.5.v.html.

4. Tacitus, *Annals*, Book xv 44. Online: http://penelope.uchicago.edu/Thayer/E/Roman/Texts/Tacitus/Annals/15B*.html.

Paul was a Jew from Tarsus (Acts 22:3), a city that was on the rise in Roman society and had many fruitful connections to Rome.[5] It is perceivable that he received his primary education there, which likely included a visit to Rome. He was later sent to Jerusalem to learn the word of God at the feet of the Pharisees, people who were dedicated to studying God's law.[6] Thus Paul was an insider of both Rome and Jerusalem, the world of the empire as well as the Jews, which becomes evident when studying his letters. In this way, he was suited and equipped for the calling God gave him on the way to Damascus (Acts 9:15–16), which was to bring the good news to the nations. Paul understood what the good news meant and how it was laid out in the Scriptures, for he had experienced it through his encounter with Christ on the way to Damascus. Also, Paul understood the need to share this good news, which could only have come from God. In Romans 1–8, he retells the story, but he contextualizes the problem for his contemporaries. Paul does not change Scripture to align it with the needs of the cultured Roman Empire, but he perceives how the old Scriptures might be able to speak to this new generation and also into a universal context. By rereading Scripture in light of his encounter with Christ, he reveals that the Scriptures have always spoken of God's intent to address the whole world with his word – not just his own people. In this process, Paul amends some of the old traditions, which many Jews thought were basic to their faith, while at the same time staying true to God's word.

We need to rediscover Scripture for our contemporaries, particularly in light of the impending world crisis. Even children are setting up protest marches to draw attention to it! The young people of our generation fear that there will not be a future for them, and so some feel they might as well squander the few days they have left through meaningless partying. Yet in the course of my re-reading, I have become convinced that when we read the Scriptures carefully and seek to understand them in our own context, they can give us guidance for real global change.

Now, some may feel this concept of global change is unbiblical. *Isn't the kingdom of God an otherworldly realm? Won't the world just go up in flames to make space for a new earth, a new Jerusalem that will come down from heaven? Surely the world cannot become the kingdom of God! It would be unfair for everyone to be saved, especially those who have squandered their lives on sin and*

---

5. W. M. Ramsay, *Paul the Traveller and Roman Citizen* (London: Hodder & Stoughton, 1895), 30–31. See also W. M. Ramsay, *The Cities of St. Paul* (London: Hodder & Stoughton, 1907), 135, 196.

6. I have attempted that reconstruction in *Paul's Territoriality*, 97–102.

making everyone else miserable! There needs to be a final judgment, and some need to burn in hell forever!

Many of us have grown up with such concepts, but have we seriously studied the Bible to investigate them and discern whether or not they reflect the truth? Or are we being drawn back into a medieval and prescientific worldview that no longer speaks to people who are honestly facing the real danger of a cataclysmic world end? Is not God telling a better story, one that he described as "the good news of salvation" from the beginning, one where heaven and earth connect in a way that has not been known before, where life begins to reign where previously there was only death?[7] Unfortunately, many Christians have given up reading Scripture, or they never even learned it in the first place. This is partially so because a multitude of contemporaries have given up reading altogether, since it is more difficult than gleaning ready-made concepts through pictures, podcasts, and YouTube videos. Moreover, the Bible is old and difficult to understand, and it takes a lot of effort to read past this old framework. The biblical interpretations of some Christians have also made it difficult for seekers to take the Bible seriously.

For instance, young women who trained as nurses in the sixties in Yugoslavia were excommunicated from evangelical churches because their school demanded that they cut their hair for hygienic reasons, but their church elders said the Bible forbade women to have short hair! For most of us today, it is unclear how short hair could have affected these young women's salvation in Christ! It is not entirely clear how the gymnastics around this interpretation developed, but it was most likely a convenient rule to make women submissive to men.

Thus any interpretation of Scripture needs to be tested, and we need to see for ourselves what the Scriptures really say, always taking serious scholarship and study into account. Unfortunately, the realms of research and pragmatic application have been torn apart, and they desperately need to come back

---

7. Anyone who has read R. Bauckham, *The Climax of Prophecy* (London; New York: T & T Clark, 1993), has had the overwhelming experience of how little thorough reading has been done of Revelation in the past. Sure, there are notions of judgment and peril in the Bible, but there is also a definitive need for action in the now, because the future, whatever it will look like, depends on the now. Similarly, A. A. Hoeckema, in his major study *The Bible and the Future* (Grand Rapids; Carlisle: Eerdmans; Paternoster, 1994), ix, wants to go the in-between way of "already-not yet," claiming that "inaugurated" eschatology plays an important part of biblical eschatology and is not only a later development, but must be seen as present from the very beginning – that is, from the "mother promise" of Genesis 3:15 (5). From there, it seems to me that the whole idea of inaugurated eschatology necessarily evolves around God's salvation. This has been developed by C. J. H. Wright, *The Mission of God: Unlocking The Bible's Great Narrative* (Downers Grove: IVP Academic, 2006), esp. 397–420.

together. For Paul, they were never separate in the first place. In the following section, I offer a re-reading of Genesis 1–3 and Romans 1:16–32 and a re-interpretation of some traditional concepts.

Looking at the Curse with Paul's Eyes
The Story of Genesis 1–2

The doctrine about the sanctity of human life is derived from Genesis 1, where God creates humans as the crown of his creation and makes them "rule over" (1:26 NIV) or "have dominion over" all other created things.[8] When we read the Genesis account and this instruction to the first people, we need to be aware of a few facts. First, back in the nineteenth century, Albert Barnes commented that "ruling over" meant "those capacities of right thinking, right willing, and right acting, or of knowledge, holiness, and righteousness, in which man resembles God," and that those "qualify him for dominion."[9] The instruction "to rule" came into a world that was still "very good" and in daily community with God. Humans reflected the goodness, holiness, and righteousness of God, and so their "ruling over" reflected the mind of God.

Second, the command in Genesis 1:26 displays God's plan about the human task even before God creates them as male and female in 1:27. To appreciate God's great design, which is forgotten in our doctrines, following is the full text:

> Then God said, "Let us make humankind in our image, according to our likeness; and let them have dominion over the fish of the sea, and over the birds of the air, and over the cattle, and over all the wild animals of the earth, and over every creeping thing that creeps upon the earth."
>
> So God created humankind in his image,
>   in the image of God he created them,
>   male and female he created them.
>
> God blessed them, and God said to them, "Be fruitful and multiply, and fill the earth and subdue it; and have dominion over the fish

---

8. For a comprehensive discussion on this doctrine, its development, and problems, I recommend D. Gushee, *The Sacredness of Human Life: Why an Ancient Biblical Vision Is Key to the World's Future* (Grand Rapids: Eerdmans, 2013), 16–36, 31. Gushee explains why it is important for contemporary Christianity to make the switch from an ancient dogma about the sanctity of *human* life towards a more biblical understanding that "all creation is sacred."

9. A. Barnes, *Notes on the Bible*, accessed online at *Bible Hub*: https://biblehub.com/commentaries/barnes/genesis/1.htm.

of the sea and over the birds of the air and over every living thing that moves upon the earth." (Gen 1:26–28)

Third, contemporaries interpret "ruling over" from the perspective of the fallen structures of sin, where everything is evaluated from the interests of a hierarchical order. In this perspective, nature is valuable, but its value is determined by its usefulness to humans. For those climbing up hierarchies, nature cannot defend itself or claim anything for itself, and so it is there to be exploited, used, and abused by humans for their purposes. Thus humans become the one "god" who rules the rest of creation. In this struggle for the god position, nature becomes a resource upon which everyone's life depends, and those who are strong and privileged enough to lay a claim on it first can, indeed, rule over all who are unfortunate, weak, or disadvantaged. Consider oil, gold, coal, and timber industries, but also, more recently, water and, in heavily polluted cities, clean air. Many theories have been developed about the "common good" and how it should be distributed and whether it should be protected by laws to ensure more righteous and equitable distribution.

But one aspect of the "common good" that we are becoming more painfully aware of than in previous generations is the fact that creation is finite.[10] As much as nature is the source of human life, there are now over seven billion people trying to survive on a relatively small planet, and so the distribution of its resources needs to be closely monitored. Just imagine all the stuff you have in your house and need daily and then multiply that by 7 or 8 billion. The earth's resources are becoming increasingly insufficient. Projections from 2014 foresee that "fossil fuel for our cars and industry will run out by 2069 and 2088."[11] Fertile land is decreasing by pollution, and the effects of global warming are more devastating by the year. Wars are not only being fought over land and oil, but over water and all forms of energy, because those who

---

10. See, for instance, G. Hardin, "The Tragedy of the Common," *Science* 162 (1968): 1243–1248.

11. A. L. Demaine, M. A. Báez-Váscez, "Bio Fuels of the Present and the Future," in *New and Future Developments in Catalysis: Catalytic Biomass Conversion*, ed. S. L. Stuib (Amsterdam: Elsevier, 2013). Penn State's student instruction in the course on Energy Markets, Policy, and Regulation claims that, technologically, we will not run out of oil, but new and expensive technologies will make it very expensive, so it will "run itself out" (online: https://www.e-education.psu.edu/eme801/node/486). However, the discussion here is about the limits of resources, which may also include the science capacities of humans and, more importantly, whether the breakthroughs can be available to all people everywhere.

rule over them will rule over the dying millions.[12] From that place of rule, they will have reached god-status.

There are other wars that humans fight with nature, trying to subject it to science, alter and meddle with its makeup, and bring it under control for their own benefit. This may soon include manufacturing humans on demand. The prophetic character of fictitious creations of future doom, such as Orwell's novel *1984*, may have missed the date of the ordeal, but global science is certainly reaching the phase in which it is scientifically possible for some people to "breed" others like farm animals in order to support their demand.[13] More recently, in *Homo Deus: A History of Tomorrow*, Yuval Noah Harari anticipates how the value of people will change as robots take over the tasks for which humans used to be valued.[14] Harari's book follows the same logic as the structures of sin, for in the end, everything – including humans – gains its purpose from the economy, and the only people who have value are those who are deemed to be useful for those who rule the hierarchies. This paradigm is gravely opposed to the story of God as revealed in Genesis. Genesis 2:15 interprets the command in 1:26 ("let them have dominion over") as "to work it and take care of it," anticipating, as it were, a stage during which humans would care for the creation. Unfortunately, humans failed in this. "Ruling over" became exploitation of the created world. If this "rule" continues to be understood as it has been – at the very least since the industrial revolution, but in actuality from the beginning – the story cannot have a happy ending.

In *Property for People, Not for Profit: Alternatives to the Global Tyranny of Capital*, Ulrich Duchrow and Franz Hinkelammert show that the history of God's people is intended as a process of liberation that points back to Israel's miraculous release from slavery in Egypt.[15] However, liberated humans continue to throw away their freedom by letting themselves be lured into capitalism. Yet Duchrow and Hinkelammert do not go far enough back in history, believing (building on Karl Jaspers) that this enslavement only arose in the "axial age" (i.e.

---

12. J. Tollefson, "The Hard Truths of Climate Change by the Numbers," *Covering Climate Now* (18 September 2019), includes charts and projections that show who and how severely people will be affected by global warming, which is fuelled by increasing emissions of CO_2, regardless of the awareness of its dangers. Online: https://www.nature.com/immersive/d41586-019-02711-4/index.html.

13. A. Regalado, "Is It Time to Worry About Human Cloning Again?" *The Guardian* (20 April 2018). Online: https://www.theguardian.com/lifeandstyle/2018/apr/20/pet-cloning-is-already-here-is-human-cloning-next.

14. Y. N. Harari, *Homo Deus: A History of Tomorrow* (New York: Harper, 2017).

15. U. Duchrow, F. J. Hinkelammert, *Property for People, Not for Profit: Alternatives to the Global Tyranny of Capital* (New York: Palgrave Macmillan, 2012), 50.

from the eighth century BCE onward, when money was invented).[16] However, categories such as capitalism or patriarchy, which describe the problems of the world in terms of economics or gender studies, do not give a full picture of the god-wars that have occurred and continue to occur everywhere throughout time. Economics, or the pursuit of financial gain, is not the only end towards which hierarchical wars are fought, for there is also a battle being waged for the right to have power and to "rule over" others. Those who work with the problems that stem from abuse and sustainability know that the systems have a defected code on a much larger scale. Though Duchrow and Hinkelammert agree that there is a spiritual aspect to the issue, historical and systematic approaches do not go deep enough and therefore cannot adequately address the reciprocal problems that are intrinsic to human nature.

Hierarchical constructs for "ruling over" creation are blind, for when confronted with the disastrous projections for the future of our children and grandchildren, those at the top continue to fight for resources, because "ruling over" resonates more with human appetites than "working and caring" for creation. Humans would rather bury their heads in the sand and continue their agendas and aspirations for conquering the hierarchy, hoping selfishly that they will not have to reap the outcomes themselves, and not caring how those at the other end of the world are affected. Let the next generation deal with it! This attitude is exactly how the Bible portrays those who rebel against God – as people with selfish ambitions.

Yet it is even more worrying when Christians play into this game by insisting that their special status as God's children entitles them to a selfish disregard for others and the future. Like the disciples in Mark's gospel, whom Jesus tries to teach a lesson about picking up their crosses and serving others unto death (Mark 8:31–10:27), many Christians just keep trying to "rule over" everything and everyone, focusing their energy on who is "the greatest" rather than seeking to become "servants of all" (Mark 9:33–35). This is far from the "good" intent that God had for the creation – and far from Christ's "good news," his path of salvation and redemption for the whole world, that they might live out of the standard of God's initial "very good."

The theological argument that God is going to let this earth go up in flames, and so why should we bother with creation care, reflects a godless entitlement

---

16. Duchrow and Hinkelammert, *Property*, 49, relying on the evaluation that "Deuteronomy presupposes an economy using money for exchange"; the term was coined by K. Jaspers, *The Origin and Goal of History* (London: Routledge Revivals, 2010); comp. Duchrow and Hinkelammert, *Property*, 45–46.

that Christians need to thoroughly and vigorously review. This attitude ignores the fact that we have been saved by the grace of God, and our salvation places us with God, who "so loved the world that he gave his only Son, so that everyone who believes in him may not perish but may have eternal life" (John 3:16). God cares so much that he "emptied himself, taking the form of a slave, being born in human likeness" (Phil 2:7), and is constantly working out the salvation of the world (John 5:19–20).

A medieval Christian mindset interprets Jesus's expressions of care as strictly "spiritual" and "eschatological." But he visited the poor; he healed the sick in mind, body, and spirit by going to where people were and working among them so that they could understand his salvation in everyday circumstances. The medieval Christian mindset also ignores Scripture's declaration that the "world is God's and everything in it" (Ps 24:1). We are not entitled to do whatever we please with the creation. God's mercy endows people with the Spirit of God, and that Spirit cares for others, for God's creation, and for the next generation. Through the Spirit of God, the creation is to be tended and cared for so that it will prosper and sustain people as long as they are on earth.

The Bible is intentionally ambiguous about the future of the world, because the fate of the world is not a human program. Only God can decide what to do with the world. Our work is to care for it. Thus it is in a Christian's DNA to care for creation. Christians need to know that people's ability to hear the gospel depends on this care, especially the young generation, who is constantly being bombarded with images of future gloom.

The blindness and entitlement of many who call themselves Christians demonstrate how people are unable to recognize and resist the deep-seated structures of sin unless they invite God to rule over them and let his Spirit work in their lives. Recent developments from #MeToo and #ChurchToo reveal that abuse does not stop miraculously at the gates of churches. Many Christians have a hard time coping with this darkness and just wish it would disappear on its own, and so they try to conceal it and treat it like an anomaly. Escaping the problem of the earth's destruction through the rapture is one such coping mechanism, but the biblical response to sin is not to sit in a church pew. Human hierarchies cannot save people, and Jesus made it clear that "ruling over" someone is never a blessing – neither for those on the receiving end, nor for those who pretend to be gods (see Mark 10:43).

The Bible also makes it clear that those who try to take on the glory of God will be judged. The word of the Lord echoes through the ages: "I am the LORD, that is my name; my glory I give to no other, nor my praise to idols" (Isa 42:8). Yet many people who call themselves Christians have no respect for this warning in their everyday living and glibly act against it by putting themselves above others and believing that God has given them permission to do so – even that God has elected them to do so!

Since the Liberation Theology movement of the 1960s, a lot has been written about the misery of the poor who are at the bottom of the world's hierarchies, and we do not need to repeat it here.[17] But more needs to be researched about how hierarchical god positions imprison and ruin humanity, both the lowly as well as those at the top who rule over others and think they are entitled to their power. In the world, success is defined in terms of material goods, finances, and economics. Thus many people believe that those who are on the top are perfectly happy, because they have everything. But, as the saying goes, "money can't buy you happiness" or love – even when you know where to shop, or when crying may be more comfortable in a house with a Ferrari parked outside. Eventually, people who presume that they are gods find themselves unable to live up to the requirements of their self-imposed divinity, such as when unexpected and unbridgeable difficulties befall them without regard for their self-importance. Or they may discover that the top position is a very lonely place when all other people become their enemies – even those who should be close, such as family. No wonder there is a long line of rulers throughout history who killed their own children and heirs because they were a threat to their power! Loneliness and detachment go against the deepest human need to belong, to be loved and appreciated.

"Intimacy," writes Elaine Storkey "has many faces but its requirements are similar in each case. It is dependent on the readiness to let go of self-delusion."[18] She notes that intimacy opens areas of vulnerability, and so it is not suitable for the corporate world of business. "It is much easier to stab a competitor in the back if he is not seen . . . as another human being."[19] Yet it is extremely sad to see this lack of intimacy in the church. Storkey warns that intimacy is "inextricably linked with an openness of sharing and a willingness to be known. It is the caring commitment that reaches out to another in trust

---

17. I thoroughly recommend the books by the initial liberation theologians, e.g. Leonardo Boff, *Jesus Cristo Liberador* (Petrópolis: Editura Vezes, 1972), and *Paixão de Cristo – Paixão do Mundo*. I read them in the German translation, *Jesus Christus der Befreier* (Freiburg: Herder, 1989). They must be read with an understanding of the context, both geographically and ecclesiastically (Catholic), and in the quest for the historical Jesus, which at the time of writing was taking a new turn. Appreciating where these discussions have led us, these books help the church to ask the right questions, featuring the lowly of the world as the focus of Jesus's ministry, and then also to find answers that speak into the present time.

18. E. Storkey, *The Search for Intimacy* (Grand Rapids: Eerdmans, 1995), 7.

19. Storkey, *Search*, 11.

and vulnerability."[20] So the lack of intimacy in the church is a direct outcome of concealment, a reflection of the culture that reigns in the world. Without intimacy, we lose our testimony about God, who cares and gives himself for the other. In intimacy, we encounter God through others.

Biblical faith maintains that people were created for community with God and with each other. The first pages of the Bible reflect God's awareness that "It is not good that the man should be alone" (Gen 2:18). St. Augustine begins his *Confessions* with the much-quoted conclusion of his own search for intimacy: "restless is our heart until it comes to rest in" God.[21] Those who set themselves up as gods are, by definition, choosing to live a life of hell, even if nobody persecutes them or challenges their position. Autocrats all around the world and throughout history have become deluded with visions of grandeur and persecution. Though they have everything, in reality they have nothing, because they constantly have to protect their status and are constantly worried about losing it. The real worth of a human life is measured by love and belonging, and those who make themselves inaccessible to others through voluntary isolation will remain unhappy. Accumulating things and people cannot change anyone's status. In the end, everyone is human, created in the image of God, for the purpose of belonging to God and to other humans. Loneliness is dangerous because it creates the urge to try to fill the heart with physical human contact, but the hierarchical structure is particularly dangerous when combined with sex.[22] A man who places his wife under his authority and does not recognize her as his equal partner only needs to take a small step to conclude that his daughters are also at his sexual disposal. Although the secret of incest has long been a strictly guarded taboo, research shows that it is far more common than one would expect.[23]

Though the Bible rebukes sexual sin, many Christian autocrats put themselves at the top of hierarchical marriages and project such hierarchical ideas onto other women in their circle, using their power not only to subject their family, but also to abuse other church members. In doing this, these men destroy individual victims in the present as well as their future families. As

---

20. Storkey, 7.

21. Augustine, *Confessions*, trans. A. C. Outler (Dallas: Southern Methodist University, 1955), Book I, Chapter I, 1. Online: https://www.ling.upenn.edu/courses/hum100/augustinconf.pdf.

22. Storkey, *Scars*, 75–95.

23. See J. Herman and L. Hirschman, "Families at Risk for Father-Daughter Incest," in P. Perri Rieker, E. Carmen, *The Gender Gap in Psychotherapy* (New York: Plenum Press, 1984), 237–258. This type of incest is estimated at 20 percent (237).

Nason-Clark observes, "Violence is learned behaviour."[24] Violating someone's body, the most intimate part of the self, is one of the most effective ways to exert power, and at the same time, it effectively ruins the future of the victim. We are constantly reminded of this through research into the outcomes of wartime rape victims.[25] But psychology shows that the impact of rape trauma is the same within family, church, or work environments in the way that it rips apart all facets of the victim's personality and often remains locked up in people's hearts because it is so difficult to face. This means that many cases don't even come through the difficult therapy process! Moreover, as Miroslav Volf has shown in *Inclusion and Embrace*, victims have a tendency to turn into perpetrators. Because of their victim status and the memory of their victimization, many victims feel entitled to revenge. "Evil generates new evil as evildoers fashion victims in their own ugly image."[26] Rather than focusing feelings of rage toward the perpetrator, the victim transfers the experience of violence to the next generation. Moreover, the perpetrator himself is devastated by his acts of violence, because he loses his humanity with every new act of ruling over a victim. He becomes a beast in the eye of his victims, and if he has been ranked high enough in worldly structures, in history as well. As such, he remains isolated from others and can find no satisfaction, joy, or purpose in his life, no love or connection. The rage that comes with these feelings of abandonment is utterly destructive, both to the perpetrator and to everyone around him.

In reflecting on the outcomes of so-called "complementarianism," it becomes obvious that this warped ideal is far from God's intention for humans – which is to live a life of mutual love within a community of service to one another. Sadly, Christians have misunderstood the biblical commands

---

24. N. Nason-Clark, *The Battered Wife* (Louisville: John Knox Press, 1997), 9.

25. Rape in wartime is most frequently a "practice," a behaviour tolerated by superiors as "self-gratification" "in lieu of wages" or even as a proof of masculinity, but often also as a "policy" in war; S. J. Woods, "Rape as a Practice of War: Toward a Typology of Political Violence," *Politics and Society* 46, no. 4 (2018): 513–537; see chart on 523. K. T. Hagen elaborates on the individual and collective outcomes of wartime rape, "The Nature and Psychosocial Consequences of War Rape for Individuals and Communities," *International Journal of Psychological Studies* 2, no. 2 (2010): 14–25, stating that "when one woman is raped the whole community is raped"; "Collectively, the society also enters into shock and grieving as they lose their mothers, sisters, and daughters through community and familial rejection, physical death, or debilitating impacts of psychological and physical wounds . . . communities in shock may not have the means of coping with the reality of events, particularly if events were linked with socio-cultural taboos relating to sexuality" (19). Unfortunately, traditional values, often also called biblical values, prevent dealing with the trauma of (war) rape.

26. M. Volf, *Exclusion and Embrace* (Nashville: Abingdon, 1996), 81.

by simplistically and partially adhering to a hierarchical interpretation without understanding God's vision for love in marriage and redemption in male-female relationships.

Reading Romans as a Reflection of Genesis 3

We can understand God's comprehensive intentions more easily from the eschatological perspective displayed in Romans, where Paul discusses how "the revelation" of God's children (Rom 8:19) – that is, the "resurrection" of their "mortal bodies" (8:11) – is eagerly awaited by the whole creation. This "revelation" is liberating for the whole creation, because it groans under the oppression of false gods. Thus the current creation has a part to play in God's eschatological purposes, a fact that has often been neglected by traditional theology. Creation, too, will be liberated from its current status of oppression under human sin – so far only partially, with the hope of full liberation at the end of history – when true believers are revealed as such because they nurture and care for the creation instead of "ruling over it" with iron fists. When this occurs, the Spirit of God will be allowed to work out the good deeds that humanity was created for in the first place (Eph 2:10).

Reading Romans as Paul's interpretation of the Genesis story about human destiny from God's perspective sheds new light on Pauline anthropology. For Paul, God's story of salvation begins with the gravity of the human condition, which is exposed in Genesis 3. In the introduction to what has been called his *Compendium Doctrinae*,[27] he writes: "For I am not ashamed of the gospel; it is the power of God for salvation to everyone who has faith" (Rom 1:16). My students think that the main question raised by this passage is, *what do people need to be saved from?* This question is often overlooked in theological deliberations that are more concerned with big doctrines about the redemption of the soul from hell, or else it is handled in passing in light of the christological debates raised by later passages. But this question is central for non-believers today, and it leads to the next contemporary question: *what is sin?* Normally, my students define sin as bad deeds, such as lying, stealing, and having sex outside of marriage. Yet the problem with this response, of course, is that Paul argues against the law and the works of the law as criteria for sin.

Paul's whole mission hangs on the unfortunate human condition as it is described in Genesis 3. Humans need salvation because death has been lurking

---

27. P. Melanchton, *The Loci Communes of Philip Melanchton: With a Critical Introduction by the Translator*, trans. Charles Leander Hill (Eugene: Wipf & Stock, 2007), 69.

to get them ever since they turned away from God, who is their source of life. No set of doctrines or good works will "save our souls" at God's judgment at the end of history. Rather, our very human existence is threatened by the basic human sin of rebelling against God. As Paul puts it, "though they knew God, they did not honor him as God or give thanks to him, but they became futile in their thinking, and their senseless minds were darkened" (Rom 1:21). The common belief is that God will judge the world at some point in the distant future and, until then, humans will be somewhat randomly affected by both good and evil.

Yet Paul understands the judgement from Genesis differently, maintaining that "the wrath of God is revealed from heaven against all ungodliness and wickedness of those who by their wickedness suppress the truth" (Rom 1:18).[28] When the first humans rejected and turned away from God, "God handed them over" to "the lusts of their hearts to impurity, to the degrading of their bodies among themselves" (1:24), to "degrading passions" (1:26), and "to a debased mind and to things that should not be done" (1:28). Then Paul adds a substantial list of wicked things that humans do to themselves and each other, which is intended as a rhetorical trap for the reader.[29] Paul has constructed this text so that whoever reads it will probably agree that at least some of the things on this list are evil: "wickedness, evil, covetousness, malice. Full of envy, murder, strife, deceit, craftiness, they are gossips, slanderers, God-haters, insolent, haughty, boastful, inventors of evil, rebellious toward parents, foolish, faithless, heartless, ruthless" (1:29). This list stirs readers to recollect the wickedness that they have seen or experienced themselves through other people. Paul's intention is not to moralise about whether or not these things are wicked, but to point the finger back at the readers' own shortcomings. For if readers have experienced anything on this list and felt that it was evil, and if they have ever sought punishment for the perpetrators, but then gone and done this same thing to others, then they have done it while knowing it is evil. Therefore, they necessarily deserve the same punishment.

Most likely, when we do evil to others, we find good and often biblical reasons for our behaviour. We rationalize our actions and try to ignore our guilt. Yet sin remains even after evil is exposed and condemned by the cries of victims. For Paul, sin is not some transcendental state of the soul that comes

---

28. The German theologian E. Käsemann interprets this revelation as already in the now, but not always recognized in his *Commentary on Romans* (Grand Rapids: Eerdmans, 1994), 35.

29. J. D. G. Dunn, *Romans 1–8* (Nashville: Thomas Nelson, 1988), 89; comp. K. Magda, *Paul's Territoriality and Mission Strategy* (Tübingen: Mohr/Siebeck, 2009), 160–162.

from the philosophical deliberations of an idle mind. Rather, it embodies itself in concrete acts of evil that tear apart the tapestry of human relations and make death the systemic principle of human existence.[30] For Paul, God's wrath is revealed in the way that God hands over a rebelling people to what they decided to do. This includes the consequences of their actions, which is the certain death of individuals, societies, and the world in general, since, as Paul puts it, "the whole creation has been groaning in labor pains until now" (Rom 8:22). In churches, we learn a simplified version of these texts, which is that Paul identifies the problem as sin and the antidote as the gospel. Both terms have been spiritualised to such a degree that the average Christian, at least in my global experience, has no ability to understand these terms as useful for their daily living. But in Romans 1:16–17, Paul makes it clear that his concern is not so much with sin, but with the outcome of sin, which is death. In Genesis 2:17, God threatens humans, telling them that if they disobey him and eat from the tree of the recognition of good and evil, death will come to people. Yet the average contemporary reader is puzzled by this, because Adam did not die at that moment, nor did he die for a long time, which may suggest that God was telling a lie.

But Paul sees the concealed threat to humanity. In our generation, as we are confronted with the pervasive global crisis of sustainability, those of us who are concerned with the wider world can see more clearly how God's "threat" has worked itself out in the world. Adam's sin was much more than a little mess-up with little consequence. The picture of him and Eve being driven out of Paradise, which may seem like a harsh punishment to us, is God's way of letting people experience the consequences of their choices: by choosing a life away from God, they separate themselves from his care and from the good for which they were created. Because they wanted independence from the Creator, they will experience what it feels like when they try to be gods themselves.

Although Adam and Eve may have lived long lives on earth, the consequences of the death that came to the world are instantly apparent. They blamed each other for the sin. They felt naked and unsafe. Their offspring killed each other. Since those first days, so much death has befallen us that we have to admit that death is a fact of life, even though our whole being longs for life. Women feel the burden of death even more strongly and earlier than men because of their capacity to bear children. So many factors of death intrude on

---

30. An excellent example of how sin works out as "redemptive violence" can be found in W. Wink's *The Powers That Be: Theology for a New Millennium* (New York: Doubleday, 1998). Wink makes a plausible case for total nonviolence as the only possible Christian way.

an unborn baby – not only in terms of abortion, but also when there is a lack of knowledge or support for unwanted pregnancies, or the growing number of people who cannot conceive due to environmental influences, or all the babies who are born into the world without a proper support system to help them grow and so end up as slaves, sex slaves, organ donors, and cannon fodder.

Even when a pregnancy is seemingly eventless, each mother wonders what will happen to her little one at the moment she first holds the baby in her arms. Her joy is immediately overshadowed by deep fear and concern. "I am so afraid," a young mother of four confessed to me. "My life is so happy right now. I have a good husband and beautiful children, but I am constantly afraid that something really bad will happen to them soon, and I don't know how I can live with that!" Unfortunately, these fears are not irrational – not even in the affluent West. In the rest of the world, they are very real.

Paul's introduction to his letter to the Romans reveals his awareness of this threat to human life. He has read the Bible deeply and has seen the threats of what on the surface appears to be no big deal. While turning away from God is a matter of serious concern, the consequential threat of death bothers Paul much more. Living sinfully would be a blast if it were not for the death attached to it each step of the way. The world is in immediate danger of extinction, and the human decision to turn away from God marks the beginning of the world's suicidal downward spiral (Rom 1:18–32). This spiral creates structures that pull everyone into the sphere of death, even "those whose sins were not like the transgression of Adam" (Rom 5:14).

Sin is bad because it brings death, but also because it does not discriminate between those who are guilty of sin and those who are not, at least an immediate sin. Even if there were innocent people – which Paul only sees as a theoretical option – death came into the world and therefore rules over all people and their environments. The threat of death is inescapable. The fact that "God gave them up to" or, from the Greek, "handed them over to" their own desires is a dangerous state of human existence, and yet humans are unaware of the danger precisely because they are self-centred (Rom 1:24, 26, 28).

Even worse, because God left humans to their own rebellion, there is no help for them. Yet God, in his mercy and against all hope, turned back to them by providing a way for their reconciliation. In Jesus, God made his face shine on his creation again. Paul's missionary urgency becomes evident in this constellation of events, which are deeply rooted in the Jewish Scriptures. Therefore, the good news that people need to know is that God turned to humans in the cross of Jesus. By turning to God in faith, death can be defeated.

The Curse of Genesis 3

The human experiment of trying to become a god is dangerous, because there is no cure for it outside of God. This is revealed in the "curse," through which God warns his fallen creation. But we need to read Genesis 3:14–24 from the perspective of God revealing to humans what life will look like without him, rather than God lashing out in anger and ordering hardships as some sort of indignant revenge. This re-reading will give us a new perspective[31] that may help us evaluate the current global human disease, which has had a misunderstood diagnosis. If we read carefully, we see that the snake and nature are cursed,[32] whereas Adam and Eve only get a lesson about their state and future within their chosen constellation of relationships away from the Creator. After the snake is cursed to belong eternally to the earth, to feed from it and constantly be threatened and crushed by humans, God addresses the woman. We may think, as many commentators do, that God addresses the woman first because she sinned first. However, God may address Eve first because she is the primary victim of future human relationships. As the one who bears children – or the only one who has the potential for birth – she needs nurture and care immediately.

God is certainly not talking about the excruciating pain of the birthing process as a punishment, though some churches ordain this for women, as if they could save themselves by experiencing the pain of birthing. (I have actually heard this taught in some churches.) Rather, as research has demonstrated, women are physically disadvantaged in the structures of society because they bear children. This disadvantage is a pain that far surpasses the temporary pain of birthing contractions. Moreover, some women have delivered babies without experiencing extraordinary pain.

In "The Economic Effects of Contraceptive Access: A Review of the Evidence," A. Bernstein and K. M. Jones find that contraception and abortion rights "can improve women's economic outcomes" because "an early birth can disrupt secondary schooling or college attainment, reducing a woman's future earning potential; each additional birth can have further financial effects especially in low-income households; and unexpected late births can impact a

---

31. This perspective, though, is not at all new. G. von Rad states it in his commentary on Genesis, *Genesis: A Commentary*, rev. ed. (Philadelphia: Westminster Press, 1972), 93; the German original, *Das erste Buch Mose*, was published in 1952. Von Rad does speak of "punishment," but he does not elaborate on his earlier claim that "it is unthinkable to speak of their malediction! [sic.]," which is of interest here.

32. Von Rad, *Genesis*, 92, 94.

woman's career trajectory during her prime earning years."[33] Moreover, there are also non-economic benefits, since women who have access to contraception can plan their lives, education, and investments, help keep their families above poverty, and improve the lives of their existing children.[34] Thus women's life-bearing capacity is at odds with the structures of death into which this life will be born. When a woman decides on motherhood, she experiences the constant pain of wishing life for her children, but seeing everywhere the threat of death and being unable to do anything about it. This pain never ends, as mothers continue to worry about their adult children and cannot ever forget them, even when they are grown and have children of their own.

The above research does not investigate the fact that women's lives are painfully affected by fertility even if they never become mothers, were never violated or abused, or have never experienced childhood trauma for growing up as girls. Women handle constant hormonal changes and regularly lose blood and suffer pain from their menstrual cycles. They are also constantly making precautions and planning ahead, because they have to live with the outcomes of sex, whether for pleasure or because of rape. Though keeping sex "safe" is a huge topic with women and girls, it is not addressed for the majority of men.[35] Women are constantly on the alert, hoping to find protection and safety throughout their childbearing years, whether they are pregnant or not. From the perspective of the hierarchies of sin, being biologically able to have children puts women in a far more vulnerable position than men, since one's progress through the hierarchical system is determined by the possession of goods and power.

This whole ordeal – rather than the proverbial birthing pains – is what is on God's mind when he predicts the woman's fate in the aftermath of the fall. God's observation about the woman, "Yet your desire shall be for your husband" (Gen 3:16), should be interpreted from this perspective. One completely inadmissible interpretation is that women have an inner urge to rule over men, which needs to be stopped by sheer power.[36] Women who bear children need to have

---

33. A. Bernstein and K. M. Jones, "The Economic Effects of Contraceptive Access: A Review of the Evidence," 9. Accessed online at Institute for Women's Policy Research, https://iwpr.org/publications/economic-contraceptive-access-review/.

34. Bernstein and Jones, "Economic Effects," 9.

35. If you Google "how to keep safe," you will get hits that are almost exclusively aimed at girls and women.

36. M. D. Gow, "Fall," in *Dictionary of the Old Testament: Pentateuch*, ed. T. D. Alexander and D. W. Baker (Downers Grove: InterVarsity Press, 2003), 289, points to S. T. Foh's argument along these lines from the parallel with Gen 4:7, but also dismisses it. The vast majority of commentators understand this verse as the woman's desire for intimacy and sexual unity. See

their partners share the load of care. Positively speaking, they need nurturing environments where they can both nurture the little ones and also nurture themselves while they take on the important, difficult, and painful process of caring for babies and rearing children in a hostile world. Any single mother can tell stories about how having someone to turn to for understanding and counsel, someone to help with her baby provides sanity when she is feeling overwhelmed. Yet even in functional marriages, women often carry the burden of raising children alone and long for caring and nurturing husbands. The dream of a happy home is a pipe dream within the reality of the structures of sin, and for nurturing environments to emerge, the entire system needs to change.

After addressing the woman, God turns to the man and tells him that he will be unsuccessful in his urge to subdue the earth and rule over it as he wishes. Von Rad notes that Adam is not cursed; rather, the earth is cursed, which plays into Adam's relationship with it. This curse

> goes more deeply to the lowest foundation of all human existence; it strikes the most elementary realm of male effectiveness ... Man was taken from the earth and so was directed to it; she [the earth] was the material basis of his existence; a solidarity of creation existed between man and the ground. But a break occurred in this affectionate relationship, an alienation that expresses itself in a silent, dogged struggle between man and soil.[37]

Again, this should not surprise us, since Adam set himself apart from his Creator and also his partner when he opted for independence and loneliness. Already in the second creation account, it was "not good" for him to be alone (Gen 2:18). So why is man now working on his own and for himself, even though God created a woman for him, who still longs for him?

Understanding the Curse through Romans 1

We have to search for the answer in the story of the fall and in Adam's motives before the fall, as Paul does in Romans 1. Yet Paul's focus is on all of humanity (not men or women in particular), and he is responding to the Jew-Gentile

---

also G. J. Wenham, "Genesis," in D. A. Carson et al., *New Bible Commentary* (Leicester: IVP, 1994), 63.

37. Von Rad, *Genesis*, 94.

divide as it impinges on world mission.[38] For our purposes here, we will look at how Paul's interpretation of and solution to the Jew-Gentile divide also impinges on male-female relationships in the church. But before we take on the gender lens, we have to take Paul's generic perspective about human sin and the outcome of death seriously, for it is basic to these considerations. Human sin in Genesis 3 is described as both male and female: they both were present at the infamous tree; they both wished to eat from it; they both wished to be "like God" (Gen 3:5–6). There is absolutely no support for the claim that women are somehow better than men, nor that the "curse" is all men's fault, nor all women's fault. As Paul points out in Romans, the core problem of sin is wanting to be "like God" (Rom 1:21). Yet to some degree, this core sin plays out differently in male and female lives because women have the biological option to bear children and men do not.

Until recently, it was popular to differentiate between male and female brains,[39] but research has shown that there is more difference between individual men and individual women than between men and women in general.[40] Thus each human is created differently. If our fingerprints and DNA are different, our particular mix of attitudes are equally different. Biology mixes into this. Yet the difference between the roles of men and women in society is a different story. These roles are pushed by the social system, which becomes problematic if we view it from the perspective of the structures and hierarchies of sin. For the evaluation here, I am presupposing that men and women are not much different aside from their biological differences.[41] Though women have the

---

38. The discussion around the occasion for Romans is far from over and has been around for a long time, but it seems to me that the issue of the Jew-Gentile divide is prevalent, regardless of the other facets of sociological environment. See my short overview of the problem in Magda, *Paul's Territoriality*, 123–153, which points to the missionary purpose of Romans, 149.

39. L. Eliot helpfully explores both positions in "Neurosexism: The Myth That Men and Women Have Different Brains," *Nature*, 27 Feb 2019, online: https://www.nature.com/articles/d41586-019-00677-x.

40. Research was conducted by Z. Krizan, E. Zell, and S. R. Teeter on more than 12 million people and published in "Evaluating Gender Similarities and Differences Using Metasynthesis, *American Psychologist* 70, no. 1 (2015): 10–20. https://doi.org/10.1037/a0038208. The study "found an almost 80 percent overlap for more than 75 percent of the psychological characteristics, such as risk taking, occupational stress and morality. Simply put, our differences are not so profound." Online: Iowa State University News Release: "Gender Roles: Men and Women Are Not So Different After All," posted on 29 Jan 2015, https://www.news.iastate.edu/news/2015/01/29/genderdifferences.

41. Mapping the similarities in biology is too complicated for a book with a different set of concerns, such as this one. But research in biology is fascinating, though not immediately applicable to everyday life. To begin looking at the extent of the problems, see A. Fausto-Sterling, *Sex/Gender: Biology in a Social World* (New York: Routledge, 2012).

capacity to bear children, both men and women are equally necessary for conception. The biblical story makes it clear that both men and women were created in the image of God to reflect God and to work equally on the tasks of nurturing and caring for the world. The differences in how we nurture and care reflect our individuality rather than our gender, for God gave all people different abilities and gifts. I have observed this in my ministry. Some fathers are gentler than some mothers, especially mothers who have been abused by male figures during childhood and adolescence. Given these presuppositions, women and men both strive to be "like God" and suffer the consequences of sin and death equally. This is where our reconstruction of the human problem begins. For even though both men and women are subjected to violence, women suffer substantially more direct violence and experience it earlier than men simply because of their biological predisposition to bear children.

> The "Global and Regional Estimates of Violence against Women"[42] claims that "Globally 35.6% [of women] have experienced either intimate partner violence and/or non-partner sexual violence. Nearly one third of ever-partnered women (30.0%) have experienced physical and/or sexual violence by an intimate partner, and 7.2% of adult women have experienced sexual violence by a non-partner. Some women have experienced both." We should note that "it is estimated that of the 87,000 women who were intentionally killed in 2017 globally, more than half (50,000 – 58%) were killed by intimate partners or family members, meaning that 137 women across the world are killed by a member of their own family every day . . . It is estimated that there are 650 million women and girls in the world today who were married before age 18 . . . At least 200 million women and girls aged 15–49 have undergone female genital mutilation in the 30 countries with representative data on prevalence. In most of these countries, the majority of girls were cut before age five . . . Approximately 15 million adolescent girls (aged 15 to 19) worldwide have experienced forced sex (forced sexual intercourse or other sexual acts) at some point in their life. In the vast majority of countries, adolescent girls are most at risk of forced sex by a current/former husband, partner or boyfriend. Based on data from 30 countries, only 1% ever sought professional help . . . Globally, one out of three students

---

42. The "Global and Regional Estimates of Violence against Women: Prevalence and Health Effects of Intimate Partner Violence and Non-Partner Sexual Violence," WHO (2013), 31, accessed online, https://apps.who.int/iris/bitstream/handle/10665/85239/9789241564625_eng.pdf;jsessionid=203523B7248B9108F17D6CB5CCED756B?sequence=1).

(aged 11 and 13 to 15 years) have been bullied by their peers at school at least on one day in the past month, with girls and boys equally likely to experience bullying. However, boys are more likely to experience physical bullying than girls, and girls are more likely to experience psychological bullying, particularly being ignored or left out or subject to nasty rumours. Girls also report being made fun of because of how their face or body looks."[43]

Returning to Romans, Paul sees the human rejection of God as God and the attempt to be "like God" as the first step toward degeneration (comp. Rom 1:21).[44] If God is removed from the picture, the god-position is open for pretenders, and as humans become more numerable, there will be more and more pretenders. As the number of pretenders increases, the wars among those striving for the top position will increase, because being god means you try to become the only one so that you are in charge of everyone else. Naturally, not everyone makes it to the top, so the hierarchies of gods and half-gods are the necessary outcome of these god-wars. Nevertheless, some people argue that such hierarchies are beneficial for humankind, because they offer at least some temporary stability for the lives of those involved. Yet people may not realize how the god-wars are at work in their everyday lives, especially those who fall on the lower end of the hierarchical pyramid. Those who function at the bottom levels of the social strata are necessary for those at the top, and they are trained to submit unconsciously through socialization. These god-wars operate in politics, companies, workplaces, and all levels of human existence. For instance, poor people in Croatia collect empty bottles to get cash, and so there is a war among those who can access which garbage bins. Woe to the unauthorized when they try to look for something in a bin to which someone else has acquired the rights!

---

43. Facts available at UN Women, "Facts and Figures: Ending Violence against Women," accessed online, https://www.unwomen.org/en/what-we-do/ending-violence-against-women/facts-and-figures.

44. Romans is often subjected to doctrinal proof-texting and often, especially in history, not much attention has been given to the context of verses or to the problem the text raises. For instance, Rom 1:19–23 is popular in the discussion about (natural) revelation (i.e. whether [fallen] people can know God and how it is possible). Often, this is done without biblical evidence. A. E. MacGrath manages to present the subject in *Christian Theology: An Introduction* (Oxford: Blackwell, 2001), 201–219, referring students only to two biblical quotations from the Old Testament. In biblical studies, texts must be read in their contexts. For Rom 1:18–23, Paul's subject is not "how" God can be known – he draws on his Hellenist and Jewish sources. (Dunn, *Romans 1–8*, presupposes this fact, dismissing Käsemann's "careful qualifications" against "natural theology," 56–57.)

Ever since we turned our backs on God, humanity has been thoroughly infected with the hierarchies of the gods. Though we may strive for equality and equity (or whatever other new term we invent for the ideal), these dreams belong to a different world and cannot be reached through our current hierarchical order.

In Romans 1:18–32, Paul's concern is not to depict natural theology, but to feature the life experience of the downward spiral of evil, which is the result of the human sin of abandoning God as their source of life and experiencing the consequences. By abandoning God, humanity abandons their own identity in creation, for the biblical story links human identity to God, creation to Creator. After humans abandon their identity, the Creator, who watches over the creation, becomes the other, a stranger to be feared. The creatures now begin to search for and build their identity alone. Yet detached from God, humans have neither a plan nor a purpose. Thus the world constantly tries to teach people how to "realize" themselves, and so they scramble around, doing whatever feels good or right to them individually. Paul describes as the "law" of the sinful "flesh" or "body" (e.g. Rom 7:14–24).[45] Having abandoned their identity in God, people run from one purpose or scheme to another in order to find affirmation as the gods they want to become. They hope that this affirmation (which could be seen as a form of worship) and the accumulation of possessions will define them as gods. But the more insecure they become about their identity, the more important it is for them to buy things and find supporters to affirm them. And though they long for support, they never really feel secure, because any support they receive necessarily becomes a threat in their quest to become self-sufficient. Thus the higher they climb, the more affirmation they will need, and the more threatened they will feel. If they cannot attract willing supporters and fans, they will coerce unwilling subjects into that role.

All hierarchies function because of the people on the bottom who support the gods at the top. Once that support ceases, the hierarchy collapses.[46] So why

---

45. Scholars have still not resolved the identification of the "I" in this passage in Romans 7. For a discussion about this issue, see Cranfield, *Romans 1–8* (London: T & T Clark, 2011), 342–343. However, I believe the way forward is to see this passage as a general experience based on Paul's understanding of Genesis 3 (see Magda, *Paul's Territoriality*, 142–143). Dunn also makes a case for this in *Romans 1–8*, 381. I am not sure why Cranfield needs to exempt Paul and the other Jews from the description, because one could argue that in every person's life, there is a time of practical living without understanding the law.

46. This so-called "imposter syndrome" was described first in higher education, but it transcends that realm. See M. Breeze, "Imposter Syndrome as a Public Feeling" in *Feeling Academic in Neoliberal University: Feminist Flights, Fights, and Failures*, ed. V. Taylor and K.

would one free human being agree to be subject to another human being? Climbing hierarchies not only require wits and strength, but also outwitting, out-cheating, and often a violent battle to the top. Rarely are the god-wars in hierarchies fought fairly. It is "every man for himself" in a battle that continues until weaknesses are exposed, or someone decides that coming in second or third is high enough for the moment. Naturally, people can be bribed into these minor positions, but it is even better if they grow up believing that they don't have the potential to be gods. Thus caste systems are invented, people are declared slaves because of the colour of their skin, and political systems are established that declare certain people to be divine by nature or "blue blood," while others are born to be subjects, servants, or slaves. These myths maintain the divine status quo and keep those at the bottom feeling weak and diminished. Some myths are actually truisms that might have helped a culture function better in the past, but many cultures simply marginalize the vast majority of people and invite only the privileged few into the inner circle. These few become the only true pretenders for the god position in that hierarchical system. I will not name any in particular, as they all function in the same manner and feed in the same way – whether in politics, the corporate world, society in general, or churches.

Churches are particularly interesting, because they do all this posturing in the name of God. God-ordained roles are given to the few popes, bishops, presidents, or apostles who rule over people in God's name. In the entire biblical narrative, I cannot find any place that overtly recommends such structures. Though hierarchical systems are mentioned and described, they are not endorsed by God, and there is nothing in the biblical teachings that would condone such stratification of authority over other people.

God does not rule and trample. God creates, gives life, and serves unto death. The Bible's basic teaching opposes human power structures. Throughout the Old Testament, God objects to them. The intriguing story of the Tower of Babel (Genesis 11:1–9) may be seen as God's first denunciation of human hierarchies, for such systems are not how God envisioned the world, when he created humans to dwell in community with him. He did not create humans as angels, who live subdued to him, but as free beings that would be like him and express his likeness in good things and through close communion with him.

Lahad (London: Palgrave Macmillan, 2018), 191–219. Breeze argues for "imposterism" within higher education, but her thoughts about how the structures may affect this feeling in individuals is interesting for our case here.

How Hierarchies of Sin Ruin Life

Because there are so many pretenders for the god-position at the top of the hierarchy, those who are opposed to God are stampeding toward that position, stirring up enormous chaos along the way. All hierarchies invent their own rules for preservation, such as exclusion and discrimination.

As discussed above, the ability to have children makes women particularly vulnerable to exclusion, because they have children to think about, and they must cope with the requirements of their bodies for breaks from so-called "productive" work. Though the ability to bear children into the world should be a blessing for the earth, hierarchies have turned it into a curse of the female body. Women have to fight constantly to overcome this biological disadvantage. Yet as hard as they fight, male hierarchies work together to exclude women from the god-wars because of the "curse of *their* flesh." While women may long for freedom and want to fight the structures, they are constantly told to submit. Thus women need open and supportive environments and mentors to sort through these conflicting impulses and ideas in order to find the freedom of God.

Many traditions around the world marginalize women and prevent them from having any direct involvement in male hierarchies. In the West, it has been noticed recently that top positions in politics or economy are not acquired, as normally presupposed, by superior knowledge, intelligence, or experience, but by being groomed and invited by those who are already in those positions and are preparing for their exit or retirement. Most often, women are excluded from such grooming – and if they end up in such positions, it is because of some error in the system.

For instance, women sometimes come into high positions during times of crisis, when holding the position would be less honourable than normal, or when the task ahead seems impossible. This phenomenon has been described as a "glass cliff."[47] To give one example, we may point to the German CDU/

---

47. S. A. Haslam and M. K. Ryan, "The Road to the Glass Cliff: Differences in Perceived Sustainability of Men and Women for Leadership Positions in Succeeding and Failing Organisations," *The Leadership Quarterly* 19 (2008): 530–543. Also online: https://web.archive.org/web/20131225013107/http://blog.aelios.com/mbawg/wp-content/uploads/2010/05/The-glass-cliff.pdf. "Glass cliff" is "an allusion to the fact that their [women's] leadership positions are relatively risky or precarious, since they are more likely to involve management of organisational units that are in crisis. Such positions . . . are potentially dangerous for women who hold them as companies that experience consistent bad performance are likely to attract attention . . . Moreover, in these circumstances the co-occurrence of two relatively rare events – the appointment of a woman and continuing poor organisational outcomes – is likely to lead them to being seen as meaningfully related" (531).

CSU coalition, who elected Angela Merkel as their first female president in 2000 in the aftermath of the great donations scandal and the all-time low of Germany's conservative party. Against all hope, Merkel won the elections in 2005 and has been instrumental in leading both Germany and the EU through the world economic crisis of 2008.[48]

We observed a similar story in Croatia when Jadranka Kosor was named as the successor for the prime minister after Ivo Sanader resigned his position in July of 2009 without stating any reason. He was later charged with leading organized criminal activities, which made his majority party very unpopular even among their own ranks. The hope was that Kosor would be an obedient puppet, but when she refused, she was replaced. The party was in such a bad state before the presidential elections of 2014 that the members decided to bring in Kolinda Grabar Kitarović for presidential elections because there were no men who could win them. The surprise worked, and Kitarović was elected, giving time to Andrej Plenković, the party's new president and new prime minister, to consolidate the party and help it win its victory in parliamentary elections in 2016. Many commented that they voted for Kitarović "because she was so beautiful." Kitarović also earned many women's voices, as it was hopeful to see a woman finally run for president. However, all along, Kitarović has not managed to make a political name for herself as president, and the general impression has been that she is a puppet at her party's hands. She herself has complained that the press rarely comments on her political statements, but always features her looks and fashion.

These examples reveal how women have often been used as scapegoats in male hierarchies. When the going gets tough and reputations could be lost, women are given an opportunity to make it or break. Though some strong women do make it to the top of companies and even politics on their own, they typically need to be twice as skilled and capable to be accepted, and they tend to face the challenge head-on, fighting in the same manner as men in the scramble to the top. Along the way, they face opposition and are warned that they are stepping into male space, where they are unwelcome. They are also called names, such as "dragons" or "bitches," and described as lacking femininity or even – as I have heard one church leader remark about a capable young

---

48. J. Abramsohn, "Chancellor Angela Merkel and Her Quiet Rise to Power" in *Deutsche Welle*, no date, online: https://www.dw.com/en/chancellor-angela-merkel-and-her-quiet-rise-to-power/a-1600411.

female leader – "having too many male hormones."[49] If women somehow make it to the top, everyone is surprised and dismayed. In my experience, capable women who step up to leadership roles in tough circumstances usually fit one of two paradigms. Either they have been victims of abuse and overburdened with responsibility at a young age, and so they learned either to stand up for themselves or die – and they stood and lived. Or, less frequently, they had fathers or male role models who believed in them and created spaces for them to flourish.

Even in the West, women grow up with an array of traditions that teach them early on that they are unfit for leadership or unable to run their lives or make decisions. They are told that they need to be led by their fathers and brothers, then their husbands, and eventually their sons. I happened to talk to a man once whose wife kept their house and garden perfectly clean and beautiful, worked full-time as a teacher, and practically raised their two boys alone, as he was rarely at home. She even went to shops for him and brought clothes for him to try on so that he would not need to leave home. This same man told me that he had to keep "strict reins" on his wife, because otherwise she would become mentally ill! As if giving her a tough life, a lot of work, and demanding submission was what she needed to preserve her sanity! I looked at him, thinking at first that he must be joking, but he was serious. I challenged his view by pointing out that if anything was killing his wife, it was the overwhelming stupidity of the way he was burdening and abusing her by adding unnecessary chores to her already full plate. Thankfully, he seemed to think this through, since I met her a few years later, and she was overjoyed with the "sudden" change in their relationship.

The traditional teaching that a woman will somehow become "damaged" if men do not manage her and keep "reins" on her is strong in many places, including those we might not expect. Sometimes it is disguised through ignorance, as the example above shows. Often, it is clothed in romanticism, such as when a father "gives away" his daughter to her husband in a marriage ceremony, or when a girl is told that she is a pretty princess. Most frequently, it is an excuse for the violent egotism of men who are trying to climb up the ladders of hierarchies.

---

49. C. Post, I. M. Latu and L. Y. Belkin, "A Female Leadership Trust Advantage in Times of Crisis: Under What Conditions?" *Psychology of Women Quarterly* 43, no. 2 (2019): 215–231, 215–216, believe that there is "Ample evidence . . . that people dislike and punish women in non-conforming gender roles" and "Despite real changes in, and favorable attitudes toward, women's access to male dominated jobs find surprising stability in gender stereotypes."

Women are important in male hierarchies as long as they stay within the traditional roles prescribed for women – and mothers often teach their daughters to stay within those roles. I once had a conversation with the mother of my daughter's friend as our girls were about to finish high school. Although her daughter was a straight "A" student, her mother was considering not letting her continue with university studies. "She will marry anyway," she told me. "That's a lot of money wasted on her education!" To make the story more interesting, the mother had a college diploma and had achieved a high position among men. However, she had seen many women rise the ranks only on account of their beauty, an experience that told her that for women, beauty mattered more than brains. As harsh as this sounds, she was a practical woman, and so she continued to impose this crippling tradition on her own daughter.

In Kenya, the Maasai women believe that girls must endure Female Genital Circumcision, now globally referred to as Female Genital Mutilation (FGM), in order to become a proper and useful part of their culture and society.[50] If they are not circumcised, the story goes, nobody will want to marry them, and it is unclear what their role would be within the culture. While the world has stood up against this painful practice, which is hazardous, often leads to medical complications that mutilate a girl for life, transfers illness, and can even cause death, the support for FMG is still strong and upheld by women. Though fathers might allow their daughters to skip the procedure, the girls have to go through their mothers to ask, and the mothers tend to refuse because they think FMG is in their daughters' best interest. The FMG initiation rites usually coincide with the end of primary education, and the girls are removed from class for a couple of months before graduation. As they recover from the procedure, they miss a lot of difficult schoolwork, which becomes impossible for them to make up. Thus their chance to finish primary school and continue to high school is diminished drastically. Many adults also tell the girls that now they can marry and have children, so who needs school anyway! In the best case scenario, the girl might get married and have a happy home and children, but this is rarely the case. Young girls who are taken from schools and taught that their only purpose is to marry and have children will hurry to do just

---

50. Of course, FGM can be found around the globe, but Kenya has been featured as an unlikely proponent. The newest contribution to this subject on Google by B. Adebayo, *CNN* (25 Oct 2019), is entitled "A Kenyan Doctor Is Seeking to Legalize Female Genital Mutilation," online: https://edition.cnn.com/2019/10/25/africa/kenya-doctor-fgm-petition-intl/index.html. See also A. Zhu, "The Woman Who Wants to Legalize Female Genital Cutting," *Bright* (8 Mar 2018). Online: https://brightthemag.com/legalize-female-genital-cutting-fgm-kenya-health-f5335243b4e2.

that. Supported by raging hormones, they will find equally eager boys, who have been taught that success is measured by going places and having as many women as possible. As noted earlier, this is an agenda for disaster.

While there is a lot to cherish and uphold in the cultures of the world, any culture, including Christian ones, needs to be evaluated critically. Does the culture benefit its people, or does it afflict and prolong suffering for the multitudes of many nations? Do its traditions help or oppress women?

Because I am writing from a Christian Baptist perspective, it may seem that this pattern is not a Christian problem. Though the BWA so far does not have an agency that monitors the status of women in Baptist churches, I have found that the tradition of FGM is still practiced among Christians and even Protestants.[51] Not surprisingly, the practice has become global and even includes some "white" territories.[52] This is just another example that reflects similar and gruesome global cultural trends that try to control women and their sexuality. I also remember my own culture shock when I was in Africa at a Baptist women's meeting and discovered that the main speaker was a divorced woman. In my background, being divorced is a major obstacle in ministry for both men and men. When I asked my host about it, she looked at me, obviously perplexed, and said, "Why would that be important for a main speaker? Most women in Africa are divorced or remarried."

Later, a young girl from South Africa approached me to ask about my talk. "Did you really mean that women can be called for something else?" she asked. "In my country, women are told that their purpose in life is to marry and have children, but men are not told that. Sometimes, they are taught that if they are truly spiritual, they will have many women, like Abraham, Jacob, and Solomon!" If we are not careful, culture will draw from various traditions, combining them into recipes for disaster. In this case, a narrative approach to Old Testament stories had taught a literal approach to interpreting the biblical text. Rather than hearing the important theological and ethical teaching of the Bible, these men had simply sanctified their inner urges with "biblical" teaching!

---

51. WHO, *Female Genital Mutilation: A Student's Manual*. Online, accessed 1 Jan 2020: https://www.who.int/gender/other_health/Studentsmanual.pdf.

52. E. Batha, "U.S. Woman Says Strict Christian Parents Subjected Her to FGM" for Reuters, 1 April 2019. Online https://www.reuters.com/article/us-usa-religion-fgm/us-woman-says-strict-christian-parents-subjected-her-to-fgm-idUSKCN1RD2LI. See also S. Moghe, "3 US Women Share the Horrors of Female Genital Mutilation" for *CNN*, 11 May 2017; online: https://edition.cnn.com/2017/05/11/health/fgm-us-survivor-stories-trnd/index.html.

By observing these dynamics in Africa, I have learned to see the potential for harm within my own traditions, even when they may sound spiritual on the surface. Though my traditions may be more subtle, they are not much different from what I have experienced around the world, particularly when it comes to the suffering of women. The whole world operates through sinful hierarchies that enforce rules and regulations on marginalized people in order to keep them enslaved – both those who live in poverty and also those who live in comfortable affluence. Being enslaved to any structure of sin only brings more death.

My own country is part of the EU and is "civilized" according to Western standards, with a high rate of literacy. Compared to the Majority World, it is not too bad off economically. Yet even here, the tradition that requires girls to marry in order to be respected is as strong as it is in the rest of the world. Many Christians here still believe that women must suffer – and not only in childbirth! Women live with men who abuse them and are continually unfaithful, which biblically speaking is already a divorce that is caused by the unfaithful husband.

In conclusion, all areas of human life are infested with the human god-delusion. The global trend to see everything through economics reveals how deep-reaching this delusion has become. We must recognize how dangerous this is for the human community and the sustainability of life. Because of this intrinsic malfunction, we are unable to recognise or accept the warning signs of a world that is coming to the end of its resources. We have inherited language and cultures that perpetuate and enforce abuse and violence, and we stand up for these practices as Christians, because we have been taught that this is the God-ordained order for the world. We fear that everything will fall apart if we rebel, and so we accept the casualties of the god-wars as collateral damage, hoping that, somehow, we will be spared.

Yet the main agenda in the Bible is the liberation of those who are captives, and God gave his son to the world to bring freedom to the captives (Luke 4:19). So why is it so easy to side-track the church?

As John Stott pointed out many years ago, the Christian life is a countercultural path that is a constant struggle and does not come easily.[53] Gerd Theißen even wonders if we should see this countercultural task as the

---

53. J. Stott, *The Message of the Sermon on the Mount* (Downers Grove: InterVarsity Press), 1978.

work of a few Christian representatives who are willing to be marginalized in societies as they seek to exemplify the rule.[54]

Envisioning a New Structure
To return to Paul's evaluation of the origin of the structures of sin in Romans 1, the human sin of detaching from God creates a downward spiral that brings death not only to those who sin, but to everyone else as well. Yet to accept Paul's evaluation of humanity and its need for salvation, Christians need to admit their baggage of sin and willingly accept that they are God's creations and God alone is God. Paul's teaching not only has enormous outcomes for a biblical theology of male-female relationships, but also, more comprehensively, for how Christians should live with each other in the world as witnesses to God, our Father.

Human trafficking, for instance, is not a criminal deviation within an otherwise well-functioning system that abhors the practice, though we may like to think otherwise. Rather, human trafficking points to the very core of how human hierarchies of sin function. Because the structures are built on the accumulation of human subjects, the "human trafficking" label simply draws lines to distinguish socially acceptable forms of "selling" (e.g. selling wives to respectable rich men or acquiring cheap adults for labour as opposed to children) from socially unacceptable forms of selling.

But the Bible has a lot to say about the business of selling souls. R. Bauckham points out that the purpose of Revelation is to unmask a system that treats people as commodities (see Rev 18).[55] When we view the problem from the perspective of structures of sin, we can see how many women try to sell themselves to the highest bidder simply to secure their positions in the hierarchy, even if they do so vicariously through a promising husband. Mothers will similarly groom their daughters for this deal. In part, FGM is upheld because the procedure makes women more appealing to men. What we need is a different system altogether – one that will not treat people as commodities, but as people who have been created to live out God's purposes in the world. This may sound like a return to Marxism or socialism, a more just distribution of means among people as equals, but I would argue that socialism and capitalism are two sides of the same coin. Both define humans in terms of the economy.

---

54. G. Theißen, *The Historical Jesus* (Minneapolis: Fortress, 1998), 398.
55. R. Bauckham, *Climax of Prophecy* (London: T & T Clark, 1993), 338–383.

Because of the power of sin, a different system is impossible without God. Only God can "buy back" his creation and give people the option once again to be his and to share in his glory. Unfortunately, this can only happen against the background and influence of the structures of sin, with all its hierarchies, myths, and rules. The difficult task for Christians is to choose to be marginalised within the hierarchies of sin, believing that by standing this ground, something new will emerge for all people and for the whole creation.

Christ Takes the Curse of the Body upon Himself

While the teaching about salvation is prominent on the lips of many Christians, our understanding and experience of what Christ meant for humanity is rather limited. More often than not, Christian churches fall into what I will call a Galatian pattern of living. They are convinced that their faith in Jesus is not enough, and so they need to add some serious rules to Christ's work so that salvation can be achieved and maintained.

Paul's Letter to the Galatians

Paul visited the Galatians on his second – and probably also his first – missionary journey.[56] The provinces of Pisidia and Pamphylia belonged to the Roman province of Galatia in Paul's day, although these Greek regions did not like to be associated with the uneducated and uncultured Celts who lived further north (and to whom they were joined by the Romans).[57] Historically and biblically, as soon as Paul passed Tarsus and began evangelizing in those regions, he crossed the line into Gentile territory. From a Jewish geographical perspective, the region belonged to Noah's son, Japhet, rather than Shem, who was Paul's nation's forefather. Although there were synagogues past Tarsus, according to Jewish geography, the territory belonged to the Gentiles.[58] The interesting development in Paul's mission, which is what brought Paul to Antioch in the first place (Acts 11:19–26), is that the Gentiles unexpectedly responded to the gospel with much more enthusiasm than the Jews, in whose

---

56. See a detailed discussion for this in R. Riesner, *Die Frühzeit des Apostels Paulus* (Tübingen: Mohr/Siebeck, 1994), 204–291.

57. Magda, *Paul's Territoriality*, 89–90.

58. M. Hengel and A. M. Schwemer, *Paulus zwischen Damascus und Antiochien* (Tübingen: Mohr Siebeck, 1998), 271.

synagogues the mission and preaching usually started.[59] Synagogues were popular places for God-seekers in the ancient world, and some evaluations have suggested that women from higher social levels were especially interested in the Jewish cult. The story about Jesus corresponded with the Jewish pursuit of the one God,[60] but because the response from the Jews was not always friendly, the new communities had to find new meeting places (Acts 14:1–7; 17:1–9).

This development in the gospel mission produced several difficulties and questions. The first question derives from the frustration that the gospel was not well-received by those for whom it was first intended – the Jews. If Jesus came to fulfil God's promise to the Jews (Rom 15:8),[61] why didn't they recognize him as Messiah, since all the Hebrew Scriptures point to this fact, and Jesus's ministry was surrounded by so much power and prophetic ministry? The first question may have frustrated the apostles in Jerusalem, because what had started so well in Jerusalem had stopped progressing. A second equally important question is, how should the Gentiles be seen within the framework of the promise to Israel? This second question raises all sorts of social and theological difficulties. Why are the Gentiles accepting the gospel and not the Jews? Has God abandoned his people and moved on to other nations? How can anyone trust God if he is so fickle and does not stand by his promise? From a practical point of view, How must the Gentiles change to fit the requirements of the (Jewish) Christian church? A huge cultural difference dominated both the Jews and the non-Jews, who wanted to maintain community in everyday life. There were also unbridgeable ethical dilemmas, for some grave sins prohibited by Jewish law were acceptable – and even welcomed! – in the Greek culture. Moreover, the practicalities of everyday church life needed to be considered. For instance, the church typically shared a meal and then added communion into this setting. The meals mimicked Jewish ways of eating because they had come from their culture. Yet the Gentiles had other norms for their meals (as can be seen in 1 Cor 11:17–34). Worst of all, how could Jews eat with people

---

59. Hengel and Schwemer, *Paulus*, 103. Japhet (the European nations) is blessed with already living in the "tents of Shem" (Gen 9:27), while Ham (whose territory is Africa) is cursed because he shamed his father, Noah. Hengel (and others) suggest that Paul is possibly driven by "territoriality" in his mission to the whole world, presupposing that Paul evangelised Ham during his time in Arabia (the "hidden" years) and that he "crosses over" to Japhet because he is driven by promises such as Gen 9:27.

60. Hengel, Schwemer, *Paulus*, 111–112.

61. Comp. K. Magda, "Unity as a Prerequisite for a Christian Mission: A Missional Reading of Rom 15:1–12," *Kairos* 1 (2008): 39–52, 50.

who smelled of pork and ate other forbidden food that was abominable to them?

Paul's first practical answer to these questions comes in Galatians, but he later adds more comprehensive reasoning in Romans. He tries to give scriptural answers to these questions, which are revealed in the person and work of Christ, and he also includes clear instructions about acceptable behaviour for all. For instance, if Christ came to die for all sinners of the world, then Adam's sin had to have a universal character (though it might be unrecognizable at first). Paul does not argue the reverse, as with the medieval doctrine of the original sin, which is that Adam's sin was transferred to all humans, and therefore Christ had to come to save them. Paul's response also has a different approach to the law of Moses – of which the Jews were so proud and which many Jews considered to be a means of salvation. Paul argues that if people could be saved by keeping the law of Moses, Christ would not have needed to come. God could have just pointed everyone to the option that was already there. But the law provided no salvation.

For Paul, even the Jewish law, which is "holy and just and good" (Rom 7:12), was not the means of salvation, but the means by which humans could recognize the greatness of their sin before God. The law reveals humanity's helplessness in view of their eternal destiny, which is death (e.g. Rom 3:19–20). The law, as Jesus reveals in the Sermon on the Mount (Matt 5–7), only touches the tip of the iceberg of God's holiness requests, and it could not be upheld perfectly even by the best Jews.

Paul knew this firsthand, as he had tried to uphold the law and had failed. The letter of the law made him persecute God's church (Acts 22:4; Gal 1:13; Phil 3:6). This does not suggest that the law is imperfect, but that it can be misinterpreted and bring death rather than life. The law condemns only to show the extent of human sin. For Paul, several things follow from this. First, all have sinned: "all have turned aside, together they have become worthless" (Rom 3:12). Surprisingly, this includes the Jews, God's chosen people, who have God's law. Second, Adam's sin must be recognized as having catastrophic consequences, for it brought about universal death on all peoples, including the Jews (Rom 5:12). Accordingly, everyone, including the Jews, needs Christ and must respond to him in faith (Rom 3:21–23). Third, Paul recognizes that if the Old Testament is read from that perspective, faith is the only access to God: "Abraham believed God and it was reckoned to him as righteousness" (Rom 4:3). Abraham was not saved by circumcision or by keeping the law. His righteousness depended on his belief in God (turning to God as his Creator and only Redeemer). Scripture repeats this idea continuously: "he who is righteous will live by faith" (Rom 1:16; comp. Hab 2:4; Gal 3:11).

For Paul, Jews and Gentiles are equally sinful, regardless of the slight advantage that the Jews have as receivers of God's promises. Therefore, the requirement for approaching God is the same for all. God can be approached only through Jesus, whom God "put forward as a sacrifice of atonement by his blood, effective through faith" (Rom 3:28). In Paul's words from Galatians, "Christ redeemed us from the curse of the law by becoming a curse for us" (Gal 3:13). Or from his letter to the Romans:

> ... because through Christ Jesus the law of the Spirit who gives life has set you free from the law of sin and death. For what the law was powerless to do because it was weakened by the flesh, God did by sending his own Son in the likeness of sinful flesh to be a sin offering. And so he condemned sin in the flesh, in order that the righteous requirement of the law might be fully met in us, who do not live according to the flesh but according to the Spirit. (Rom 8:2–4)

Therefore, besides Christ, none of the other requirements of the law can be considered as God-ordained or mandatory for salvation. Paul argued his case before the apostles in Jerusalem, and it was accepted by the "brothers" there (Gal 2:1–10; comp. Acts 15:4–35). Yet this teaching was not easily implemented, as demonstrated by Paul's rebuke of Peter (Gal 2:11–14). Culture and tradition have a mighty grip on people and prevent them from changing. Paul's letter to the Romans was written because the dispute about the law persisted and seemed to escalate as the years passed. Eventually, Paul was imprisoned for his teaching in Jerusalem and delivered to Rome (Acts 21:27).

Paul's theology is difficult for us to accept because of our sinful nature. We don't easily accept salvation, because we want to be "self-made" and demonstrate our importance. God's gift in Christ requires us to submit with humility as creatures before our Creator. But humans are like a "living sacrifice" (Rom 12:1), able to jump off the altar when we don't like the process. We were created with a free will to accept God, or not. Yet when we fail to accept God as our Creator, we have to accept the death of a non-being, one whose life has been emptied of its purpose.

In *God in Creation*, Jürgen Moltmann, the famous German theologian, paints a philosophical picture of what it looked like when God created the world. As someone who encompasses everything, God had to withdraw from some space within himself, or "empty himself" (Phil 2:7), so that the other, his creation, could live independently of him. In order for the creation to live, God had to give himself up. By giving the other a free will, God simultaneously opened up space for potential enemies within himself, and in so doing, he opened himself up for suffering.[62] What Jesus goes through in our world is much more than a ransom, for it is a symbol of the eternal pain of creation, which can be relieved only by staying in voluntary connection with God, accepting him as Creator, connecting to his Spirit, and becoming one with him. This imagery is all well-known from Jesus's conference with the disciples in the Gospel of John (John 15–17).

Moltmann's model has been criticized for some flaws – one being that it is bound to the human experience of earth and body.[63] Yet this may also be an advantage, since the picture is similar to the experience of women and their biological "predestination" to suffer by bearing a new life. First, women seem to be at the forefront of this birthing process of equality. They feel the pain it brings to nurture life within the structures of sin, or within the territories of the enemy. Thus women need to address it first, which is very countercultural. Second, when we apply Paul's discussion about Christ's work to male-female relationships in the church, we have to say that Christ is enough. Women do not need to add motherhood or submission to their husbands in order to attain salvation. If women believe, they are lifted from the curse and into the community with God. Though they are different biologically, they can be one with God. Their function is not determined by biology, but by the Spirit of God that moves within them. Because women carry the Spirit of God equally, they cannot be placed in a subordinate position to men.

---

62. J. Moltmann, *God in Creation* (Minneapolis: Fortress, 1993), 80–89.

63. In a review of *God in Creation* published shortly after the book was published in English, P. S. Fiddes, *Journal of Theological Studies* 38, no. 1 (1987): 262, notes that: "Moltmann has frequently provided theological support for activism, such as political effort on behalf of the oppressed." Fiddes also hits on several of these criticisms, such as Moltmann's "Trinitarian concept of God as community," who "is open to relationships with others" and which "will foster a view of the whole world as a ... spiritual ecosystem in which man is called to participate rather than dominate" (262). However, Moltmann's anxiousness "to preserve divine initiative" in this does not offer much freedom to the creation, as it only seems to play a role towards God's own rest/Sabbath ("the crown of creation is not man, but Sabbath," 263). Fiddes has some questions about Moltmann's pneumatology because it seems to "dissociate" the Spirit from the Son, as the Spirit's kenosis is perpetual (happening in the Creation throughout) and the Son's is particular (265). Others have suggested that by concentrating on eschatology, Moltmann loses ecclesiology altogether. E.g. W. K. Key "God in Creation: A Reflection on Jürgen Moltmann's Theology," *Rural Theology* 2 (2005): 75–84, 81.

Galatians 3: Christ Redeemed Us from the Curse by Becoming a Curse for Us

In revisiting Galatians 3, it is important to pay careful attention to the language of the curse and the body: "Christ redeemed us from the *curse* of the law by *becoming a curse* for us" (3:13). This means that in a Christian community, we cannot apply the principles of the curse to anyone in particular, including women, since Jesus took our curse on himself by "*becoming a curse* for us." Generally, Christians do not have a problem with this, since it is basic to the doctrine of salvation and Christology. However, Christians easily transport the equality aspect of our redemption into eternity because we are currently living within the structures of sin that challenge it. Biblically, both salvation and the equality of men and women have implications in the now, which means that both have to be visible here, within the structures of sin, and not only in an eternal future.

Just as it was important for the Jews to understand that social differences could no longer be maintained in Christ because his sacrifice overruled them, we in Christ must live as if "there is no longer Jew or Greek, there is no longer slave or free, there is no longer male and female; for all of you are one in Christ Jesus" (Gal 3:28–29). Interestingly, Paul adds "male and female" here, even though this was not a weighty discussion in his culture, nor is it a primary concern in his letter to the Romans.

Again, paying close attention to the language of the curse and the body, consider Romans 8:2–4:

> ... because through Christ Jesus the law of the Spirit who gives life has set you free from the law of sin and death. For what the law was powerless to do because it was weakened by the flesh, God did by sending his own Son in the *likeness of sinful flesh* to be a sin offering. And so *he condemned sin in the flesh*, in order that the righteous requirement of the law might be fully met *in us, who do not live according to the flesh* but according to the Spirit.[64]

Body language is also important in 1 Peter 2:24, especially for the case of women: "He himself bore our sins *in his body* on the cross, so that, free from sins, we might live for righteousness; by his wounds you have been healed." Jesus "bore our sins in his body" (1 Pet 2:24) so that we, "who do not live according to the flesh but according to the Spirit" (Rom 8:4), can be fully righteous – regardless of our bodies and regardless of whether we are male or female.

---

64. Emphasis added.

This is important for the discussion of the role of women in the church, because those who live by the Spirit, whose sin is crucified with Christ, can no longer be judged by their flesh, but only by the Spirit. Women's biological differences cannot be the ground for determining women's roles in the church. Rather, the system has to be changed to accommodate her equal standing.

If we continue to look at the implications of Paul's concern about Jew-Gentile relationships in the early church, the difficulties become visible for male-female relationships as well. The problem that Jewish Christians had with Gentile Christians was very tangible and material: Gentiles had a different approach to life. Thus the Gentile element destroyed the peace and uniformity of the Jewish experience and approach to the early church, where the core (Christ) and the contingencies (culture and religion) were conveniently mixed. The question about the law and proper regulation becomes even more important given the huge differences in the ancient world between Jews and Gentiles.

The law determined how the Jews needed to live, eat, and relate, but this was not how the Greeks and Romans lived out their lives and relationships. Of particular concern were the strict Jewish eating habits and sexual ethics as well as keeping Shabbat and, of course, circumcision as a sign of belonging to God's community. The first Christians in Jerusalem were all Jews. All had this unifying cultural and ethical framework. Now, people with different ideas, needs, and urges were joining the congregations.

While the Jews may not have thought that the requirements of the law of Moses saved them, it was necessary for them to hold onto them as an outward sign of their status as God's chosen people.[65] Thus they felt that if the Gentiles wanted Jesus, they had to adapt to these Jewish Christians' requirements first. After all, up to the end of the first century, Christianity was officially part of the Jewish religion.[66] But the Gentiles did not know any of this when they accepted Christ, and so they testified that salvation in the form of God's miraculous Spirit came to them as they were. Paul argues with the Jews in Galatians 2:16:

---

65. It is now generally accepted that E. P. Sanders' book, *Paul and Palestinian Judaism* (London: SCM, 1977), triggered a revolution in how Paul's theology (in particular in Romans) is viewed. Before Sanders, it was generally accepted that Paul's problem with the Jews was the same problem that M. Luther had with the Catholic church – namely, salvation by works rather than faith. Now, most Pauline theologians accept that the Jews considered themselves obliged to the law of God because of their election as his people, which came when they were still slaves.

66. The split of Christianity from Judaism is a process rather than a moment in history. In literature, the Jewish council of Jamnia at the end of the first century has been identified as one moment where the clash became evident through an alleged "Blessing against heretics," meaning, primarily, Jewish Christians. Comp. S. T. Katz, ed., *The Cambridge History of Judaism: The Late Roman-Rabbinic Period*, vol. 4 (Cambridge: CUP, 2006), 291–292.

"We ourselves are Jews by birth and not Gentile sinners; yet we know that a person is justified not by the works of the law but through faith in Jesus Christ. And we have come to believe in Christ Jesus, so that we might be justified by faith in Christ, and not by doing the works of the law, because no one will be justified by the works of the law." Why did we need Christ if the law could have saved us?, Paul asks. He concludes that the law is obsolete for salvation, because Christ accomplished salvation for us all.

From the perspective of male-female relationships in the church, we also need to step back and realize that our salvation is in Christ, and therefore there is neither "male or female." This means that the different ways we experience our physical life, culture, and society are contingent and have no bearing on our salvation or, consequently, on living in the community of God. This is difficult to live out in the everyday experience of people who have been subjected to the hierarchies of sin and trained within hierarchical myths about female ontological inferiority.

I have seen many expressions of this, but one story in particular comes to mind. In my hermeneutics classes in Osijek, Croatia, we used to have many students from the surrounding countries of what was then the "Eastern Bloc" come to study with us. I taught the class all the hermeneutical rules about how the Bible is interpreted, particularly that no doctrine should be determined by just one verse, and that every interpretation should be judged against the framework of the great doctrines of the Bible (such as Christology). However, when the time came to apply this by interpreting 1 Timothy 2:15, "Yet she will be saved through childbearing, provided they continue in faith and love and holiness, with modesty," all of my students argued that women will be saved by childbirth!

After all the lessons and examples I gave in class, what the students had learned in their churches and cultures stayed firm and seemed impossible to uproot. They forgot the whole array of exegetical questions that precede hermeneutics. What could the author and first readers have understood by "being saved"? How does Christ and his work impinge on the problem at hand? From a practical point of view, they were not even bothered by the difficulty of those women who could not have children. They simply replicated what they had learned early on. Both men *and* women alike wrote the same thing.

Understanding Christ's work within the structures of sin in which we live is a difficult task. Like the Galatians, we get swiftly and easily side-tracked by practical questions, rationalisations, and learned "truths." For the Jewish-Christian community, the logical (and justified) question that followed was, can everyone then live as they please?

Galatians 4–5: Adopted as Children and Heirs of God

As 1 Corinthians shows, some nasty things were going on in the churches of the Gentiles! Paul has an answer for this, too. In Romans, he argues the grounds of Genesis exegetically, as a rabbi would, but in Galatians 4, he uses the example of the ancient family. I cannot remember ever hearing a sermon preached on Galatians 4 in the church, perhaps because the example about Sarah and Hagar (4:21–31) is complicated, but the first example (4:1–10) is clear, even to us today.

In Paul's example, there are three categories of "dependents" who are living in the father's house: (1) slaves, with no access to inheritance; (2) minors, who have a promised inheritance, and (3) adult sons who have full access to the father's business and inheritance.

Paul describes an interesting difference between the minor children and those who have come of age. Minors are practically slaves in the house, as they have a pedagogian (in the Greek world, this was a strong slave with a stick) who makes sure that they behave in line with the father's expectations and that they take their learning seriously. Paul calls the Law a "pedagogian" for the Jews, whom he calls "minors" in God's household.

Children who have come of age, on the other hand, sit at the father's table, have a say in how the business is conducted, and even have access to all of the father's resources. The same goes for those children who have been adopted as "sons." In Paul's thought, they represent the believing Gentiles. Paul explains that those who have believed in Christ have been baptised into this relationship of adoption as "sons" with the "Father." They have full access to God; they share in his Spirit; they even have the freedom to co-create the father's business. People who are "of age" and have the Father's Spirit know that freedom in God's house comes with responsibility for what is no longer the Father's possession alone, but has also become their heritage. "For *this* freedom Christ has set us free!," Paul exclaims (Gal 5:1). You can do anything, of course, but if you are an adult son, aware of your heritage, you will want to do what is in the best interest for your home and business. You will want to do what is in line with the Father who made you an heir, what is in line with his Spirit that is now also in you.

Minors, however, are still in the process of learning their father's business. Their mind is scattered, and their attention span is ruined by the things of the world. They need someone to remind them when they are up to mischief. Slaves, who functioned as pedagogians, needed that big stick to help them beat sense into the minor sons (at least, this is what the old nations thought was required for education). For Paul, the Jewish law was such a pedagogian, there to teach those who did not obey through punishment. But things are different in Christ. Even the Jews can "come of age" through faith in Christ and outgrow the law as they participate in the community as adult children and heirs.

Slaves had no standing in the house, for they could perform well and still be sold on. Only full adoption as sons gave slaves the right to belong to the family. Paul expands on this picture in Romans 8. Once the Father decides (or lets his Son decide) to adopt these slaves as sons, they are allowed to share equally in the family business and become a permanent part of the household of God.

All God's children, both those who have come of age through Christ and those who have been adopted as sons from among slaves, now have God's Spirit to guide them into "all truth." Now they can all sit together at God's table and share in his thoughts directly. An adult heir would never want to bring back a pedagogian to instruct and abuse him. For one, those rules are infinitely inferior to the full revelation of God's will through the Spirit of God; moreover, the Father's wisdom is now available to them at all times.

From this perspective, consider the illogical request of the Galatians. As slaves in the universal household of God, they have now been adopted as sons and heirs. They are invited to God's table, where they can participate as equals and have the Spirit of God permanently dwelling in them. But all of a sudden, someone tells them that this is not enough. They need a pedagogian to teach them. They should know that this is regressing rather than progressing on the way of faith. No wonder Paul exclaims with frustration, "Oh you stupid Galatians!" (Gal 3:1).

This distinction applies equally to men and women, but it can be frustrating for women to read the Bible, especially in languages such as Croatian, where "people" can either include or exclude women. Luckily, Paul specifies in Galatians 3:28 that he means *all*. Paul is not just speaking to men in Christ, although he does talk within his particular social experience about "adoption as sons" in Romans 8. Yet he obviously means *all* who are in Christ Jesus, and he considers *all* as "sons" and "heirs" of God, including women. For Paul, a women's biological predisposition changes nothing, for now they, too, equally sit at God's table, equally participate in the Spirit of God, and equally contribute to the business of God as it is fit for the profit of God's (and their) household and business. One could say that for Paul, God now has "sons" of both genders, although "heirs" or "children" would be a more fitting category in our environment.

Patriarchal Language and the Marginalisation of Women

The patriarchal language of the biblical writers is often a stumbling block to contemporary readers, as it may seem that patriarchy is the preferred social expression of the Bible and that biblical women are second-class citizens. The church has often perpetuated this misunderstanding by prescribing patriarchy as a divinely ordered social system for the church.

However, a careful reading of the Bible testifies to the contrary. While most of the biblical writers were – to our knowledge – men, there are amazing and unexpected game turners, such as Paul's words in Galatians 3:27–29: "As many of you as were baptized into Christ have clothed yourselves with Christ. There is no longer Jew or Greek, there is no longer slave or free, there is no longer male and female; for all of you are one in Christ Jesus. And if you belong to Christ, then you are Abraham's offspring, heirs according to the promise." Though Paul elaborates on this passage from the perspective of the patriarchal family arrangement, where only sons count, he nevertheless identifies women as equals, even though including them is not necessary for his argument.

Moreover, the evangelists who wrote about Jesus were all living in patriarchal systems, and yet they did not hide Jesus's countercultural relationships with his female followers, but revealed their importance. John, for instance, depicts true faith almost exclusively through female figures (Jesus's mother, the Samaritan woman, Mary of Bethany, Mary Magdalene), while most men are featured as either unbelieving, half-believing, or as traitors (Nicodemus, the man at the pool in John 5, Peter, Judas Iscariot, and the Jewish leaders). While the Twelve Apostles were all male, they were not the only "apostles" among Christ's followers. Women were the first witnesses to the resurrection, and they were sent out (*apostellō* in Greek) to announce it. The Twelve may represent the twelve sons of Israel to the Jews, but Jesus's mission transcended that as well.

So even though the Bible was written by men, it has been inspired by a different Spirit that pays attention to women and features them against the odds of the surrounding patriarchy as equal receivers of God's mercy and equal participants in the kingdom of God. Though the Bible reflects the patriarchal system in which it was written, it never supports the hierarchical systems that men use to rule over others, nor does it support violence, especially violence against women.

Rather, as we saw in Galatians 3, the Bible is full of unexpected challenges to patriarchy – whether through unusual female God-fearing leaders, such as Deborah (Judges 4–5), or the missionary call to a "lost" Samaritan woman in John 4. Though her name is not remembered by the church, the evangelist is eager to state twice that it was God's particular will that brought Jesus to her well. This little detail, which is evident from the Greek and expressed by "divine necessity" language (John 4:4; 4:34), is often overlooked.

Let us also not forget Paul's list of women in Romans 16, "who risked their necks for my life, to whom not only I give thanks, but also all the churches of the Gentiles" (16:4), who like Mary "worked very hard among you" (16:6), who like Junia "were in prison with me," and who were "prominent among the apostles" and were "in Christ before I was" (16:7). There were also women like "those workers in the Lord, Tryphaena and Tryphosa," and Persis, "who has worked hard in the Lord" (16:12). Paul does not commend them for potluck dinners here! All these women are led by Phoebe, a prominent leader and far more than a "deacon" (as it says in the NRSV) in the Corinthian church of Cenchreae (16:1). This – and so much more – evidence reveals how the incipient church was a movement that confronted the surrounding patriarchy, something that has been historically and socially reconstructed in Elisabeth Schüssler Fiorenza's theological milestone *In Memory of Her*.[67] But the question of language is serious when we consider women's experience in the church. For instance, it is unusual for men to sing a worship song that is written by a woman from the female perspective. Yet it is considered normal for women to sing hymns that were written from the male perspective. When reading the Bible in patriarchal church settings, a woman reading the Bible has to read selectively, asking (either consciously or subconsciously) whether the text applies to everyone or just the men. The problem becomes even more complicated when we realize that most readings and public teachings on the Bible have been done by men – and so men decide which passages include or exclude women. Women are expected to receive whatever is taught to them by men as a divinely ordained instruction.

Reading the Bible with this prism in mind may open new ways to challenge the structures of sin. I recently wrote a short article on the role of women in the church, showing that the role of women is usually defined negatively, both in terms of what women are not allowed to do in the church, and from negative examples, such as Eve or Jezebel. The only positive role that is offered is that of a self-giving mother. My male editor was a kind Christian academic, and he was shocked by the article. "I could not believe the experience of women in the church is so negative, and I had to run the article by my wife and teenaged daughter." He was surprised when they affirmed my experience.

---

67. E. Schüssler Fiorenza, *In Memory of Her: A Feminist Theological Reconstruction of Christian Origins* (London: SCM, 1996).

Sadly, this negative experience is rarely up for discussion in the Christian church. Most church boards would not even consider it – and if they did, they wouldn't understand it. Rarely, someone, like one friend, wrote a letter of apology for "being so blind to such immense suffering of my sisters." Why do women keep quiet about their suffering just to protect male egos? Have they bought into the teaching that they are born to suffer, or has their experience taught them that things will never change? Many believe that "rocking the boat" will make things worse by opening them up for more insults and abuse about their "true" standing before God as sinful females.

I would like to suggest that the issue of the Bible and patriarchy is only a secondary issue, which becomes important when the hierarchies of sin are challenged. No amount of political correctness can solve the dreadful suffering caused by hierarchies for all marginalized people, including women. Political correctness is often like passive aggression; it moves the insult deeper and makes it harder to recognise or address it. Laws will not solve the problem either, as any good law will either stumble or stand through implementation. Laws are dependent on the good will of the people who administer them, and yet those who administer them often want to rule over others rather than serve others according to the law.

In my country, bureaucracy is a dreaded institution of small gods that makes people's lives miserable through paperwork.[68] Files appear on top of piles or disappear in drawers for decades, and there is always the phrase that "all has been done by the law." Whatever the language or system, everything can be abused by human hearts. There are not any "corruption free" areas in the world.[69]

Resurrected Heirs of the Kingdom of God

So how can we work out the theory of equality through practice? Paul says that the word of Christ's gospel was confirmed by the power to change people (Gal 3:1–5; comp. Rom 15:18–19; 2 Cor 6:7). So how are the "children" of God to live as "heirs" if there is no law? Isn't it dangerous to give such freedom to sinners? If we don't try to control them, won't they go astray and abuse their absolute freedom? Yet the changed inner being of those who are part of the church

---

68. Both GAN and Transparency International place it among the more corrupt places in the world, pointing in particular to bureaucracy (e.g. online: https://www.ganintegrity.com/portal/country-profiles/croatia/).

69. Even Canada and Sweden are only at 81/100 by Transparency International; see online: https://www.transparency.org/cpi2018.

have the seal of the Spirit of God, which cannot be regulated by law or issued through orders. Rather, the Spirit of God works within his children to make changes from within – or, as Paul puts it, he resurrects their mortal bodies.

So how can Christians change and become one as Jews and Gentiles, women and men, poor and rich? This question is connected with the inner potential for transformation, which is initiated by God's Spirit in the lives of believers. The world tries to persuade us that change is almost impossible, that racism, nationalism, and genderism, segregation, and xenophobia are the norm. With globalization, all these attitudes become increasingly appealing because people feel overwhelmed by the scope of the challenges and threatened by foreignness. Violence and war, on the one hand, and cowardice and flight, on the other, seem to be the only options.

Yet Jesus requires a "third way," as Wink describes it. Rather than "nonresistance" to evil, "Jesus counsels resistance, but without violence. The Greek word translated 'resist' in Matt. 5:39 is *antistenai*, meaning literally to stand (*stenai*) against (*anti*)."[70] The requirements of God for the new community of believers are therefore totally countercultural, both in their faith in the love of God and their experience. Yet if we surrender to God, we fear that it will disintegrate our individualism and create structures that will somehow work against our best interests. Can the new reality of God be lived out within the structures of sin? Won't the structures of sin try to crush it? How can Christians even be certain about how to live when history has found the church to be guilty of promoting even more structures of sin? To give one example from the past, some of the missionary movements in the eighteenth and nineteenth centuries turned out to be imperialist impositions of foreign culture rather than proclamations of the gospel to free people. How can we discern what is divine and what is cultural? In the next section, we turn to these questions, using Paul's theology of the "body of Christ" (*soma* in Greek), which he juxtaposes with the sinful principle of the "mortal body" (*sarks* in Greek) to guide and challenge us as the church.

---

70. Wink, *Powers*, 99. This is the kind of standing that Daniel exemplified when urged to worship the king. It shows the right behaviour and makes the powers take charge to finish their ugly work and to be exposed as what they truly are: violent imposters.

Bearing Fruit: The *Sarks* and *Soma* Dichotomy in Paul

Though Paul was a trained theologian, who dedicated years of his life to the study of Scriptures, he did not write about theoretical problems, but the concrete problems being experienced within the churches he founded. His solutions drew from Scripture and applied it to living out of a faith in God in daily life.

The Works of the Flesh, the Spirit of Resurrection and the Fruit of the Spirit

When most Christians hear the word "resurrection," they tend to think about a transcendental, divine sphere that is endlessly different from our reality. Faith instructs us to believe in this sphere without seeing or having much proof of it, and church tradition gives us creeds to recite about this eternal realm. Though we live in the valley of death, we wait for the time when "the Lord himself, with a cry of command, with the archangel's call and with the sound of God's trumpet, will descend from heaven, and the dead in Christ will rise first" (1 Thess 4:16).

However, a careful examination of the Scriptures reveals that resurrection is much more than a final eschatological event. Resurrection was inaugurated with Christ's coming, and its power was visible already in Christ's ministry to the demon possessed, the sick, and the hungry. But it was fully revealed in Christ's resurrection from the dead. Since resurrection happens whenever people acknowledge their standing in relation to God and return to him by believing in Christ, this moment is called a "new life." Evangelicals call this "conversion" and often describe it as a change in life's direction – the way we live life, our philosophy of life, or, in my part of the world, a conversion "from" a traditional church to evangelicalism.

In short, we tend to define conversion in terms of our own personal experience, neglecting the fact that, biblically speaking, the decisive point in this event is the change in *how* we stand with God. Though it is easier to define "conversion" from the perspective of an earthly change that can be defined by a concrete set of practical rules, it is much less fruitful, for it closes our eyes to the riches of God's promise and the power of his resurrection – not only in the future, but already in the now. The theological concept of the "already but not yet" approach to eschatology in the Bible has been adopted in evangelicalism as a "futurist" eschatology of the synoptic gospels merged with a more "realized" eschatology of the Gospel of John. Though the full potential of eternal life will only be realized at the end of history, the "already" does not only suggest a theoretical adherence to a philosophy about God. But the presence of a visible power of life shines through the darkness of the present time – a light, as the Gospel of John puts it, that already shines in the darkness.

Unfortunately, throughout the history of the church, Christians have not paid much attention to the experience of life in the present, an oversight for which they have been criticized. Though training the children of Christian parents and baptizing them without waiting until they can hear and respond to God's call personally may have helped the church's political standing, Christian education is ambiguous territory. Naturally, Christian parents want their children to follow in their footsteps, because they know how valuable faith in God is for life. Baptists, in particular, have been known for their consistent instruction through Sunday school. Yet paradoxically, experience reveals that it is often more difficult to find your own faith if you have grown up in the church rather than a secular background.[71] Though I grew up as a Baptist in a dedicated Christian home, where church and all of its activities were mandatory, I still struggled with the idea of sin or being sinful myself. Like the rich young man (Mark 10:17–22), "I have kept all this since my youth." Moreover, I did not go to parties and discos, did not wear trousers (a huge sin in my church), and did not smoke or drink. Rather, I cleaned the church with my mother, baked many cakes for events and guests as a young girl, started teaching Sunday school to children when I was fourteen, because "there was nobody else," and took care of my younger brothers and sister because I was a girl.

My "conversion prayer" went something like this: "God, I will accept that I am a sinner, because you say so. Please forgive my sins." It was difficult to see a change in me, because I was such a good girl already (based on what people saw). The change that happened was on the inside and atypical for how conversion was described in my church. I could see it through my changed interests, the ease with which I began ministering to others, the fact that friends came to seek my advice about life issues, and the way people seemed to sense that I had something that could help them in their need. I also had a love for Scripture. Looking back, I can see how God started to prepare me for the path of ministry by teaching me what sin was – and how much was still in me! This

---

71. According to research done by the organisation HOPE, only 50 percent of children brought up in Christian homes in Great Britain became Christians themselves. Online report on their research *Faith in Our Families*: https://www.careforthefamily.org.uk/wp-content/uploads/2017/03/Faith-in-our-Families-Research-booklet.pdf. While this still represents the majority of the next generation of Christians, and only 19 percent of those in Anglican environments come from non-Christian backgrounds, it still shows that for 50 percent of churched children, the obstacles to faith in the church are too big to overcome.

book is the result of that teaching, which has opened my eyes to things that my childhood church did not – and probably could not – teach me.

Paul's definition of conversion is the picture of "a seal" or "a first instalment" (2 Cor 1:21–22; 5:5) of God's Spirit into a convert's heart. In other words, "God's love has been poured into our hearts through the Holy Spirit that has been given to us" (Rom 5:4). We know these words, but they are technical terms within the transcendent, spiritual realm that we assign to faith. Yet Paul tries to explain to the Corinthians that what really happens at "conversion" is a first instalment of God's Spirit, so that they will experience God's power of resurrection regardless of the structures of sin, just as he did. Paul elaborates on this in Romans 8 (and elsewhere):

> But you are not in the flesh; you are in the Spirit, since the Spirit of God dwells in you. Anyone who does not have the Spirit of Christ does not belong to him. But if Christ is in you, though the body is dead because of sin, the Spirit is life because of righteousness. If the Spirit of him who raised Jesus from the dead dwells in you, he who raised Christ from the dead will give life to your mortal bodies also through his Spirit that dwells in you. (Rom 8:9–11)

Then Paul juxtaposes two life styles: one "in the flesh" and one "in the Spirit" (Rom 8:12–13). As he addresses the Christians in Rome, he wants to make sure that they understand that the Spirit of God dwells in them already. They received their first instalment of the Spirit when they first trusted God through Jesus's work of salvation. Paul reiterates this in the negative: "Anyone who does not have the Spirit of Christ does not belong to him" (Rom 8:9). This is not a warning, as it is sometimes understood – as if someone could be a Christian and not have the Spirit – but a statement of fact.[72] Christians need not worry about the Spirit, because it is God's gift and promise. Yet Christians are right to be concerned when the Spirit is not visible in people who claim to be Christians. Earthly things are more prevalent in their lives, and they often behave as non-believers. In Romans 8, Paul explains this in terms of an "already but not yet full" redemption. As Christians continue to live within the structures of sin, they can quench the Spirit of God by not allowing him to do his work through them. This results in many crippled and useless Christians, which is a very real threat to the life of the church. Paul says that those who "live according to the flesh set their minds on the things of the flesh" (Rom

---

72. The Greek suggests, as Dunn points out, that if you indeed are Christians, having the Spirit is a fact (*Romans 1–8*, 428).

8:5). Thus they do not have the Spirit, because it is impossible to have the Spirit God but still prefer the "flesh."

Galatians 5: the Works of the Flesh (*Sarks*)

In many places, Paul refers to people without God as "dead meat" (*sarks* in Greek). In Galatians 5:16–21, Paul explains how those who are "dead meat" (corpses) behave according to their own laws, doing things that promote death, because the principle of death is in them. This picture is helpful for our deliberations about life in the church and within the hierarchies of sin, as it explains how you cannot order a corpse to stand up or to stop stinking. It is dead. One can recite the Ten Commandments to it, and it will have no effect. A corpse "lives" by its own law, the law of death that resides in it and creates more death in it and around it.

When I think back to my own Christian experience, much of our evangelism consisted of such attempts to order "corpses" to stand up and walk. We explained to people how sinful they were and how they should stop doing what they were doing (cursing God or smoking). If someone nice came along who did not curse or smoke, who like the rich young man from Mark 10 already kept the commandments, we thought that all they needed was to be baptized. The fact is, a person without God cannot do the things of the Spirit. This is also true of our own children in the church. Whatever we have taught them is not "life," but our own testimony of life. Evangelizing means accepting people in their dead existence and bringing them to God. Only God can put the Spirit of life in them, which will bring about change and restore them to life.

Paul's strict, almost black and white, juxtaposition of the "flesh" and "Spirit" in Galatians 5 is a stark contrast to the practice in most churches. Paul issues a striking threat to the Christians in Galatia early in his mission: "I am warning you, as I warned you before: those who do such things will not inherit the kingdom of God" (Gal 5:21). His emphasis is not on Christian ethics, but his experience of the power of becoming a new creation in Christ.[73] As Moses Silva remarks, "It was truly ironic that these Christians who were seduced by a message of law-keeping, should fall into behaviour that blatantly contradicted their faith. Their emphasis on the flesh – literally through circumcision but more importantly through their dependence on their own effort – led them indeed to perform the works of the flesh in another sense."[74] The Spirit exposes

---

73. H. Brandenburg, *Der Brief des Paulus an die Galater* (Wuppertal: Brockhaus, 1961), 112.

74. M. Silva, "Galatians," in *New Bible Commentary*, ed. D. A. Carson et al. (Downers Grove: InterVarsity Press, 1994), 1219.

where there is lack of life. Paul's initial proclamation to the Galatians included this warning before they were Christians (in that he was teaching them that salvation is in Christ alone), and he repeats it now in view of the new developments in the church, which were probably initiated by some Jewish Christians who did not understand the relationship of Christ and the law.

To believe in Christ means to follow his Spirit. There is no other way. Martin Luther remarked that people either live in the flesh or in the Spirit and both will be evident by the work they do or the fruit they bear.[75] Yet there is an "in-between" state because of the flesh into which the Spirit of God dawns and because of the structures of sin, which impinge on that flesh. For Paul, the "already and not yet" principle is displayed in the fact that God's Spirit is infused as a "first instalment" into this "living" corpse, almost like when paramedics come to an accident scene and shock life into a clinically dead casualty on the side of the road. Though this person may not be defined as "dead" anymore, he or she still has a long way to full recovery and usefulness. I believe, along with John Calvin, that this is similar to Paul's claim in Romans 8:11: "If the Spirit of him who raised Jesus from the dead dwells in you, he who raised Christ from the dead will give life to your mortal bodies also through his Spirit that dwells in you." From the context, Paul cannot only mean future resurrection,[76] for as John Calvin rightly suggests, Paul's subject is the sanctification of those "corpses" that have now been infused with the first instalment of God's Spirit. That is, they have been given a new law, a new principle, and a new potential for life.

At conversion, the Spirit of God is infused into Christians (2 Cor 5:5), who continue to live within the structures of sin and therefore to experience the challenges of their "sinful flesh" as in a foreign country (2 Cor 5:6), even though they now belong to God's eternity through the Spirit. This Spirit of life is the same Spirit that raised Jesus from the dead in the historical event of

---

75. M. Luther, *Kommentar zum Galaterbrief* (Göttingen: Vandenhoeck & Ruprecht, 1989), 326.

76. E.g. Dunn, *Romans 1–8*, 432, believes that the future tense *zōopoiēsei* must be understood as referring to the final resurrection (as in 2 Cor 15:22). Calvin, on the other side, comments: "By mortal bodies he understands all those things which still remain in us, that are subject to death; for his usual practice is to give this name to the grosser part of us. We hence conclude, that he speaks not of the last resurrection, which shall be in a moment, but of the continued working of the Spirit, by which he gradually mortifies the relics of the flesh and renews in us a celestial life," (*John Calvin's Commentaries*, Christian Classics Ethereal Library, online: https://biblehub.com/commentaries/calvin/romans/8.htm). Dunn reads too much eternity into the future tense, as what the Spirit will do in the life of a person already here is equally "futuristic." Paul's line of reasoning in 2 Cor 5:4–5 is very similar to what Calvin, rightly, sees in Rom 8:11.

resurrection (Rom 8:11). Nothing is impossible for this Spirit of resurrection. Therefore, it can fight the aftermath of death in the believers' "deadly bodies" – their own sin and the sin that others have inflicted on them. The Spirit takes on all our broken bones, brain concussions, paralyzed limbs and spines as a divine healer. The illustration of an accident scene is helpful here, because it conveys the long and ongoing process of recovery.

A few years back, the daughter of our good friend was hit by a drunk driver. Thea was swirled into the air and fell head first, left for dead on the side of the street with a fractured skull, broken hips and legs, totally disfigured, covered with bruises. Luckily, the paramedics arrived swiftly and managed to revive her. But her recovery took more than two years, requiring a series of operations and intense physical therapy. I watched Thea fight for her life and experience a lot of physical pain. She repeated the aching movements that she was able to do over and over again with each visitor who came to see her. The pain of trying to repeat these movements contorted her face, but she did not give up until it stopped hurting, and her mobility fully returned. The pain continues to resurface when the weather changes, and her scars hurt sometimes, but she was very brave as she went through risky operations, painful procedures, and many months of painful physiotherapy. She lived through looking like a wreck, joking about all the stages of her new hairdo – including her shaved head. Thea is fully back to her normal life now, doing very productive work.

If we imagine this in the spiritual realm, we have many obstacles to being resurrected from the "dead." Through the structures of sin, some of us have been hurt more drastically than others, although this is hard to measure. Some have been abused physically. Others have been manipulated by passive aggression. Some have been sexually abused by a close relative. Others have been deprived of an education and forced to sell their bodies. Some have had to endure intense pain and loss. Others have had to cope with extreme poverty, illness, slavery, and impossible life situations. They do not know life, only death. They live without trust. Unable to love or care for themselves and others, they often perpetuate the cycle of evil by destroying the next generation through the trauma that lurks in the spare room, where they have tried to hide it away.

Through the recent war in Croatia, I have seen how poverty perpetuates its traditions, just as the rich perpetuate their traditions through entitlement. Both situations abuse, exploit, and manipulate others for their own purposes. When the Spirit of God breathes into situations of darkness, it is initially covered up with the debris and pain of the previous life. It takes time to sort out that "spare room" of trauma and clean out the house (Matt 12:43). First, one has to have the will to endure some tough operations that will straighten our bones and fix our muscles so that life can return to our bodies.

I have seen many people come into the church seeking help, but they turn away when they realize that they need to do something hard – such as work for a living, or accept the job they already have, or own the hurt they have inflicted on others by asking for forgiveness. Obeying the Spirit's call to change is not easy. Just like Thea had to struggle physically through operations and therapy, the spiritual revival of a "dead body" depends on the willingness to listen and obey the inner urge of the Spirit towards new life.

Romans 7–8: Resurrected by the Spirit
Paul refers to this process when he speaks about the resurrection of the mortal body in Romans 7–8 (comp. 2 Cor 3:18; 4:16–17). His concern is that there are people in church who seem more dead than alive in their daily living. Resurrection – the initial reception of the Spirit of life that saves us from certain and eternal death – is indeed a miraculous event that is worthy of celebration. But when we dwell on the moment that we first became alive, we shift our focus from our spiritual development back to the old principle of sin, which hinders us from becoming fully alive. We are expected to keep running with the Spirit so that our own resurrection will start to resurrect our environment, bringing forth a sweet smell of the kingdom of God in a rotting world.

People love the attention they get when they first believe, just like those who are trapped in hospital beds with severe trauma appreciate frequent visitors. Others need to wheel them away to operations and therapy procedures, do things for them, keep them company, and provide them with everything they need. But when patients leave the acute phase, they need to begin moving forward on their own. If they expect to continue being the centre of attention and refuse to take responsibility for their recovery, they are not patients anymore, but needy nags. The church is full of people who whine about the lack of love without recognizing that they are the ones who need to be extending love through their lives. Jesus's question to the sick man at the pool in John 5 is a question for all who have received the Spirit and been resurrected to life: "Do you want to be made well?" (John 5:6). This essential question is followed by clear instructions: stand up, take your mat, walk, and do not sin any more (5:8, 14).

Women are particularly prone to living vicariously through others in the church, since they have been taught from an early age that their role is to submit. Because they are unable to make decisions on their own, they expect others to care for them and become a burden to the church. After listening to a report on global work by and for women, a brother from India came to us and complained, "I wish there was more of this kind of thinking among our women. You should come and teach them! All they want to know is getting married and babies!"

This is not God's intention for the church. The Spirit of God resurrects people so that they can join in the work of the kingdom of God, which is to resurrect the whole world. This does not exclude an eschatological resurrection at the "last day," but it is an instrumental testimony in the life of a Christian who continues to live within the structures of sin. If the Spirit of God cannot demolish the structures of sin within a Christian and within the Christian church, then any testimony about the power of God is jeopardized, and the world has no reason to believe.

In Romans, Paul makes it clear that the required outcome for the life of a Christian is to reflect the glorious life of God's Spirit in the midst of the structures of sin and death more and more each day by allowing God to resurrect our mortal bodies. Paul reveals God's amazing plan, which is not only for the personal resurrection of the individual Christian to his or her full potential, but for the cumulative effect that a community of resurrected believers will have on the whole creation of God. In Romans 8:19–21 he claims,

> For the creation waits with eager longing for the revealing of the children of God; for the creation was subjected to futility, not of its own will but by the will of the one who subjected it, in hope that the creation itself will be set free from its bondage to decay and will obtain the freedom of the glory of the children of God.

This is why the "suffering of this present time" has to be endured (Rom 8:18). The glory that will come from those who let God work out his resurrection in their mortal bodies is well worth the struggle.

I once met a Roma family at a Christian camp who were full of grace and God's character. I imagined they were probably a little better off than most, as they seemed to have a good education. But when Biljana shared the story of her life with me, I was taken aback. It was as bad as it gets among Roma women. "You know," she told me, "my mother did not love me. I don't know why, maybe because she hated my father who left her pregnant. She forbade her other daughters, my half-sisters, to be kind to me." The only person who cared for Biljana was her grandmother, who took her to a church on occasion when she was a little girl. She remembered some of the hymns that they sang. "They were beautiful hymns, but did not mean much to me."

Biljana's mother married her off when she was fourteen. Neither she nor her new husband were happy with the marriage, as they did not know each other and did not want to know each other. She was beaten and abused in her husband's family, both by him and others. Finally, she decided she could not bear the abuse any longer and left, but she was pregnant. She roamed the streets and ended up with a much older man, who promised to take care of her and her child, but then she found herself in an even worse situation.

One night, she fled and spent the night in the park, holding her baby boy close to her. A hymn came into her mind from long before, and she sang it to her boy, praying for God's love and shelter. The next day, she went to her mother to ask her to take them in. Her mother agreed to take the baby, but not her. "You have a home and a husband, so you have a place to go!" she said. When Biljana came for her baby the next day, she learned that her mother had delivered the boy to his father. So there was nowhere to go, and she ended up in the initial place of abuse once again, living as a beggar in the streets of the city with her children, which kept arriving one after the other.

The change came when a Christian woman made a business arrangement with Biljana. She agreed to give Biljana a coin every third time she saw her and her children in town. Biljana started looking out for this lady, and a relationship developed. The woman invited her to come to church. Whenever she came, Biljana would get some food or things she needed for her babies. At first, she did not like going to church, but gradually, the meetings became more important than the things she was receiving.

As Biljana got to know Jesus, her thinking and priorities began to change. She accepted work opportunities rather than begging, doing odd jobs at her church and for her Christian friend. Eventually, her husband, Đeno, started coming along and working on small repairs in the church. As he, too, got to know Jesus, their life started to sort itself out. It was a long and painful path of resurrection for Biljana and Đeno, and it is still continuing. They have to fight prejudice and rejection within church. Sometimes people tell jokes without noticing how hurtful it is for them, and yet they grow and spread life around them. As they take up one challenge after another, they are learning to live in love and peace and to teach their children in the same way. It has not been easy to school their children, as neither Biljana nor Đeno finished their basic education. But they have taken every opportunity to learn and also to give themselves to others in their community through service.

When I met Biljana and Đeno, they were already leading a Roma church plant as pastors. They were at our retreat because they wanted to learn and grow more. I have been amazed by Đeno's natural insight into biblical texts. He rarely speaks, as he is still shy and self-conscious, but when he does, the Spirit of God shines wisdom on us through Ðeno. He was the kindest soul in the camp, collecting the children and caring for those on the fringes. Meanwhile, Biljana and Ðeno are working on the first Bible translation into the Bajash dialect of their Roma tribe. Biljana has started writing children's books and has already had two published.

This story shows the amazing resurrection potential of the Spirit of God in an overwhelmingly disadvantaged and pain-filled life. Just as Paul promised the Romans, Ðeno and Biljana reveal the promise that the "the sufferings of this present time are not worth comparing with the glory about to be revealed to us" (Rom 8:18). Many have seen God's glory in this couple, first in the way they learned to love and care for each other. But life continues to reveal itself through them, as they are survivors who listen to the urging of the Spirit and understand that "the Spirit of him who raised Jesus from the dead" dwells in them and is resurrecting their mortal bodies for the glory that will be revealed to the world. The world is changing as "death is swallowed up in victory" (1 Cor 15:54).

The Fight between the Flesh and the Spirit: The Suffering of These Times

Romans 8 has been used and sometimes abused for all sorts of teachings, but we must never lose sight of the fact that Paul is writing Romans to Christians – not non-Christians. In 8:9 he says, "But you are not in the flesh; you are in the Spirit, since the Spirit of God dwells in you. Anyone who does not have the Spirit of Christ does not belong to him." In this verse, Paul is not saying that there are Christians who do not have the Spirit, nor that another act of the Spirit is needed, nor that certain Christians will receive it if they pray for it earnestly (though many people do explain the passage this way).[77] Rather, Paul's aim is to encourage Christians in Rome to change their attitude toward the Spirit, who is already in them – for if it weren't, they would not be Christ's. Paul wants them to grow in the Spirit for the benefit of the world and possibly, more concretely, for Paul's mission to Spain, which would complete the circle of the then-known world.[78]

---

77. J. W. Ward, "Pentecostal Theology," in S. G. Ferguson and D. F. Wright, *New Dictionary of Theology* (Downers Grove: InterVarsity Press, 1988), 503. This other act of the Spirit is called the baptism in the Holy Spirit or the second blessing.

78. There is a long list of scholars throughout the centuries who have seen the immense theme of mission driving Romans. For a discussion, see Magda, *Paul's Territoriality*, 125–130.

Spain was the "end of the world," and today's Morocco was called the "island in the West" because it was only accessible through the sea. During the time of Paul, no roads had been built through the Atlas Mountains on the northern coast of Africa. While the discord and immaturity of the Roman Christians may not be as evident as it is in 1 Corinthians, it is present. Therefore, we should not be misled by Paul's theological emphasis in Romans 1–8 to consider the rest of the letter as a circumstantial addition or even a set of parenthetical interpolations.[79] Paul is a missional theologian and does not write theology for the sake of theology. Rather, his theology is occasional and is always grounded in the practical issues that churches are facing, including the church in Romans.

Paul's earlier theological deliberations on the "deeds of the flesh" and the "fruit of the Spirit" in Galatians 5 become clearer when we understand the story about the Spirit of God resurrecting the "mortal" body of believers, who choose to live the life of Christ within the structures of sin in the world. If we interpret Romans 8:11 as a "spiritual" resurrection that is happening already in the now for the life of Christ within the structures of sin (as I believe we should, given the context), we can easily understand Paul's notion in 8:18 about "the sufferings of this present time" and why Christians cannot escape them. As the Spirit within us urges us to stand firmly against the structures of sin and death in our mortal bodies and in the world, we experience life as a constant struggle. Although it may seem pointless and even crazy, the Spirit urges Christians to believe in and trust God as they seek to love people in the midst of the sinful structures that are trying to climb over everything and everyone in order to serve their own interests. Whoever has tried to live by the Spirit understands the ongoing pain of this position.

Thus it is illogical for someone who has the Spirit and has been liberated from slavery to want to return to the experience of being enslaved to the structures of sin that are not of God. Yet as soon as the Israelites, God's freed people, hit the desert on their way to the Promised Land, they remembered all the cucumbers, melons, and garlic that they had eaten in Egypt (Num 11:5), and they wanted to go back. While in Egypt, the Israelites experienced the crushing yoke of slavery, and so they cried out to God for salvation for decades, but when they finally obtained freedom, the desert scared them, and they wanted to go back to what was known – even if it meant slavery.

---

79. This is especially true of the "old" perspective on Paul. M. Reasoner, *The Strong and the Weak: Romans 14.1.–15:13 in Context* (Cambridge: CUP, 1999), 41–42, has shown extensively that Romans 14:1–15:13 is not only an integral part of the letter, but addresses a real situation of division in Romans.

Paul warns the Galatians that by trying to add the law to Christ, they are turning their backs on God and returning to slavery. It is like wanting to become a child again, after having been accepted as an adult heir at God's table – like asking for that abusive slave with a big stick to beat the father's will into you, after you've already been communicating with the father directly. Isn't it better to sit at the table with God? Isn't it better to contribute to the household of God with all that we have? Isn't it better to live in a close relationship with God and get to know him and his business through his Spirit that is within us? Why leave the freedom and fulness of God's executive table and exchange it for a slave's interpretation of God's will? There is no logic in abandoning the higher position of an adult heir to return to the life of a minor child.

In pondering Paul's illustration about the household of God, we can see more clearly the abuse of the legalistic system in our churches. Slaves and minors in the house have the same status. They neither know the father, nor his business, nor his character. They have to depend on others to instruct them in the name of the father, but these pedagogians end up being abusive, because their minds do not cooperate with the father's mind.

Yet the pedagogian is also a slave. He can do practically anything in the name of the father, but there is no way to know whether he is acting out the true will of the father or just lashing out on the minor because he has been given the authority to do so. Even when the father's will is interpreted well, the partiality of the instruction feels imposed and is therefore a burden. The law is never complete, as Jesus shows in the Sermon on the Mount: "You have heard that it was said to those of ancient times . . . but I say to you . . ." (Matt 5:21, 27, 31, 33). Doing another person's will is overwhelming, and everyone rejects such an imposition. People were not born to be slaves. Without knowing or caring for the father, his will seems like a random and senseless set of impositions that go against our own ideas about what we would like to do or not to do at any particular moment.

Yet when we come to the table and make decisions as equals in our own house, we finally see the business that our father is in and how what we do affects the whole household, for better or worse. We are invited to share in the family resources and means, and we are also asked to contribute our own gifts, insights, and potential. Eventually we realize that we have come to understand the mind and character of the father.

Our relationship in this setting is so different! Sometimes, we have an idea, and the father may say, "Well, go out, try it!" Or he may say, "Now, that may not work – we have tried it in the past, remember?" Sometimes, we will go and try it anyway, because we have the freedom to make that decision, and we will realize that the father was right. But because God is God, he will refrain from saying, "I told you so!" So we will grow from this bad decision, and we will become more like our father. Within this framework, we can easily see that not everyone who sits at this executive table, discussing the business of the father, does so at the same level of engagement, energy, know-how, or experience. There is a growth process for everyone.

When Paul continues the discussion in Galatians 5 in theological terms, he speaks of the "works of the flesh" as being opposed to the "fruit of the Spirit." Those who are slaves or minors are unaware of God's business, so they only have themselves to please. Thus they do "works of the flesh." This is what the principle of sin looks like in each of their "mortal bodies," the *sarks*. The body wants to have fun, sleep, get drunk, get their own way by being violent, scheming, or lying – even when other people's lives are at stake. For Paul, people who have no notion of God are dead to God. You can recite the law of God to them as much as you want, and nothing happens. Rather, it feels like talking to a corpse. You can order it to stop stinking, but because it is in its nature to stink and decompose, it cannot hear or understand you.

Something drastic needs to happen for the *sarks* to become a living creature, a new creation. This change cannot come from the corpse itself. It has to come from outside, as a miracle of life infused into the dead body. Then a resurrection process can start. As this body now has the living Spirit within, it can take up the fight against decay and death. Paul emphasizes that living up to the requirements of the Spirit is a process that is similar to bearing fruit. A victim that has been heavily bruised, who is a newcomer to the father's executive table, will need to go through a process of learning or "growing" into the role that has been assigned by God. We do not need to be surprised by the hardship of this process, "the sufferings of this present time," as Paul describes them. Those who "have the Spirit of Christ" now live by a new law, though the law of sin and death continues to surround them with its networks and hierarchies. Often, the growth process requires operations or many repetitions of the same movements (practicing a new life and building godly character). Eventually, after enduring the pain of therapy, we can take care of ourselves, and then we will hopefully become useful to our environments.

> Theologically, this would be the place to discuss the undecided issue of human involvement in the process of salvation, the extent of human defilement through original sin, and predestination. But from the perspective of biblical theology and Paul's theology in Romans, these questions are alien to Paul's

> pragmatic approach to the problem at hand. He is unconcerned with medieval ontological questions and concerned with the real questions of being a Christian community. While ontological questions have their place in theology and have been important, Paul's theology in the letters is not systematic. For instance, A. J. M. Wedderburn has suggested that instead of arguing for original sin in Adam, which finds its cure in Christ, Paul's mind works the other way around: the universality of salvation in Christ makes it necessary to see that Adam's sin did not impact him alone, but the whole world, even though there may have been people who did not sin as he did.[80] Similarly, the exposition on the "predestination" in Romans 8:29 ("For those whom he foreknew he also predestined to be conformed to the image of his Son, in order that he might be the firstborn within a large family") must be read within the context of a Christian address and not as a discussion about the ontological problem of God's pre-knowing and predestining people. Paul does not discuss how God handles people's free will and how the will of God relates to the will of a free human. I agree that it is difficult to reason how humans contribute to the reception of the seal of the Spirit that makes them alive, since this is the Spirit of God and only subject to the will of God. A biblical solution would be that Paul speaks to a Christian community. His discussion is with people who have received the Spirit and not with non-believers. His concern is with the lack of Christlike fruit that is being revealed in their life as a community even though they have all received the Spirit. As such, they have been sealed, and because they are sealed, they are also predestined and chosen. He does not argue about how they got there.

It takes a lot of training for a thirteen-year-old Jewish boy who has gained access to his father's executive table to learn the business well enough to be fully useful. In the same way, becoming like Christ and finding our place in the body of Christ – the church – will take an exercise of our will, time, and effort. God initiates this process and expects us to grow. He knows how we function and the circumstances of death that continue to enslave us. We live by grace. God didn't invite us to his table because he needed us (as if God couldn't make all the decisions by himself), but because his love makes space for us in his life, work, and family. Though we are impatient, God has all the time in the world to get us to where we need to be. Though the process will feel like suffering, it

---

80. Comp. Rom 5:14; Magda, *Paul's Territoriality*, 139–141.

is not useless or senseless, but about finding our true identity in Christ so that we can become useful to the household and the mission of God.

In his letters, Paul illustrates the difference between a sinner and a believer as the difference between "living in the flesh" (*sarks*) and "living in the body [*soma*] of Christ." As we saw before, the *sarks* for Paul carries the principle of death because it strives to remain dead and to drag everything it touches toward death. These people live according "to the flesh" (Rom 8:4–9) and produce the "works of the flesh," which are "obvious: fornication, impurity, licentiousness, idolatry, sorcery, enmities, strife, jealousy, anger, quarrels, dissensions, factions, envy, drunkenness, carousing, and things like these" (Gal 5:19–21).

Psychologists tell us that there are good people whose goodness is a reflection of their own need (for instance, being accepted and loved) and nothing else. So why is there such a high toll on apparently innocent things, such as carousing, so that "those who do such things will not inherit the kingdom of God" (5:21)? What's the problem if we're not doing any harm to other people, just having some fun ourselves?

But intoxicated people often bring pain to other people – at best, they make them feel uncomfortable or threatened, and at worst, they rape, hurt, or kill others through drunk driving. Our fun becomes the point of death for others when the pain is carried into the next generation: the trauma of loss, the hurt of verbal abuse and damaging words, the doubt, the chaos of alcoholism and drug abuse, which makes children unable to cope with the demands of life without becoming addicts themselves, or the total disintegration of those who have been raped. They will never gain the feeling of belonging. The "works of the flesh" are notorious for bringing death into the world. They are directly linked to the human desire to be a god over others, imposing oneself and one's own "fun" on others so that the perpetrator who has "fun" is exempt from reaping the consequences himself.

On the other hand, those who have the Spirit of God know that they belong to God and understand – to speak in popular terms – "the heart of God." They live out of the will to worship God in whatever they do, and this bears the "fruit of the Spirit" in their lives. The trouble is, when they do this from within their "mortal bodies," they can be pulled toward the deeds of the flesh, which corrupt the nudges of the Spirit of God, who inspires them toward works of life and freedom. As we grow in the Spirit of God, we begin to listen to the Spirit rather than to the mortal body. While the "deeds of the flesh" are immediately revealed, the "fruit" of the Spirit starts as a heavenly seed sown into the heart, which slowly emerges as a shoot from the ground, and then starts to grow, producing fruit very gradually after a long time until the full glory of God is revealed. As Isaiah prophesies:

> They will be called oaks of righteousness,
> > the planting of the LORD, to display his glory.
> They shall build up the ancient ruins,
> > they shall raise up the former devastations;
> they shall repair the ruined cities,
> > the devastations of many generations. (Isaiah 61:3b–4)

In a godless world, bearing such fruit is countercultural. Fruit brings sustenance and life, not the death of the world. Although the seed of the Holy Spirit has life and potential – as Jesus makes clear in Mark 4 – the Spirit works with the individual's process, waiting for growth and, in some ways, fighting for it.

Paul expects this to be a hard process – he calls it "the suffering of this present time" (Rom 8:18). This suffering comes in many forms and can be mild or extremely severe, almost apocalyptical, or otherworldly. It may include parting ways with people who think we're weird because we're too ethical. We may no longer find pleasure in the death-dealing things in which everyone else is engaged. We may experience marginalization when we speak against the immoral treatment of others, or when we care for those who have been written off by society. We may feel pain because we choose a life of voluntary poverty or to cut down on our consumption. In many places, we might be persecuted severely because of our faith, facing abduction, torture, rape, incarceration, assassination, and acts of terrorism, such as church bombings.[81] Living a countercultural way in this age is extremely demanding, for we will need to study the Bible thoroughly as we think about how to love our enemies and those who are working against us, trusting in the sovereignty of God and the eternal safety of our lives in him. We will need to grab evil by the horns wherever we are placed. This may mean staying in a church as a "prophetic presence" after the pastor (who has no training or knowledge) decides that you "have not proven yourself useful to the church," even though you've had a public and recognized ministry for thirty years. Or he may announce that he does not believe that women should be in leadership, or preach, or receive

---

81. The persecution of Christians is projected to be stronger globally in our time than ever before. According to Open Door's World Watch list for 2018, 245 million Christians live in places where they will experience persecution, which reflects a 14 percent rise between 2017 and 2018. Online: https://www.opendoorsusa.org/christian-persecution/.

visions from God. The pain will be even more intense when you notice that all the men on his team are not being evaluated by the same criteria.

Even more difficult, you will see young women selling themselves out for a myth about love and subjection to their husbands, and nothing you say will change their minds – until it is too late. Or you may have to watch your daughter – a bright, fantastic, and gifted girl – walk the same road of pain and humiliation in the church that you have walked. As she serves with her undeniable gifts, you fear for her soul, wondering if she will be able to bear the suffering of the present time?

One of my current "present time sufferings" is that I have been advocating for justice for women for so long, and yet it seems – in spite of all the learning, energy, and increased awareness – that we have been unable to instruct the new generation. They are taking their freedom and right to education for granted, and they are discarding it and finding their way back into slavery. For me, the suffering of the present time also includes looking at the girls in my classroom who are much more concerned with their looks, make-up, and how the boys will evaluate them than with learning and developing their skills. They are afraid to be smart.

I know also that my husband has suffered much by trying to balance the need to speak up against my unjust suffering in the church, which he has witnessed firsthand, and the desire not to rock the boat in order to prevent a church split. This situation has caused a lot of pain to both of us and to our children. The suffering of the present time, of course, is not only gender specific. It will attack anyone who tries to live up to God's standards by opposing the structures of human gods in any environment. Yet it is most painful when it happens in the church and is inflicted by those who are called "brothers" and "sisters."

As grave as this may sound, Paul urges the Christians in Rome not to lose perspective. Christians must expect suffering if they want to live by the urges of the Spirit, as the Spirit challenges sinful structures, which have many ways to inflict pain and even death.

In the story about the two witnesses in Revelation 11:3–11, the two witnesses prophesy in "sackcloth" to a fallen world that is trampling the sacred grounds of the temple of God. They are deliberately poor, since sackcloth is a sign of humbleness before God. Their strength is not in complying with the norms of the "inhabitants of the earth," but in their story, which they use to "torment" the godless public as they challenge their way of living. Their strength is also in the power of God's word, which is affirmed by God's signs. People who live by the Spirit are truly different, and the witnesses scare the inhabitants of the earth with their story. Thus it is a great relief when the witnesses are done in by the "beast" from the "bottomless pit."

However, after their resurrection – that is, their vindication by God – the unbelievers "were terrified and gave glory to the God of heaven" (Rev 11:13). To my knowledge, this is the only place in Revelation where unbelievers give glory to God. None of the other methods that God uses to afflict the unbelievers in Revelation (the cycles of "tribulation," the seals and the trumpets) are truly effective, for they only make the people more rebellious as they "curse God" (Rev 9:20–21; 16:21). God's good news is sweet when we have first tried it, but it does upset the stomach, as John found out (Rev 10:10), along with other prophets before him (Ezek 2:9–3:14). In Romans 8:18, Paul describes this experience of countercultural witness and the pain of the structures of sin as the "suffering of the present time."[82] If Romans 10:11 is understood as the process of the present "resurrection" of the "mortal body," Paul also seems to have this in mind in 2 Corinthians 5:4: "For while we are still in this tent, we groan under our burden, because we wish not to be unclothed but to be further clothed, so that what is mortal may be swallowed up by life." Thus the sufferings of the present time are another way of describing the process of bearing the fruit of the Spirit (Gal 5:20) in a world that is consumed by death and decay. The sufferings are growth pains that will eventually reveal the glory of God in his children. Just as a woman's contractions bring a child into the world, this suffering may feel dreadful and unbearable for the present time, but God's glory is promised to all who endure the process.

Too many sermons have been preached to scratch the ears of Christians who want to escape the suffering in the world, and too many prayers have been issued in churches for people to be able to dodge suffering. As Jesus prayed in Gethsemane, we can always pray to God, our Father, to ease our burdens. Yet Christians must be aware that trying to have an easy life within the structures of sin and death is an oxymoron. There is nothing easy about living within the structures of sin. Rather, each encounter with sinful structures will hurt and challenge us to recognize that our life is in Christ – not our homes, cars, clothes, watches, leisure, money, or whatever else the world is trying to sell as valuable.

In effect, it is in a Christian's DNA to oppose the structures of sin and the hierarchies of death. When we live as equals under Christ, a different system

---

82. Although Dunn says that 8:11 "clearly refers to the final resurrection" (*Romans 1–8*, 432), he is ready to speak of "a period of overlap between 'this evil age' and the age of resurrection life *already* shared 'in Christ'" (*Romans 1–8*, 468, emphasis mine). Käsemann concludes his extensive discussion by claiming, "Christ is already risen and we are on the way thereto, whereby our new obedience reflects on earth the future glory" (*Romans*, 224).

is being revealed already on this earth – one with Christ as the head of the church. The only effective witness to the unbelieving "inhabitants of the earth" is countercultural living. Though it may irritate unbelievers, they will see the truth of the gospel of God after the structures of sin have had their games with such witnesses and left them half-dead on the side of the road. In other words, unbelievers will only see the gospel if it is lived out in the church of God.

When I am talking about this suffering of the present time, I am not talking about medieval ideas that Christians have inherited from their songbooks and traditions about a tearful valley, where we need to accept our lot as victims of evil and condemn our poor, poor souls, which are powerless in the face of such a harsh lot. This is not what Paul means by the "suffering of the present time." Rather, *because* Christians dare to challenge the structures of sin with God's good news and eternal life, they will experience suffering.

The structures do not like to be challenged, and those who work against them will be attacked – whether by setting up medical care in Karen refugee camps in Thailand against all odds while living there as a refugee, as Dr. Cynthia Maung did; or by establishing birthing huts in the mountains of Papua New Guinea, as Kaa Simon did; or by leading a women's job corp in South Africa, as Patricia Ihlenfeld did; or by doing research on violence against women in evangelical churches, as Dr. Nancy Nason-Clark did – to mention just a few of the amazing (Baptist) women I have met. Their work required a willingness to take on the suffering of the present time as the structures of sin continued to fight back, always trying to hold their ground so that no one – especially women – could escape.

The suffering of the present time will include thinking for ourselves, an activity that many people give up on as students, because it is too demanding and impractical. Why bother with reading the word of God when you have mouths to feed? In many places, women have not been taught to think in the first place. An education is the first step in facing extreme poverty, and education is becoming less accessible as the system is becoming more high-tech and complicated. Think about how easy it is to trick old people into buying smart phones that they will never use, or to keep track of their expenditures in the jungle of new bank products. It is especially important for Christian women to take up the education of women and girls around the world, which is very countercultural in many places.

Back in the sixteenth century, when the printing press was invented and the Bible was printed and distributed more broadly than ever before, the reading of Scripture by ordinary people brought about a worldwide revolution – and not just a Reformation. We cannot rely on what we have been taught alone, though the teaching of truly Christian preachers is valuable. Everyone needs to read Scripture for themselves, as Paul encourages the Thessalonians: "Do not despise the words of prophets, but test everything; hold fast to what is good" (1 Thess 5:20). Women especially need to hear this direct call and study the Bible for themselves so that they will hear the voice of God, rather than messages from the structures of sin, which are often imposed on Scripture. One of my big concerns is the fear of theology that I see in many women's groups. Men have given theology a bad name by burdening it with strife and division in the past. But this past division only makes it more imperative for women to study and understand the will of God for themselves. A deep and thorough study of the Bible, including formal education whenever possible, is necessary and freeing for all Christian women.

The suffering of the present time is also experienced when we feel like small nobodies attempting to challenge the structures of sin and the bullies that perpetuate them. It is challenging for anyone to find a voice, but particularly for women. We need to realize that the structures of sin train people to be imitators rather than challengers. We're told to compare ourselves with others, to give up our sense of self so that we can fit in with the hierarchical model. The structures do not want us to become who God intended for us to be. They want us to blend in so that we don't rock the boat of the hierarchy of sin. Perpetuate the status quo. Do not point to where the structures create pain and death. Keep quiet. Hope for the best. Be satisfied with little.

So what exactly does God want us to challenge? Where do we need to step back, and where do we need to step up? Our discernment of these questions will not be as difficult if we make it a habit to ask some of the following questions. Am I trying to serve someone else rather than God? Do I need to make someone else happier than God? Do I fear someone else more than God? Am I accepting someone else who is imposing on me as God? Figuratively speaking, is someone trying to unload their trash in my life's living room? Are they dumping their emotional baggage on me through abuse and violence? Have I been putting up with it for so long because I fear them? Have I accepted the stench that this has brought into my life, even though I know it is tearing apart my family and ministry?

We need to address these impositions and stop them – even if it is dangerous, since violent, emotional people are not pleasant to be around. But when we accept their behaviour and affirm it by staying, we are just enforcing their god-delusions, on the one hand, and treating them as a god, on the other. The problem is not just that they are unloading their trash, but that they think everyone else is going to accommodate them. Violence in the home is also a form of idolatry. If you accept it because you fear the man, rather than God, you are not serving God. You are fearing the idol that has sold himself to you as a god.

To give another example, some people come in and want to rearrange your garden.[83] They might profess that they know what you should be doing, and so they set up your schedule and make you fit into their plans. In severe cases, they might run over you with their bulldozer. But you know what they're doing is not what you want, and so you are frustrated, but you cannot say "no" because you respect or fear them. In extreme cases, our parents, particularly our mothers, may try to do this by living their lives through us. I am writing this portion on Mother's Day, and as much as I believe that we should give tribute to our mothers because their work is so hard and devalued in the structures of sin, Mother's Day teaches us that mothers are some kind of semi-gods that need special worship. They have given themselves for us, and so now it's pay-back time. Yet mothers have chosen to become mothers (or should have chosen to be mothers). They did it (or should have done it) out of their free will. No child asked to be born, and so it is the choice and duty of the mother to bring up the children she set into the world. No mother was called to give herself up in the process. If she did, that was her own decision, and her attempt to manipulate others by pointing out her eternal victimhood to her children is wrong. It is not biblical and does not count as honouring your parents. Instead, the Bible says, "for children ought not to lay up for their parents, but parents for their children" (2 Cor 12:14).

This brings us to another form of suffering of the present times. Christians have to refrain from being in charge of everything and everyone. Yet we (and not God) often want to enlarge our tents and territories inappropriately, moving into other people's homes and gardens. Such Christians establish themselves as a god for other people by intruding into their lives and making decisions for them. Sometimes, in Christian circles, we call this carrying other people's burdens, but, in fact, it is nothing but meddling. We try to sort out other people's problems because it makes us feel good – not because we are helping them.

Many mothers do not help by constantly cooking and babysitting for their adult children, though many people in my culture believe that this is what life should look like. While the young new parents may have the blast

---

83. This illustration is built on H. Cloud and J. Townsend, *Boundaries: When to Say Yes, How to Say No to Take Control of Your Life* (Grand Rapids: Zondervan, 1992), 31.

of an extended youth by relegating their children to their mother, people who have children should embrace adulthood by accepting the self-imposed responsibility of childcare.

Grandmothers, too, sometimes take on the feeling of extended motherhood when they are burdened with caring for a grandchild, but they should be stepping into a new phase of wise maturity. As a new grandmother, I appreciate the clear "no" I get from my daughter when I overstep. Nobody profits from these deficiencies of growth, because we just love to get stuck in whatever feels good for the moment. Unfortunately, many cultures respect this meddling and make space for it in their traditions. We need to recognize this as a psychological deficiency and a lack of faith so that we can move into new territory.

To give another example, possessive mothers have relegated their gifts to the realm of serving their families. Because they have given up and failed to live their own dreams, they have learned to live vicariously through others, who are not allowed to live their own lives – mostly their husbands and children and particularly their sons. These mothers count their husband's and children's successes as their own, and they carry their failures with shame, even though they had no say in the decisions that brought about those successes or failures. But people hate it when others try to live through them. They feel that this person who is trying to own their successes and failures is a permanent squatter in their house. They cannot evict them, because the squatter plays the role of an angry and demanding god. Whenever the subject is brought up, the mother plays the manipulative card of self-sacrifice. There are no winners in this constellation.

My mother-in-law is an amazing woman, but she never had the opportunity to live her own dream. As a German in post-World War II communist Yugoslavia, she and her mother and siblings ended up in a concentration camp. When they were miraculously released on one Easter morning while the rest of the camp was destroyed (together with all the other people in it), she was tasked with working for her fatherless family by baking bricks in a brick factory. She has always been tiny and skinny, but strong. She did not learn to cook until she was thirty. Finally, after her siblings finished school, she could live her own life.

She never considered herself as a victim, and I have never heard her complain or ask for recognition. She took life as it came. She married a kind man, and they made a good life together. It was not easy, but she worked with him on construction, and as my father-in-law was a lay preacher in Romanian village churches in Yugoslavia, she joined him and had the trust of the brothers to care for the administration of that ministry. She was always a learner. Even now, in her nineties, she reads daily.

However, while she worked to put her siblings through school, she was never able to finish the school that she wished to attend. Instead, many years later, my husband says, she made an "executive decision" about what school he should finish "because she always wanted to go to that school." Unfulfilled dreams often come back to haunt us. Also, as much as my mother-in-law wanted her son to finish "her school," she could not understand why I was pursuing my studies towards a doctorate. She thought that, just like her, I should let go of my dreams to tend her grandchildren, who needed their mother! This is the flip-side of the same problem. We expect all other people to live up to the same sacrifices that we made.

We have been making fun of my mother-in-law because of these things. She is the kind of person who understands fun, and yet it is hard for her to understand my life. She is a great Christian character, and the gifts of the Spirit in her always trump the prevalent traditions, because the Spirit of life in her always trumps the spirit of death. But we need to understand that wherever the circumstances of the structures of sin are harsh, and wherever there is a chronic lack of life and fruit of the Spirit in a Christian, there will also be more suffering, and the pain will be carried forward into the next generation.

To give another example, a woman I knew never attempted to live her own life. She let herself be pushed into the role descriptions by her environment and her mother, who was a rebel for a short time, but then returned to the myths of her culture. This woman got married in her thirties, believing that she was an old maid and the last choice. She took no initiative, other than being passive aggressive when her family and other people were not living up to her expectations. She was very proud when her husband became an elder in the church and said, "I feel like this is my own achievement. You know, there is always a great woman behind every successful man!"

But then the impossible happened, and her husband was unfaithful to her. She went through counselling and then decided that she wanted to keep their family together. Although her husband repented, she had a hard time forgiving him. Just like his success, she also took on his sin, as if it were her own. Because she had no life on her own and had lived through him, she felt he had ruined her, too. No word could remove this belief from her. She continued resenting and grieving, wishing for a different life, as if someone else could give it to her.

It is hard to live through other people – both for the one living that foreign life and for those who have to endure it. After finding myself in the role of a Christian counsellor for a number of years, I can fully understand why middle-aged women are recognized as a group as hysterics. J. M. Charcot and S. Freud defined hysteria as a "psychological scar produced through trauma or repression," and Freud later thought that it was produced primarily through "the loss of penis" in women.[84] It seems to me that women's "hysteria" is better explained by the structures of sin, which either abuse women, or force them to lose themselves by becoming nurturers of husbands and children – and who are then stuck in the impossible task of trying to be happy by living vicariously through others and then being resented for it. Necessarily, children need nurture and sacrifice by the parents, but there is a difference between a couple that decides what they want to do and how they will divide the chores once the children come, taking into account both of their gifts and dreams, and such that just dump everything on the mother. Biblically speaking, there is no such gift as motherhood, only a commitment to care and nurture what we have accepted as God's gift to us.

There is another neglected sermon text in Luke 11:27–28, which is at odds with our traditions about motherhood. A woman blesses Jesus's mother for giving birth and nursing him, but rather abruptly, Jesus answers that such people who listen and do the word of God are more blessed than her! Evidently, each of us needs to live up to what God has put in us – regardless of gender – and motherhood is not the highest calling in God's kingdom. Children are God's gift, but nurturing them is to be shared by the parents based on the gifts they bring into the relationship. Children are a gift to both parents, and so both are equally responsible for raising them.

If this is difficult to understand, consider it from a practical perspective. Today, women are not even in childbearing age for more than 60 percent of their lifetime. If we relegate them to motherhood, what do we expect them to do during these "free" years, and how can they use their neglected gifts? If they hang on to their calling as eternal mothers, they will probably meddle

---

84. I am not a psychologist nor an approved psychotherapist, and so I cannot unpack Freud's thoughts in detail. Ideas reflected here on women's "hysteria" can be tracked in A. McVean, "The History of Hysteria," online at McGill's Office for Science and Society, 31 July 2017: https://www.mcgill.ca/oss/article/history-quackery/history-hysteria, passages 4–5. J. Breuer and S. Freud, *Studien über Hysterie* (Leipzig; Vienna: Deuticke, 1895), 2, describe a long line of hysteric expressions. Although the authors point out that childhood trauma is often the trigger, they continue on the same page with examples of adult women's lives and episodes that frustrate women. They also admit that hysteria does not necessarily depend on one big trauma, but can be the result of a sum of smaller events – fear or shame (3), the inability to react to a trauma or frustration adequately (5–6), or even a laborious suppression (*mühevolle Unterdrückung*, 9). The authors do not make this a female problem, but the examples they use in the book are all female.

in their adult children's lives, resenting people (particularly women) who are living their dreams, resenting their children (particularly their daughters), resenting their husbands and their neighbours, who seem to have it all. I have seen a lot of this in my ministry to women. Gifts that are not being used for the benefit of the wider community become bombs that destroy communities and put strain and hardship on families.

Children are a wonderful gift and part of life, and they provide a great learning experience, especially about our relationship to God as his children. By having children, we learn more easily how God is our parent, what it means for him to love us unconditionally and show us mercy. Children are not only expensive to raise. They cost us our lives, and we seem to die many times over as we first respond to our own children and then, with much more insight, to our grandchildren.

In fact, both men and women need this experience. Success in life happens through a happy exchange of the gifts God has given us. Children need mothers and fathers; they need to see how two different people manage to stay together and work together, bringing up a family and releasing it to God. This is a principle everywhere in the Bible and does not only concern children, but all areas of life. We are called to come together and not to segregate. When we are different, we need to trust that God wanted us all. Something wonderful happens when people with different gifts and experiences start working together for the blessing of the world and the glory of God, bearing the fruit of the Spirit.

Coming Together under Christ: The Lord's Table

Yet this coming together is countercultural in our hierarchical world, since hierarchies thrive on finding ways to segregate people and assign them to castes so that they will be unable to challenge the power structures. The world loves to discuss the ideal of community, but in reality, community does not fit into the agenda of the hierarchies of sin. When we let go of our fear and striving, we can see the amazing potential of community, but only idealistic young people are usually willing to try such experiments.

Those who believe God, however, do not need to fight for space in hierarchies, because we believe that God has a place for us. We are called to accept others equally and to offer ourselves to one another freely. We know that our needs are met in God at the right time and that our lives are safe because they are hidden in Christ. We do not respond out of fear for our lives or fear of death, as the writer to the Hebrews points out (Heb 2:14), and so we can live a relaxed life in community. If God cares, we do not need to fight or be afraid.

However, many Christians struggle to embrace this attitude. They feel pressured by the circumstances of life and disappointed by backstabbing friends who have used them for their own promotion up the hierarchies of power, sometimes even in the church. Christians can be easy prey for the power thirsty, because they depend on the word of God, and so their behaviour is predictable, and they are easy to manipulate. The Bible carries testimony to people who are not perfect, but still coping with sin in their mortal bodies, and so churches become entangled in the structures of sin.

Paul exposes one example in his letter to the Corinthians, a much-read chapter that many of us know by heart: "I have no praise for you, for your meetings do more harm than good" (1 Cor 11:17–34). A historical reconstruction of the situation in Corinth points to a number of things. First, Corinth was a city with two harbours, which meant that commerce and communication were the basis of everyday life. Second, the society was not close-knit, because many people were just passing through and had no family or community ties. Thus the Christian community that formed in Corinth was probably also very diverse.

There has been a long debate about whether Paul's churches belonged to a lower social class,[85] but it is generally agreed today that they were diverse – "mixed strata, ambiguous status" according to Meeks.[86] This diversity was particularly true for the Corinthians, and their differences are featured in this passage. There were people in Corinth who were well-off enough to sit around all day, eating, drinking, and having fun (1 Cor 11:21–22), while others had to work and so arrived late to the assembly only to find their brothers and sisters drunk. From its beginning, the Christian church professed universality,[87] not only with regard to geography – people of all nations were welcome because the church belonged to the whole world – but also with regard to other dividing factors, such as social status, race, nationality, or gender. To accept this universality in salvation is to acknowledge God as the sovereign Creator of the world. Ideologically, this is exciting. We like to think in these romantic

---

85. W. A. Meeks, *The First Urban Christians: The Social World of the Apostle Paul* (New Haven: Yale University Press, 1983; repr. 2003), 51–73.

86. Meeks, *Urban Christians*, 72.

87. This is evident from Jesus's Great Commandment in Matthew 28:19 and Paul's *catena* in Romans 15:7–12 (along with other places), and it is affirmed in the Nicene Creed: "We believe in one holy *catholic* and apostolic Church," where catholic (from the Greek) means "general," which includes "universal," and thus no one is excluded.

terms about being equals in the eyes of God, but to put this belief into practice is a different story, as there are many factors and traditions that disrupt the ideal. This struggle is made evident in the Corinthian church.

In Corinth, many cultural traditions flooded into the church. Commentators mention ways in which people came together for meals in the ancient world. The houses of the rich had atriums that were used for feasts, where friends came together to hang out and celebrate.[88] Thus the Christian idea of an agape meal was not a revolutionary or new concept. The old tradition of coming together and hosting a meal was easily translated into the new practice of sharing an agape meal that included the Lord's Supper. Yet that the old tradition had some elements that did not measure up to the Christian requirement.[89] Food was very important in the Mediterranean – and it still is today. The rich had time on their hands and could bring as much food as they wanted, enjoying fellowship all day long. Yet their fellowship was only with people who belonged to their same social level, because the poor people could only come after they finished their day's work, all sweaty and hungry. Some commentators even suggest that the custom in Corinth was for the rich to invite the poor to come at the end of the feast to pick up the leftovers from the table, so they could ridicule their poverty and low status, helping the rich feel even better about their affluence. "Do you despise the church of God by humiliating those who have nothing?" Paul asks the rich Corinthians (11:22).

Clearly, they were not thinking about the church of God, because they were just living according to their old traditions of segregation. Paul turns this tradition upside down, but he does not suggest that they share their riches with the poor.[90] Rather, he criticizes the Corinthians, saying, "when the time comes to eat, each of you goes ahead with your own supper, and one goes hungry and another becomes drunk. What! Do you not have homes to eat and drink in?" (1 Cor 11:21–22). Paul relegates social eating and drinking to people's own homes in order to free the Lord's table from social divisions. "Paul's present concern is not with penury or gluttony, but with being truly together at the

---

88. See G. D. Fee, *The First Epistle to the Corinthians* (Grand Rapids: Eerdmans, 1987), 541–542, particularly fn. 55.

89. K. Magda and M. Wachsmuth, "'Discerning the Body' in Cross-Cultural Relationships: A Critical Analysis of Missional Partnership in Southeastern Europe," *Kairos* 1 (2014): 25–43, 28. See also W. Schrage, *Erste Brief an die Korinther* (EKK., Zürich: Benziger, 1991).

90. Fee suggests (reading Martial and Pliny) that the issue can be seen as "from above" ("the rich should eat the same fare as the others") or "from below" ("the poor should eat the same food as the rich"), which are typical solutions to the problem at hand by "contemporary social ethicists," but Paul's concern is not with distinctions about the rich and poor, but with "being truly together at the common table," *First Corinthians*, 544.

common table, with no class distinction being allowed . . . Paul attacks the system indirectly, but at its very core."[91] Everyone eats and drinks at home, but when they come together, they come together around the Lord's table. The shared table reminds them of Jesus's sacrifice on the cross, the abyss that has been bridged between heaven and earth so that a most unlikely community with God could become possible. This obstacle could not have been bridged in any other way but by God becoming a human and dying on the cross, so that equal access could be given to those who did not and could not deserve God's glory in any way. What are human social differences by comparison?

When we come to the Lord's table "in remembrance of" Jesus's work, we are reminded of our status compared with the divine status of Christ. Where would we be without Jesus's sacrifice? Who would we be if not the body of Christ? Paul believes that there is great uniting power when we come together to the Lord's table, and therefore it is impossible to respond with any segregation. We are to accept each other with the love that Christ showed us by dying for us all equally. We are measured only by how God sees us in Christ – not according to any human hierarchies. Our earthy possessions are not a factor in the community of God.

Returning to the situation in Corinth, the people were coming together as a diverse people of God, but they were still caught up in the worldly structures of sin because they believed that social strata were important. But Paul does not respond by engaging the typical discussion about equity, which is often preached from the moral pulpits of this world. Paul's first step is not the pursuit of justice from a human and legalistic perspective, because Paul knows that justice and equity cannot be commanded, and nothing can be achieved when the rich are forced to share their riches. They may comply to some degree so that they won't lose face, but their charity will be driven by self-promotion or some new way to get even richer.

I have lived through a war, a large-scale flood emergency, and at the gates of the refugee highway through my country in 2015. I have observed the fertile soil of human tragedy firsthand and seen how it can be used to promote organizations and politics. Unfortunately, it is easy to make humanitarianism about ourselves and to rationalize it so that, in the end, the poor are sold yet again. Even for Christian organizations, it is difficult to avoid falling into this same trap. The world sets up criteria for help, and people sometimes feel that if they don't bend their Christian ethical standards just a little to fit into some

---

91. Fee, *First Corinthians*, 544.

category "as everyone else does," they will miss out on a good opportunity to further their work.

Thus Paul is right. Equity cannot be commanded; it can only come from a heart that is free from preoccupation with the self because of faith in God. Paul recognizes that the only place to achieve true equity among Christians is at the Lord's table. In the Corinthian setting, it needed to be stripped of all distinctions about social inequality. The double command to eat at home is therefore not an incidental instruction (1 Cor 11:22, 34). Rather, it is a necessity in order to remove worldly distinctions from the place where human differences become irrelevant in view of the great abyss that Christ bridged to make it possible for humans to meet a holy God.

But Paul also wants the Corinthians to learn another lesson from the Lord's table. It not only reminds them about the great abyss that was bridged by Christ, but also about the outcome of Christ's work: the old, sinful, death-stricken "flesh" has been replaced by the body of Christ – his new *soma*. If Christians fail to recognise this new *soma*, the Eucharist will be understood as a place of judgment for the participant (1 Cor 11:29, 34).

Traditionally, at least in Western culture, the instruction to Christians to "examine" themselves "before they eat of the bread and drink from the cup" (1 Cor 11:28) has been understood in terms of an internal spirituality.[92] In many churches, people are called to examine any personal sins that might prevent them from coming to the Lord's table, because approaching the table unworthily, with sins in their hearts, will cause their ruin. Yet from the perspective of the doctrine of salvation, this teaching is wrong. People are not sinners because they sin; rather, they commit sins because they are sinners at heart. The self-examination that is required in many churches suggests that we can know ourselves and our sins fully – that our sins are bad deeds that can be counterweighted by good deeds and/or repentance. This is a simplistic

---

92. E.g. A. Barnes presents what is regularly taught in many churches in the context of the Eucharist: "Let him search and see if he have the proper qualifications . . .; if he has true repentance for his sins; true faith in the Lord Jesus; and a sincere desire to live the life of a Christian, and to be like the Son of God, and be saved by the merits of his blood. Let him examine himself, and see whether he have the right feelings of a communicant, and can approach the table in a proper manner." From A. Barnes, *Notes on the Bible* (1834); accessed online through *Bible Hub*, https://biblehub.com/commentaries/barnes/1_corinthians/11.htm. Fee concludes that 1 Cor 11:28 "along with v. 27 has been the cause of untold anxieties within the church," but also says, "This is not a call for deep personal introspection to determine whether one is worthy of the Table. Rather, it stands in contrast to the 'divine examination' to which unworthy participation will lead" (Fee, *First Corinthians*, 561).

and superficial view of sin, and it is not compatible with Paul's theology of systemic structures of sin.

As Christians, we are invited to participate in God's new reality through the Spirit of God, which is given to us as a gift. This does not mean that we stop sinning, but that our salvation is not determined by our acts, but by the fact that we belong to God in faith. It is certainly important for us to evaluate whether we are glorifying God[93] with our lives and how the Spirit who lives in us might be leading us to change, and the Eucharist is a good place for this mindful evaluation. But Paul's main agenda is to show the rich Corinthians how wrong they are when they insult the church of God by their leisurely, unthoughtful lifestyle. Paul does not condemn them for *not* sharing, but shows them how they are failing to discern that they are part of the body of Christ along with the poor, whom they are belittling, despising, and judging according to the world's labels. For Paul, the inner problem of the rich Christians is bigger than the outward sign. In Christ, the people they despise are worthy parts of the body of Christ, to which they also belong, and the body cannot function without all its members. If they despise them, the body will not function properly. For this reason, many in Corinth are weak and dying. When we distance ourselves from – or deny others a connection to – the body of Christ, our life is in danger. It would be like not having a kidney to cleanse the body of toxins. If you cut out the kidney, the whole body will be dead within a week. Jesus presents a similar picture in John 15, describing the branches of the vine that try to live apart from the vine. They become worthless chaff and will go up in flames.

Positively, there is immense didactic potential in Paul's instruction to eat meals at home and come to the Lord's table without worldly expectations. For one, people are less receptive to the traditions of the world that work on the principles of social strata. At the Lord's table, the world is turned upside down, because God came to earth to give himself up for people. As those assembled observe the great miracle of God's self-emptying in the bread and the wine, they view themselves from a new, divine perspective. Whatever the world thinks of me and wherever it places me, I am a child of God, and therefore I belong to the family of God, the body of Christ with others. My value is not in myself, nor is it defined by the structures of the world; rather, my value is in Christ and my function, along with my gifts and experiences, is determined by the Creator, who made us all.

---

93. Fee helpfully suggests that there is a "judgment theme" in 1 Corinthians "since they will be examined by God in the end," but their present behaviour towards the Lord's table and those others around it requests a very concrete examination (*First Corinthians*, 561–562).

When I was last in South Africa, I saw what a great project the church is conducting there by trying to live out this Eucharistic community in their post-apartheid context. How do you combine diverse traditions of living, worship, values, and languages into one body of Christ? This is only possible when Christ becomes more important than our individual traditions or the ways that we used to live. When we fail to make space to embrace the other, our life will be affected. I loved the lush colours of this rainbow nation, which is showing the world the beauty of diversity as they seek to come together in Christ. It is by no means an easy project, and it is only on its way, but it becomes easier when our eyes are firmly fixed on Christ, and we have been "joined and knit together by every ligament with which it [the body] is equipped, as each part is working properly, promotes the body's growth in building itself up in love" (Eph 4:16).

Christ, the Head of a New Body: Global Christianity

Within our action-based humanitarian tradition and our concern for justice, it may sound oddly inappropriate for Paul to send the rich back to their own homes to eat and drink rather than calling on them to share what they have with the poor. But Paul is not a lover of human revolutions, since they only tend to upset the hierarchies of sin without much hope that any reassembling will bring a better world order. Instead, Paul urges churches to pray for "a quiet and peaceable life in all godliness and dignity" (1 Tim 2:2).

As we have noted earlier, Paul expects an inner change in Christians, from which a deep-going, quiet revolution will spread as they voluntarily submit to one another and take on one another's suffering. This kind of revolution is hardly imaginable without a close and strong attachment to God in faith, a faith that keeps our lives safe as we struggle against the structures of sin. Paul's *soma* language – being the body of Christ in the world – has a revolutionary potential to benefit the world, bearing eternal light into the darkness of the structures of sin and death. This vision of the body of Christ offers a true change of paradigm.

In her book, *Gender or Giftedness*, Lynn Smith helpfully highlights the difference between a system that fights for justice for women and the justice that comes from recognizing Christ as the head of the church. To describe the search for justice in male-female relationships, she uses a seesaw to depict the constant power struggle. Someone has to give up some power in order to make the seesaw balance, but that balance is always unstable. When we focus on justice and rights, Smith concludes, there will be wars that will never cease.[94] Feminists often point out that men have been privileged long enough and should step down, but this will not happen without a fight, for no one gives up privilege without a fight.

In economics and politics, this experience is generally called a "shift to the right,"[95] but it can also be seen in the area of human rights for women. Yet what was accomplished for women's equality in the last century is crumbling as conservative forces gain more support and "security" becomes more valuable than development. I have been taken by surprise to see many attitudes about injustice and violence resurface, which we thought had been eradicated. So many political movements want to put women back in the kitchen under the strict authority of men. But the seesaw effect should not be surprising, for it has been aided – and possibly triggered – by terrorism and globalization phobias. Efforts towards equality in the twentieth century have been imbalanced by these new considerations, which challenge the position of "Egalitarians." Some believe that men are finally retrieving their naturally "wild" hearts from the "feminized" selves that were imposed on them by feminists. A good number of young women feel that it is much easier if the husband brings in the money and provides a nice and peaceful existence for the family, and they are glad to be relieved of carrying the double burden of work and family. But these women (often from the entitled West) forget the downside of this deal, which often permits abuse and excludes those who do not fit within the narrow role descriptions – or find themselves feeling unfilled when they enter their forties.

Smith sees a different way for Christians, which she calls a "reconciled" paradigm of male-female relationships under Christ.[96] When Christ is the head and Christians are his body, all the different parts have an equal standing, regardless of their function or visibility. Moreover, Christ determines how each

---

94. Marilyn B. (Lynn) Smith, *Gender or Giftedness* (Manila: World Evangelical Fellowship Commission on Women's Concerns, 2000), 8–9.

95. P. Patnaik, "The Global Shift to the Right," *People's Democracy* 22 (2019), accessed online: https://peoplesdemocracy.in/2019/0602_pd/global-shift-right, describes the problem for politics and economics. But the women's issues also develop in such circumstance, since after September 11, 2001, M. Khan insists, "Global: Shift to the Right," *San Francisco Examiner* (23 Dec 2002), accessed online: http://www.glocaleye.org/shift.htm. S. Milne, "Women Are Now to the Left of Men: It's a Historic Shift," *Guardian* (5 March 2013), online: https://www.theguardian.com/commentisfree/2013/mar/05/women-left-of-men-historic-shift, notes that these circumstances are moving women to the left – he believes for the first time in history, at least in Britain, due to the position that women have gained with public services.

96. Smith, *Gender*, 6.

person will function as part of his body, and so we are not assigned gifts for the building up of the church based on our biological sex.

Though many of us grew up with this logic (and many people still grow up within this paradigm), there is nothing logical about it. A mother of 2.4 children may spend up to fifteen years in immediate motherhood, where staying at home with the children may be a good idea both for her and for the children. Yet within her seventy-two years of average life expectancy (on the global level), she has thirty-five years when she will not be needed as a full-time mother. These will probably be her best years, as she will have learned amazing skills that will be transferrable to leadership roles, and she will have learned a lot about herself in relation to other people. Why do we expect her to waste all of her wisdom and potential on cleaning things that have not been made dirty, because the children are out of the house? Why are we surprised when she meddles in her adult children's lives and interferes with the way they are bringing up their children? Why is her husband upset by her frustration about being useless? In church settings, we will blame her for being a gossip when she talks about everything that needs to be improved. How can we blame her for all the psychosomatic illnesses that will be caused by all this frustration? The questions become even more complicated when we take into account the explosion of the world population.

Both women and men are created for the glory of God, and only God can determine the diverse purposes for which they have been created. Mothers are often discarded from leadership even though they have successfully led the smallest and most vulnerable people to adulthood, a job that requires intuition, teamwork, and the capacity to handle diverse chores and people. Being an involved parent should be counted as an invaluable skill in job interviews because it also demands endless resourcefulness and maturity.

As already observed, the creation account does not distribute the tasks of men and women on the grounds of their sex. In the New Testament, and already in the Old Testament prophecies about the amazing times when the Spirit of God will be poured out freely on "every flesh," there is no distinction between the gifts given to men and women (Joel 3:1-3; comp. Rom 12:1-13; 1 Cor 12:4-31). We also saw that in spite of the heavily patriarchal background in which the Bible was written, there is a strong affirmation of women. Deborah is made a judge and army leader (Judg 4:4-5:31). Jesus accepts female disciples against the rules of the environment (e.g. Mary; Luke 10:38-42). Paul identifies women as the amazing leaders of early Christian house churches (Rom 16:1-16). Thus from God's perspective, we can conclude that there is not one prescribed role for women. If they are called to submission, so are the men

(Eph 5:21). Submission is a trait of those who are part of the kingdom of God, as modelled first by Jesus (Phil 2:5–11).

So what makes our church practice so difficult? First, the structures of sin, along with traditions, cultures, and values enforce gender distinctions because they are driven by the need for superiority and the desire to rule over others. But Jesus explicitly says to the disciples when they fight about the positions in the kingdom of God: "it should not so be among you" (Mark 10:43).

There has been a recent discussion among Bosnian evangelicals about whether women can serve as pastors and leaders. From an outsider's perspective, this question is redundant, as evangelical witness in Bosnia has grown to a large extent from women, who have been pastors and leaders from the beginning of church there. Even public documents bear witness to this, since they were signed by women who were serving as pastors. This was never questioned while the work of the church was in its beginnings – merely a "movement."

Now that the church is more established, some people are insisting on structures so that everyone can know "who is in charge." This has involved a process of eliminating people from the structures, where only a few are deemed "fit" for leadership. If all the strong women are removed, men will rise more easily to the top. Though the work has been carried by women for almost thirty years, this discussion about the "biblical" position regarding women in leadership has been introduced now. Some men have even suggested that the women who have served as pastors all these years should not have "authority" over the men in their congregations. This raises several interesting questions. How can women serve as pastors if none of the men in their churches recognize their authority? When do men become men? Can women have "authority" over male children? Exactly what kind of authority do these men think that pastors should have over people? Doesn't this whole discussion reveal a worldly perception about "ruling over" others rather than a biblical one? Biblically speaking, this language reflects the curse – and Jesus explicitly prohibits it within the church.

I am not using this example to pick on the Bosnian church, for it is hard work to grow a church from scratch within an extremely hostile environment. But because it is a relatively young church, the developments can be more easily observed than in other places, where traditions and practices have been obscured by spiritual talk. Churches often follow the trend of the structures of sin, even though God established the church to be a countercultural presence of resistance to such structures. Our best intentions easily get corrupted by superficial readings of Scripture, and so women have suffered greatly from the structures of sin that have been transported into the church.

Women and Bible Study

We have recognized already that women often play alongside such unjust traditions because they believe it will be easier for them to survive or at least to reach a goddess status. This makes them easy victims in the power struggles, where they often become collateral damage, along with their children. By yielding to the hierarchies of sin, women also fortify the myths of male structures for the future by educating their children within them. Men often ignore women when they speak or refuse to heed their suggestions.[97] Women often grow up thinking that they have no voice in society, and so they willingly give up their voices for some minor gratification of vicarious power or an empty promise of security by a man. This is particularly sad in view of biblical interpretation. By conducting historical and literary research of the New Testament, Bible hermeneutics has been greatly enhanced in the last century – though the process is far from finished. There is nothing particularly new about the approach – and it is certainly not some liberal agenda! The Croatian Reformer known as the father of hermeneutics, Matthias Flacius Illyricus, insisted on similar principles for the correct understanding of Scripture.[98] It is extremely important to attempt to comprehend a passage of the Bible as it would have been understood by the first recipients of the text within their setting, because such an understanding frames an interpretation and safeguards it from ones that are rooted in sinful structures. Throughout history, a lack of proper biblical research has brought the church – and the world – much pain. Regarding women, men have read certain biblical passages and interpreted them to mean that God orders submission for women and identifies men as

---

[97] The extent of this problem is presented in S. Chira, "The Universal Phenomenon of Men Interrupting Women," *New York Times* (14 June 2017), accessed online: https://www.nytimes.com/2017/06/14/business/women-sexism-work-huffington-kamala-harris.html; M. Riechers, "How Women's Voices Get Silenced and How," *The Best of Our Knowledge* (27 July 2019), accessed online: https://www.ttbook.org/interview/how-womens-voices-get-silenced-and-how-you-can-learn-speak; V. Rueckert, *Outspoken: Why Women's Voices Get Silenced and How to Set Them Free* (New York: HarperCollins, 2019).

[98] According to Matija Vlačić Ilirik, *O načinu razumijevanja Svetoga Pisma*, trans. Ž. Puratić (Zagreb: Hrvatska Sveučilišna naklada, 1993), 124–147, these principles include the right spiritual approach to the Bible, a knowledge of the Bible's original languages and historical settings, a good grasp of grammar in both Greek and Hebrew as well as one's own language, an understanding of the broader context of the passage being read, including the scope and intention of the whole book, and an understanding of the structure of the passage or discourse. All these requirements are still very relevant and basic to the reading of Scripture. Flacius wrote his seminal work *Clavis Scripturae Sacrae seu de Sermone Sacrarum literarum* in 1567. Unfortunately, Flacius has not been translated much from the original Latin, but there is one recent attempt to make him available in English, M. Flacius, *How to Understand the Sacred Scriptures*, trans. W. R. Johnston (Saginaw: Magdeburg Press, 2011).

the enforcers of God's will. This misconception has resulted in abuses of all kinds: physical, psychological, financial, material, and spiritual. Throughout the ages – and in some places in our present age – ignorant men who have been enslaved by their carnal desires have interpreted the Bible inadequately and have established their ignorant ideas as validations for the abuse of women.

Unfortunately, few have stood up to correct or challenge them, and equally ignorant women have often served as disinterested bystanders to such abusive interpretations, accepting them without bothering to read the Bible for themselves. A lot could be said about lazy, carnal Christians – both women and men – who live out the illogical option of being freed in Christ and having an amazing life-bringing Spirit of God in them, but continue to choose death over life in their "mortal bodies." Searching Scriptures is difficult, but when we fail to do so, God is defiled by strife and bondage to worldly flesh in the church.

Christian women in particular must study and read the Bible for themselves, discussing the outcomes with others and looking for the implications in their lives. As I travel around the world, I am amazed by how little love for the word of God I see among women – and how very basic their knowledge is. So many women relegate life-giving Bible reading to men, often arguing that theology ruins everything. I have even known students in theological institutions who thought the Bible was boring! By transferring our responsibility to hear the word of God to someone else, we open space for our own enslavement – and thus the enslavement of others.

When I studied the Bible lectionaries a few years ago, I found that most of the gospel readings did not include passages about women. It is possible that the men who assembled the lectionaries did not think about this. Or in fact, people who put together Sunday School material for kids. But a small girl in my Sunday school class wondered if God loved women, because she only heard about the "men of God" in her class. When I began to read for myself about the women who met and followed Jesus, it was an important step towards my affirmation and faith.

Women are called to make up for the many centuries we failed to listen to the word of God directly. We need to discover all the facets that the church has missed in order to challenge the partial and incorrect interpretations that marginalise women in the kingdom of God. By presenting to the world the healing power of the kingdom of God as we partner together to fill our full potential within the church, we can model the different world that is possible with God. Women need to take responsibility for nurturing and encouraging other women to learn the Bible, making space for them and inviting them to share what they have read and learned in order to enrich the church and strengthen its mission to serve the world with the good news of Christ.

However, reading the Bible from a female perspective is difficult, because the Bible was written in a system that was ruled and established by men. Men have continued to enforce the myths and traditions that keep men in power, often identifying their perspectives as infallible. This fact of the patriarchal system needs to be taken into account.

The hardship begins with the language, since women are implicitly excluded from the word "*man*kind." In some languages, including mine, women are automatically excluded from the word "humans" unless they are explicitly mentioned (*ljudi i žene* means "people and women"). Thus when women read their Bibles, they must decide whether a verse includes or excludes them. For instance, 1 Corinthians 12 and Romans 12 recall the gifts of the Spirit, and women often exclude themselves from the gifts of "teaching" or "preaching," since they were taught that women must be silent in the church and cannot teach men (1 Cor 14:34; 1 Tim 2:15). Yet these passages in Corinthians and Romans do not distinguish who can have which gifts, since the Spirit of God is responsible for distributing them according to the free will of God.

Women also read the Bible through the social roles that have been assigned to them by male leaders. If a girl with a potentially outstanding gifting as a pastor is taught in Sunday school by a male teacher and told that only men can become pastors, chances are that she will withdraw from the gift that has been given to her by the Spirit. It is rare for young girls to challenge their teachers by arguing for their strong inner persuasion about God's calling, particularly if she is showered with abuse by the teacher in order to "put her in her place." From a young age, many women have been "encouraged" through such clear instructions about the proper roles for women in the church. No wonder women have had such a hard time finding their place in the church and fulfilling their gifts to the glory of God!

For the past twenty years, I have heard a lot about the pain that has been inflicted on women by these false and ignorant interpretations of Scripture. For instance, women have been told that they have to "submit" to adulterous and physically abusive husbands who also abuse their children – something the Bible strictly identifies as sin and therefore must be challenged. Women are told they have to "submit" because that is their God-ordained place, and the family is "sacred" and needs to be preserved at all costs. Yet an adulterous man has already broken up a family, so there is nothing to uphold!

These men need boundaries, and they also need to be challenged – not only by their victims, but also by the church. Yet in the hierarchies of sin, "a house is a man's own castle," and other men have no business interfering, even if a man hits and abuses his wife and children in public. The way one man disciplines his wife and children is his own business, because he is the God-ordained head of the family. Yet in speaking about those who expose the deeds of the flesh, Paul says "those who do such things will not inherit the kingdom of God" (Gal 5:21). And Jesus said that ruling over others has no place within the context of Christian leadership.

Yet Christians around the world cling to this myth about male authority regardless of all the sins that have been committed, both in the home and the church. These abuses of power have become evident in all denominations, and Baptists are no exception. A man who believes that he is a god in a social system has no boundaries, particularly when no one can challenge his interpretations of Scripture or his behaviour. We need to challenge the idea of male (divine) headship in family and social structures by a thorough re-reading of Scripture.[99] Although I have said a lot about Ephesians 5:22–33 already, I would like to turn to it again to demonstrate what can happen when we read the Bible with new eyes. The following interpretation is divided into three parts: first, the grammatical dependence of 5:22 with the previous section; second, identifying submission as a framework for all Christians in the church; third, the implications of the grammatical analysis of the text, especially when taking social and historical data into account.[100]

Reading Ephesians 5:22 in Context

In some older translations, such as the so-called Zagreb Bible, which is popular in my context, or the English Standard Version, the section about the "Christian Household" begins with 5:22: "Wives, submit to your own husbands, as to the Lord." Thankfully, most newer versions have revised this to reflect the original Greek, where 5:22 does not have its own verb, but is dependent on 5:21, which

---

99. S. Titkemyer, "Male Headship and the Problem of Power," in *Pantheos No Longer Quivering* (27 May 2014), accessed online: https://www.patheos.com/blogs/nolongerquivering/2014/05/male-headship-and-the-problem-of-power/; W. Luimes, "Love and Power – or Powerful Love: Submission, Headship and Abuse," *Mutuality* (Summer 2016): 18–20.

100. I will not refer to the traditional "complementarian" view, as this is well known in most churches. If you need a reference, see the commentary by J. MacArthur, *Ephesians* (Chicago: Moody, 1986), 279–305.

says, "Be subject to one another out of reverence for Christ, wives to your own husbands..."

Even more broadly, the whole section is grammatically dependent on the context of 5:18: "... be filled with the Spirit." In the Greek, the participles that follow this main clause all describe what being filled with the Spirit looks like in everyday life – namely singing psalms and spiritual songs to the Lord and to one another, being thankful, and submitting to one another. Though the submission of wives is repeated here, the point is not to single them out as the only ones that need to submit,[101] for Ephesians is about how the life within the church should be an example for the world as a testimony of the kingdom of God. Paul prays that Ephesians might see how great it is to belong to the church of Christ (Eph 1:17–23). This privilege necessarily carries with it some responsibilities, which are described in this section. In the immediate context, Paul urges the Ephesians to walk in the light and to "live as children of light" (5:8) as compared with the non-believers, who "are darkened in their understanding" (4:18). Because believers are "light in the Lord" (5:8), they need to live like "children of light" and "be careful how" they "live, not as unwise but as wise people" (5:15). Wise, pure living is proof for Paul that the Spirit of God is alive within a Christian. Christians have to put all their effort into such living.

We have already seen this when Paul brings up the fruits of the Spirit and how they differ from the "deeds of the flesh" (Gal 5:19–22). From the Ephesians, Paul expects to see the fruit of the Spirit when he says: "Do not get drunk with wine ...; but be filled with the Spirit," (5:18). Then he adds how this can be accomplished, which is not through some mystical blend of transcendence and hyper-sensuality, as some people define spirituality. And clearly the church at Ephesus seemed to see the work of the Spirit as being completely out of their minds, as if drunk, unaware, and out of control.

Yet in 1 Corinthians, Paul suggests the opposite: "... the spirits of prophets are subject to the prophets, for God is a God not of disorder but of peace (1 Cor 14:32–33). The Spirit is revealed through godly living that requires us to control our urges, and such living includes singing psalms (instead of mumbling), giving thanks to God in all things, and being "subject to one another out of the reverence for Christ" (5:21). All these actions are grammatically dependent on the main verb and expressed in participles. When we take those participles and translate them as individual imperatives, an important connection is lost, and we are left with a moral code rather than a life that streams out from the Spirit of

---

101. This is noted by P. T. O'Brien, *The Letter to the Ephesians* (Grand Rapids: Eerdmans, 1999), but later downplayed (405, particularly fn. 178).

> God. Because Christians are filled with the Spirit, they sing psalms, give thanks, and are led to be subject to one another because of their reverence for Christ.

Being Subject to One Another: A Paradigm for the Church

The theme of being subject to one another is not new for Paul, nor for Christianity in the first century. We can find a similar request in Philippians 2, where Christian submission is modelled on the example of Christ. In Romans 12:1, Paul speaks about presenting "your bodies as a living sacrifice," and so on. Life in the church is dependent on Christians being subject to one another as a reflection of Christ, because egotistically seeking one's own will creates factions and strife, which are clearly defined as "works of the flesh." Being "subject to one another" is a general call to all Christians, because it testifies to the love of God. In the church, all people – regardless of race, nation, or gender – should be accepted as they are, build each other up, and carry each other's burdens and shortcomings for the greater growth of all. Moreover, those who lead do not rule over others, but must be subject to all (Mark 10:44–45). The line about submission to all is not from Paul, but Jesus.

Being "subject" in Ephesians 5:22 is not a matter for theological deliberation. All Christians need to embrace submission to Christ as the first imprint of a Christian life. Yet being "subject" becomes a problem in both the family and the church when it is seen as an exclusive directive to women. Submission is for everyone in the church of Christ. When the principle is applied to families (as in Eph 5:21–33), wives are to be subject to their husbands, and husbands are to love their wives and to give themselves up for their wives. The life that Paul is describing is based on mutual submission. He who loves lets go of his own interests as he seeks to benefit the other.

Submission and the Family

The family is a primary battleground for the Spirit. If people can function as children of God in the family, where they reveal who they really are, no other environment will be difficult. Therefore, it is important for pastors to pay close attention to what is going on in families. If there is mutual submission and love in the family, this will be transferred into the community. If there is strife and violence, the trauma will burden the church. Paul knows this, and so he binds his discussion about submission to one another to the family.

In this passage, the longest, strongest, and most persuasive instruction is directed to the men. Paul seems to anticipate that his male readers will have the greatest problems with his request for submission and his instruction to husbands to love their wives as Christ loved the church. Paul naturally begins the discussion on submission with women, since the patriarchal environment in which he was immersed would not have had any problems with what he was saying. Bruce Winter points out that some women, widows in particular, were breaking out from the dominant role of submission in the Roman world of the Mediterranean as New Women.[102] Yet we can still maintain that the majority of women during this time would have accepted (or been forced to accept) their role as submissive wives. In Ephesians 5:22, Paul handles women as a sideline within a sentence fracture: ". . . wives to your husbands, as to the master . . ." (from the Greek). NRSV translates this verse, "as you are to the Lord," picking up a common trend in interpretation, which is that women's submission to their husbands somehow mimics the adoration and worship they bring to Christ. This further implies that the man is the divine representative in the marriage and that women should worship their husbands as they would worship God. Spelling this out exposes its idolatrous nature. Clearly, this is not what Paul had in mind, even within his own hierarchical social setting.

The feel for the text is somewhat different when the Greek is translated literally: "Wives, be subject to your husbands as (house) lord." While the singular "lord" is grammatically awkward, it transits into the model that Paul sets forward with Christ and the church. With this legitimate translation, Paul would simply be affirming the social rules in Ephesus and the Roman Empire.[103] A similar concept is found in 1 Peter 3:6: "Sarah obeyed Abraham and called him lord," which the Living Bible interprets correctly as, "Sarah, for instance, obeyed her husband Abraham, honoring him as head of the house." The lord of the house had to be obeyed by women, children, and the slaves, because he had the right over their lives. Paul simply calls on Christian women to accept this fact. We may be surprised by this conformity, but it does not reveal a glitch in Paul's thinking. Rather, it seems consistent with Paul's advice elsewhere for people to "remain" in their status rather than trying to change it.[104] The slaves are to remain slaves, even when they have the ability to become free (1 Cor 7:21), and Christians should be subject to every authority (Rom 13:1). Paul is

---

102. B. Winter, *Roman Wives, Roman Widows: The Appearance of New Women in the Pauline Communities* (Grand Rapids: Eerdmans, 2003), 21–34. Winter's intent is to show that independent women existed in the Roman Empire and could have been taken as a model for some women in Christian churches. However, that does not seem to have been the case in Ephesus when Paul was writing Ephesians, and it may have changed with the Pastorals (97).

103. Winter, *Roman Wives*, 39–58.

104. Fee, *First Corinthians*, 268 points out that this "remaining" is "the singular theme" of 1 Cor 7.

not a social revolutionary. He believes that the Christian goal is "a quiet and peaceable life in all godliness and dignity" (1 Tim 2:2).

As discussed previously, nothing but suffering is gained by open wars, because replacing one hierarchical system with another will not bring about anything new. Christians who find themselves in a lower status can concentrate on the inner changes that will redeem the structures of sin and bring about peace. When wars rage, people get sidetracked by their survival instincts. According to Paul, there are no distinctions between systems. In all of them, Christians are caught up in certain circumstances within the structures of sin that will cause them pain. The inevitable change of society described in Romans 8 will not come from the outside through revolutions; rather, it will come from the pain of living out the freedom of Christ within these sinful structures.

To understand Paul's instruction in Ephesians, it is vital to understand the distinction between "Christ" in 5:21 and "lord" in 5:22. While everyone should be subject to one another out of reverence to Christ – or, more literally, out of "the fear of Christ" – the submission of wives in Ephesus is socially defined as their duty towards the lords of the household, which is also the duty of slaves (Eph 6:5). If Christians are called to be subject to one another, it should not be difficult for wives and slaves to respect the head of the household, as custom requires. Yet husbands are not "half-gods" who should be feared and revered as godheads, because that would be idolatrous.

This reading reveals two important things. First, wives are called to be subject to their husbands based on the general principle of submission to one another as part of the Christian faith and spirituality. Second, the wives in Ephesus are being called to accept their husbands as their "house lords" without challenging the authority that was vested in them within the social setting of the Roman Empire in the first century.

Regarding the first, the instruction about submission is not given to women in general or to men in general, but to the wives of husbands. Naturally, Ephesians 5:21 calls all Christians to submit to one another because of their reverence for Christ, reflecting their knowledge that God is in control. While we are always called to point out things that are wrong within the community, we sometimes must wait on God and not push for changes in ways that might ruin the unity of the community – in other words, to have it done our way, when we want it, and how we want it. Sometimes God works differently and we need to wait on him.

The second point introduces the fact that the church in Ephesus was in a different social situation from ours today (at least in many places). In many contemporary societies, wives and husbands share a house that they bought together. They both work jobs outside of the house, and their household consists of them and their underaged children. Paul would still tell them both to submit to one another out of reverence to Christ – even in their marriage. However, he may have had totally different words of caution about how to treat each other well in social circumstances of relative equality.

Love as Submission

There have been many debates about the meaning of "head" in this passage. "Head" in the structures of sin necessarily means "the one in charge," "the one to be obeyed," or "the one with god-status." Unfortunately, such notions about the "head" greatly contribute to authoritarian readings of Ephesians 5:22. Thus some have argued that "head" connotes "source of life" rather than "authority over," though this doesn't change much in terms of status for wives.[105]

Yet Paul diminishes the power that he seems to have given to men by the concession that follows this instruction: "Just as Christ is the head of the church, the body of which he is the Saviour" (5:23). Because Christ's authority comes through his self-giving love, so a husband receives his authority through the love that he extends to his wife. Paul frames the submission "in everything" with the requirement that husbands are to act as "saviours" for their wives. A husband's actions should seek to save his wife, not hurt her. His decisions should be made to please his wife, not to fight her or trample over her and treat her as a maid for his selfish, fleshly desires. So just as wives need to submit to

---

105. Some authors – mostly from the egalitarian camp – argue that *kephalē* in texts about husbands and wives means "source" of life (in the sense of the Gen 2 account, i.e. that she is taken from him). Others – mostly from the complementarian camp – go to some length to show that *kephalē* means "authority over." E.g. W. Grudem, "Does Kefalē ('Head') Mean 'Source' Or 'Authority Over' in Greek Literature? A Survey of 2,336 Examples," *Trinity Journal* 6, no. 1 (1985): 38–59. From the perspective of the context of these passages, I find this discussion obsolete and lean towards letting *kephalē* mean what most people hear today, as they did in the past, which is "boss" and "master." I don't think that insisting on "source" as the translation really solves anything and, in fact, it could make things worse for women if they are told that husbands are not only their bosses, but also their "source of life." This could suggest that wives have no life of their own and are practically nothing without "their source." Paul is very aware of this possible misconception in 1 Cor 11:12: "For just as woman came from man, so man comes through woman; but all things come from God." And yet, it seems that in 1 Cor 11:7–16, Paul's idea of "head" is based on Genesis 2, which would exegetically (from canonical criticism) make it a case for "source" as the meaning. Yet Paul himself resolves this by pointing to the mutuality of men and women, especially in Christ. From rhetorical criticism, 1 Cor 11:7–16 is even more interesting, as it seems that Paul himself is overwhelmed by the misconceptions that could be read into his words, and so he adds (somewhat agitatedly), "But if anyone is disposed to be contentious – we have no such custom, nor do the churches of God."

their husbands, so also husbands must submit to their wives by loving them and looking out for their interests. To serve the interests of others, we have to talk to them and ask for their input and not assume what they need or decide for them what is best for them.

Paul elaborates on biblical love in 1 Corinthians 13, revealing how it takes initiative and assumes responsibility for the relationship rather than seeking its own rights, privileges, or comforts. This description is completely opposite to the ideal of a complementarian marriage that is promoted in many churches, where an authoritarian husband is met at the door of his home by a wife that has fixed herself up, having laboured to keep the house, tend to the children and prepare a meal. She then gets the children to bed so he can have his peace and quiet, anticipating his every wish as she tiptoes through the house so that nothing will disturb his football match. This is what complementarian husbands have in mind when they hear Paul's call to wives to submit to them. Yet Paul's instruction to husbands to love their wives is countercultural and completely overthrows the complementarian ideal.

Thus Paul expects that he will be challenged by this instruction, and so he pulls out his rhetorical heavy artillery to drive his point home. If wives need to submit to their house lords, then those lords need to show their wives the love that Christ modelled when he gave himself up for our salvation. The insistence on "male authority" in our day and age bears witness to the scandal of Paul's request. Instead of loving their wives, Christian men order their wives (and women in general) to submit, because they need to rule over them in order to be above them as their "head." They expect full obedience and subservience, often restricting women's personal piety and involvement in church.

Authoritarian husbands find it very difficult to love their wives and certainly don't make things "safe" for them. The statistics about abuse in Christian homes are devastating. A. Weaver claims that "domestic violence is probably the number one mental health pastoral emergency."[106] Nancy Nason-Clark's research has shown that even though Christian men do not abuse their wives more than other religious men, Christian wives have fewer options about how to respond, and their abuse is less likely to be recognized.[107] Pastors estimate that one in five families suffers from domestic violence; most pastors have counselled at least one battered woman in the past year; almost all

---

106. A. Weaver, "Psychological Trauma: What Clergy Need to Know," *Pastoral Psychology* 41 (1993): 402, as quoted by N. Nason-Clark, *The Battered Wife*, 14.

107. N. Nason-Clark, *The Battered Wife*, 14.

Christian women have talked to a woman who has been battered.[108] Since all of this happens in the name of Christ, we must ask, where do Christian men learn that abuse is a valid way to treat women?

Though Christ has absolutely nothing to do with such violence, violent men (most perpetrators are men)[109] have been exposed to the works of the flesh in their families, which degrades Christ's message of love. By living according to the "deeds of the mortal flesh," these men are distorting the good news and veiling the glory of God from the family, from the next generation, and therefore from the church and society at-large.

By calling the Ephesian husbands to love their wives as they would love their own bodies, Paul is proclaiming a truly countercultural message. His message about marital relationships flips the role expectations in his culture on their head. But until recently, his words have been unacceptable to most men. Though his words conform with traditional cultural expectations for wives, he transforms the "headship" of the husband into a servitude of self-giving love and respect for the wife, which is modelled on the way Christ offered himself for the church, submitting himself to the needs of others.

Yet Christian men around the world and throughout time have believed that Ephesians 5 instructs them to force their authority on their family and behave like gods towards their wives (and towards other women). In Ephesians 5:25–33, Paul sets forth Christ's self-giving love as an example to follow, granting no permission for husbands to force their wives to submit to their silly, egotistical wishes and pleasures. He in no way suggests that husbands are divine agents within the home.

---

108. Data from The Rave Project by the Muriel McQueen Fergusson Centre for Family Violence Research, accessed online: https://www.theraveproject.org/resources-categories/looking-at-the-data/.

109. There is a trend in researching violent women and sometimes, it will be observed that women and men show "similar rates of physical aggression," but these numbers must be taken with care. Women's Aid, an English charity dealing with family violence state, based on research, that "there are important differences between male violence against women and female violence against men, namely the amount, severity and impact." Women are much more likely to experience extreme violence (up to death) at the hands of their partners. "In the year ending March 2018 the large majority of defendants in domestic abuse-related prosecutions were men (92%), and the majority (66%) of victims were recorded as female (13% of victims were male and in 21% of prosecutions the sex of the victim was not recorded)" online: https://www.womensaid.org.uk/information-support/what-is-domestic-abuse/domestic-abuse-is-a-gendered-crime/; Violent women are usually reacting to violence S. C. Swan, L. J. Gambone, and D. L. Snow, "A Review of Research on Women's Use of Violence With Male Intimate Partners" online: https://www.ncbi.nlm.nih.gov/pmc/articles/PMC2968709/ under: Women's Motivations for Violence.

Theologically, this interpretation of husbands as "divine agents" is fundamentally wrong.[110] First, identifying men as "divine" in marital relationships takes away from God's glory, suggesting that women need to worship their husbands just as they worship Christ. But the transcending biblical message of God's holiness is that he does not share his glory with anyone (e.g. Isa 42:8).

Second, this idea about male spiritual leadership prevents women from living their own lives as believers. Often, men will not let women serve, and women who are so dedicated to serving their house lords have no time to serve God in the church or society. If wives have a responsibility to worship God directly (and not via proxy), then they must be able to make their own decisions about their spiritual life and walk with God. Of course, one can argue that a true "head" will see this and discern that it is in the best interest of the family to support it, but this would reflect the character of Christian men who are able to submit to others out of love for Christ. The danger with the idea of spiritual leadership is when men who cannot submit to others in love are given permission to "rule over" and therefore abuse their wives.

Third, the wife's role can easily be reduced to a house slave for the man who assumes a god-position in his family. This neglects women's gifts, impoverishing both women and the church. Unused talents can become a foul ground, where dissatisfaction grows as weeds, poisoning not only the life of those who have suppressed their gifts, but also those who cannot benefit from them. The only role for women in this constellation is as "mother," since that is the only area where men need women.[111] In such circumstances, women are degraded, because they are regarded as birthing machines that, paradoxically, do not share common humanity with men.[112] This was not as problematic in

---

110. See, for instance, the Focus on the Family Q & A contribution, "Submission of Wives to Husbands," accessed online: https://www.focusonthefamily.com/family-qa/submission-of-wives-to-husbands. While this article (like many on the Focus on the Family website) takes abuse seriously, the insistence on the spiritual (God-ordained) leadership of husbands undermines all the concern for equality. If husbands are the God-ordained leaders, they alone can interpret what is divine, and the women cannot. Such headship will inevitably disregard or mock "her opinions and feelings." Moreover, the general statement – "the sexes have different needs for love and respect: Men need to feel respected by their wives, and women need to feel loved by their husbands" – is, scientifically speaking, a myth, as we have shown elsewhere.

111. Origen, *Homilies on Genesis* 1:14; see also Ambrose, *Paradise*, chs. 4 and 6. In 6:33, he argues for woman's ontological inferiority from creation because she was unable to recognize what she had done; in 10:48, he argues that the woman is a good help, but of inferior status. For Ambrose, her inferiority comes from the fact that she was not created from Adam's soul, but from his rib, a part of his body (11:50).

112. Interestingly, proponents of "complementarity" never think through the end of this argument, as medieval church leaders did. A council in Lyon in 584 was, apparently, devoted to the question of whether women had souls, that is, whether they were truly human. By only one

the past, when bearing children was important for the agricultural society's wellbeing. But today, as the population of the planet is challenging the earth's sustainability, the role of motherhood is being diminished.

We must see the boundaries of Paul's Christ-husband analogy for even more reasons. For one, Paul himself knows that there is a boundary. The husbands themselves are called to submit to loving their wives as Christ loved the church. In this, they should be proactive. But there is a part of Christ's work on behalf of the church that they cannot do, which is "to present" the wife "in splendour, without a spot or wrinkle or anything of the kind – yes, so that she may be holy and without blemish" (5:27). That is, the husband cannot save the wife in a soteriological sense. Paul warns the Ephesians that he is talking about the church here – not marriage (5:32). He is instructing husbands to love as Christ loves, but Christ alone can make the church perfect – that is, all men and women who believe in him. A husband cannot sanctify his wife, and she cannot be subject to his instruction in faith. Rather, their relationship of mutual submission and love is a glimpse of eternity with God, which people can see in them.

In Ephesians 5:21–33, Paul does not allow for spiritual abuse, though women have historically experienced this from both their husbands and other men. Rather, Paul focuses on the need for mutual submission and love. This is not the only countercultural biblical instruction for men, as the Bible also requires them to leave their fathers and mothers when they cleave to their wives (Gen 2:24). This contrasts starkly with traditions around the world that expect a woman to leave her family and join her husband's family. In my culture, men often remain as their mother's sons, and so wives experiences double abuse, both from her childish and egotistical husband, who refuses to grow up, and from her mother-in-law, who hovers over him. Mutual submission is at odds with the culture of men who do not listen to their wives because it is somehow a sign of weakness and with a culture that teaches men to be distant, absent, and violent, because they are "wild" at heart.

---

vote, the council concluded that women were equal with men in their humanity. Some sources doubt the historicity of this council, because details on the council are unavailable. However, it is easily imagined that it is probably true and that the Lutheran scholars who support or reject the theories discussed there have not invented this council. Compare Dan Bulter, "Church Decision Whether Women Have Souls. Results," accessed online: https://groups.google.com/forum/#!topic/net.women/PtEmp8kJC4A.

Christ as Head of All

Submitting to one another out of reverence for Christ brings us to our conclusion for this chapter. Because Christ is the head of all Christians, all things happen in him and through him, and he is the one we seek to imitate in all of our relationships. Through our faith in Christ, we can submit and let go of our sinful independence, which drives us to work hard in order to serve ourselves. Faith opens us up to new and creative possibilities as we step out of our comfort zones, unleash the gifts that are inside us, and trust God to reveal our full potential in his time. Through faith, we trust that Christ is guiding us and will lead us to the fullness of his glory as we walk the path of self-sacrifice and submission. We do not walk in fear, but trust. We can leap into love, offering all our resources – in our marriages, the church, and society – because all that we have is from God, and all abundance is in him and is available to all, who are equally his.

This depicts a different kind of life on all levels – individually, within marriages and families, in the church, and also in society.

4

The Church as New Creation

Challenging the Structures of Sin

How did the church, which is indwelled by the mighty Spirit and lavished with so many gifts, become so calcified that most Christians in our day feel it's utterly impossible to bring about change? Throughout the centuries, the structures of sin have continued to be sanctified by the church because they have "felt good" to those at the top of the hierarchy. Moreover, the lowly and marginalized majority have clung to the romantic idea of an orderly "old time religion," where even though things might be gloomy in our present reality, "true" Christians will be doing fine in heaven. The Marxists rightly criticized Christians for such a misconception. Moreover, because Christians have struggled to understand the sin that still reigns in their "mortal bodies," those in power have covered up rather than healed the ulcers of violence and the abuses of power, sex, and money.

Yet our contemporary culture is refusing to buy into distant visions of eternity because most people are no longer moved by otherworldly ideas about heaven and hell. History has taught us a thing or two about what happens when people accept abuse from others, and so we want to see change now. We are desperate for the hope of a power that will bring about that change.

As victims continue to speak out, exposing more hidden ulcers of ugliness in the church, their testimonies are becoming enormous obstacles for those who are searching for God, particularly within the biblical tradition. Though many people long for the biblical promises of love and peace, they cannot deal with the ugly worldliness of the church. Many have been trying to escape such ugliness in the world – particularly women! Thus the gospel teaching of the church, which is being sold amidst a plurality of views in our global world, is not working. If the Christian faith is not going to be abused, we need to reconsider Paul's teaching to the Corinthians:

> For we are the temple of the living God; as God said,
>
> "I will live in them and walk among them,
>   and I will be their God,
>   and they shall be my people.
> Therefore come out from them,
>   and be separate from them, says the Lord,
> and touch nothing unclean;
>   then I will welcome you,
> and I will be your father,
>   and you shall be my sons and daughters,
> says the Lord Almighty." (2 Cor 6:16b–18)

We also need to reflect on what Paul means when he insists that his preaching always needs to be backed by God's power of change.[1] The good news of God through Christ is not only concerned with eternity! If the church is going to challenge the hierarchies of sin, Christians not only need the word of God, but the power of the Spirit to display faith, courage, and an outpouring of gifts within Christians so that they will reveal God's glory.

Before turning more generally to how the church can lead the transformation of the structures of sin, I will address particular concerns for both men and women so that they can forge a path of cooperation rather than competition.

A Biblical Word to Men

Because I come from a culture where women do not address men in the church, it is unusual for me to write this section. I hope male readers can refrain from thinking this is unbiblical, since many women in the Bible have spoken to men. Though I am not pretending to be a Deborah or Prisca, I do hope that

---

1. In Gal 3:4–5, Paul speaks of the miracle that the Spirit "works among" them. In Phil 2:13, he points out the power of a changed personality. In 1 Thess 2:13, he features the word of God that they accepted, which works its power among them. The whole of 2 Cor is a testimony about the glory of God exposed in Paul's ministry. In Rom 8, as we have already seen, Paul expects a crescendo of this glory in the resurrection power of Christ through the Spirit – real change that will affect creation, although it is eschatological in nature and its fullness will finally be revealed at the end of the times.

men will learn to hear women's voices so that, together, we can draw towards the Lord's table and the love of God.

Meek Is Not for the Weak: Mark 10

Many recent popular books about male identity suggest that it is difficult to be a man in the contemporary global society. I think this is true, particularly in evangelical circles (though not exclusively). My experience among global Baptists reveals that the pendulum of concern in many churches is constantly swinging between the fear of weak, feminized men and the fear of violent perpetrators. Unfortunately, a lot of blame for this havoc in the male identity has been cast on women, particularly feminists, for ruining the hierarchical order in traditional homes. Though this might seem to be a logical diagnosis, our biblical investigations point to a much more serious root problem. Both women and men are the victims of the structures of sin, and so their battle for identity needs to be sought elsewhere – it is a symptom rather than the cause of the problem.

As noted previously, church structures often blamed single mothers for the male identity crisis in the world. Yet father figures have always been conspicuously absent from the everyday life of children, including male children, until their teenage years. In many places, the rearing of children is still relegated to mothers or their surrogates, nannies. Even today, mothers are rarely asked whether they want to be the primary caregiver – or, in the case of single mothers, the only caregivers. Also, in terms of historical social models, going "back in time" hardly ever offers a solution. History may help us learn how *not* to do things if we are willing to listen and learn from it, but if we are honest, most people don't really want women back in the kitchen. The world has moved forward, and there is no going back to the way it used to be. Even more importantly, we have been there, and we moved away from it because it did not work!

Encouraging dads to be present in their children's lives may seem to be a contemporary attitude, which we may interpret as an outcome of feminists who have challenged hierarchical structures in society. Yet the model appears first in the Bible, where fathers are tasked with instructing their children along with mothers.[2] Thus husbands need to work with their wives to find new

---

2. E.g. Deut 6:4–10 sums up the fathers' responsibilities to the children, presupposing constant contact with them, taking them along wherever life leads. In several places, biblical parallelisms indirectly include both mothers and fathers as instructors, since the child is instructed to listen to instruction from both (Prov 1:8; 30:17; Deut 21:18).

ways of partnering together to raise children in order to benefit the world, the church, and the family.

Yet some women do not value the presence of men in the family. In fact, some women even discourage men from getting involved, thereby keeping them away from women's "traditional" realm. I can still hear the patronizing voice of the nurse in the maternity ward when I was in labor with my son, explaining to my husband that there was no need for him to be present at the birth.

But tradition also expects men to find life outside the family, where positions are held, money is gathered, and history is made. "Outside," you make a name for yourself, your worth is evaluated by your peers, and wars are fought. Family is the place where you come home to lick your wounds, where you are pampered and cared for after your clashes with the titans of the world. In the home, you want peace and quiet, and your position should not be questioned – in fact, no one should question you at all. Everyone in the family should know your needs and respond to them quietly and swiftly, being seen but not heard. This is the picture that women assume when they hear the term, "head of the house." The home is a place that men pay for, and so it should work to benefit them. Many women only cook what their husbands like, the way they like it. Their preferences are less important, and the children have no say whatsoever.

Even worse, some men feel that home is a place where they can let go of their guard and release their frustration, lashing out in violence against their wife and children because "they had it coming." Many Christian men are told that it is biblical for men to use the rod! But in the Bible, the rod is used to discipline, and it is only a metaphor. When men lash out in frustration and anger, they are not disciplining their children. Rather, they are revealing how undisciplined they are, because they are unable to control their feelings of inadequacy, fear, frustration, isolation, being overwhelmed, and all the other feelings no one has taught men to identify. Boys are often taught to suppress their feeling and to hold back tears in order to be a real man! Men need to stop passing this broken teaching onto their sons.

As Paul puts it, do not "provoke your children to anger" (Eph 6:4). Men who teach their children "discipline" when they don't have it themselves only continue the cycle of violence and pain and prevent their children from knowing themselves and learning to handle their feelings without hurting others or oneself. The frustration men feel in the outside world reveals the downside of the hierarchy. Whatever position we are able to reach as an adult is our own decision. When our choices backfire, no one else is to blame.

To make decisions on behalf of others – or to be a leader – we need to cultivate character. In the Gospel of Mark, Jesus explains what greatness looks like in the kingdom of God. Three times, he teaches the disciples about the necessity of the cross for the Messiah (Mark 8:31–32, 34–38; 9:31;10:33–34). The first time Peter hears this teaching, he rebukes Jesus (8:32). Jesus has made a name for himself as a teacher and a healer, and the disciples want the establishment to recognize his power! They don't want to follow a loser! Whenever Jesus talks about service, suffering, and death, the disciples express their hope that they will receive an earthly glory (Mark 9:34; 10:35–37).

After Jesus hears them discussing "which one of them is the greatest" (9:34), he invites a child into their midst to teach them that those who are the greatest will know how to minister to the smallest (9:36–37). Yet this lesson does not fit their expectations. The disciples are so focused on their own greatness that when children are subsequently brought to Jesus, the disciples try to protect Jesus from the nuisance of noisy little children and utterly fail to heed Jesus's teaching about caring for the smallest (10:13–16). In 10:14, Jesus harshly rebukes the disciples, driving home his teaching that greatness can only be tested by our attitude towards little ones – which includes our own children. Thus on two occasions, Jesus uses children in his teachings about the agenda of the kingdom of God, because children are considered insignificant by the rulers of the world – and also his own disciples. This attitude is still common among the rulers of the world and also within the church.

Next, a rich and influential young ruler catches the disciples' attention when he asks Jesus, "What shall I do to inherit the kingdom of God?" (Mark 10:17). Though this young, rich ruler seems ready to submit to Jesus, Jesus is not impressed. Much to the disappointment of the disciples, Jesus tells him to "sell what you own, and give the money to the poor, and you will have treasure in heaven" (10:21). After the rich ruler goes away, grieved because he cannot follow Jesus's teaching (10:22), the disciples ask, "Then who can be saved?" (10:28). They still don't understand why Jesus keeps teaching them about his own death, because John and James (*Boanerges*, the Sons of Thunder, as Jesus named them) discuss their own greatness yet again and ask Jesus to give them a position of authority above the others when Jesus comes into his glory (10:37).

Of course, the other disciples are furious when they realize what John and James are talking about with Jesus (Mark 10:41). They all deserve such positions of honour! Jesus concludes his lesson on greatness in the kingdom of God by teaching the disciples, yet again, that the rulers of the world exercise power over others, "but it is not so among you" (10:43). Rather, in the kingdom of God, whoever wishes to become great shall serve everyone, give themselves up for others, and suffer for the little ones (10:44–45). This requirement is the same for both men and women. Yet human culture has relegated the care for children to women and kept them away from the public, arguing that men need special training to learn how to "sacrifice" themselves for others.

Men need to pay particular attention to this single-minded urge to climb to the top of hierarchies, because they tend to have direct access to power and privilege. The kingdom of God needs leaders who will use their power to serve others rather than rule over and exploit them. For sinful people, servant leadership is not a natural state. Men who practice such leadership will be ridiculed by other men – not only in the world, but also in the church. Yet Jesus's word has been sealed by the example of his own death. If Jesus lived this way, the church needs to live this way – even when church culture encourages men to wage war and hunt because those are their "natural" realms. Forsaking ourselves for little ones is not weak or "feminized" behaviour, but strong behaviour that imitates Jesus!

In Moldova, I met a Christian man who had taken it upon himself to cook Sunday dinner for people with special needs in his church. Moldova is a European country with one of the lowest GDPs, and these people were living at the brink of existence. This brother believed that on Sundays, at least, these poor people should have a break – *shalom*, if you will – and so he cooked a lunch for them every Sunday. In his culture, he should have delegated this task to his wife and two daughters, but he decided that Jesus had called him to serve these people, and so it was his ministry. I observed this man serving everyone with the kindest attitude. While Moldovan Baptists tend to be conservative regarding male-female roles, the question of "headship" never comes up in this man's house. There is only one who rules, and it is Jesus! It is a blessing to see such strong men humbly respond to God's call to serve people with love in all circumstances and environments.

Embracing Women as People

In Croatian and many other Slavic languages, women can be excluded from the word "people" because the culture is so severely patriarchal. Men who want to serve women in the family and the church (and anywhere else) must consciously and intentionally seek to include women in their language. Inclusive language is not feminist gibberish, but an important reflection of God's intentions when he created male and female in his own image to work together to keep and care for the earth.

As we have already discussed, human culture (including women) has a hard time accepting women as people. In fact, human hierarchies keep trying to exclude certain people groups *a priori* from the battle for the top position because of their gender, race, nationality, or any other distinctive that the hierarchy can use to identify them as weak, small, or unworthy. Interestingly, Jesus calls for a different attitude from those who follow him. Those who want to be great in the kingdom of God cannot exclude, but must seek ways to include those whom society despises. Christian greatness is measured by how we approach the little ones – and this always includes women.

Social blindness is an interesting phenomenon. Though some Christians may firmly believe that they are "colour-blind" when migrants of other colours come to their borders, they suddenly judge certain people to be terrorists because of the colour of their skin. Many Christians believe that if we don't think or talk about gender, race, or social status, we're unbiased. But any form of blindness suggests a failure to see and understand the suffering of others. When we emphasize and seek to see life from the perspective of the little ones in society, we can begin to take steps towards fairness.

In Christian churches, we have only scratched the surface of the suffering that women have had to endure. In the following sections, I touch on some of the most common wounds that have come out of church teaching: first, in the way that "fallen" biblical women have been used to teach bad theology; second, in the way that strong biblical women have been neglected; third, in the way that Jesus's teachings have been ignored; and fourth, how Paul's instructions about women have been misunderstood.

Using Eve as a Femme Fatale

First, churches need to stop using Eve as an example of female fallenness. Some may consider this teaching biblical, since it surfaces a couple of times in the bylines of the New Testament. However, in some traditional arguments, humans are regarded as the "crown of God's creation" because God created them last, and from that perspective (as the joke goes), Eve would be more perfect than Adam, upon whom God was still practicing.

The reports on creation – or rather, the one report about creation and the possible wedding sermon of Genesis 2 about why men get enchanted with women and marry them – have so much more potential than the traditional game of blaming Eve.[3]

---

3. Kvan, *Eve and Adam*, 27–31 and 69–95 expound on all the options that Christian and Rabbinic theologies have read from the text in Genesis 1–2.

Because the woman is equally created in the image of God, she is equally equipped to help care for the world. In the New Testament, women are given the gifts of the Spirit to serve the church. These gifts are never identified as gender specific, regardless of the various social environments within the churches. (In some early church contexts, women were restricted from public speaking or from teaching men.) Rather, the New Testament church identifies women who speak publicly and teach both men and women. Godly men who want to extend the kingdom of God need to explore and reflect upon these examples.

> The Old Testament, especially Genesis 1–12 (which is primeval), needs careful exegesis. The first step is to notice that Genesis 1 and 2 represent not one, but two accounts with totally different emphases in terms of the questions they want to answer. First, the oldest manuscripts have no divisions between chapters or verses. These manuscripts are from the medieval times.[4] The exegete must determine where themes end. There are two conclusions in Genesis 1–2. The first, "Thus the heavens and the earth were finished, and all their multitude" (2:1), presupposes that what the author had in mind was a "real" account of creation by God. The second, "Therefore a man leaves his father and his mother and clings to his wife, and they become one flesh" (2:24), suggests that the author is answering a question about why man feels compelled to leave his father and mother to cling to his wife, the other, who is foreign to him. This looks like a deliberation about marriage.[5] Pulling the two accounts into one, which has been done since the middle ages, is problematic. If it is done, the "real" creation account should govern the creation of the woman, which (as it has been pointed out in rabbinic literature) comes with an emphasis on equality, although some authors point to anachronisms concerning the issue of equality, which was not a topic for the biblical author. The priestly account is therefore "neither for nor against women's equality," Phyllis Bird claims.[6] Yet the traditional, hierarchical interpretation is equally inappropriate.

---

4. See for example, S. Macauley Jackson, ed., *The New Schaff-Herzog Encyclopedia of Religious Knowledge*, vol. 2 (New York: Funk & Wagnalls, 1908–1912), 113–114.

5. See K. E. Kvam, L. S. Schearing, and V. H. Ziegler, *Eve and Adam* (Bloomington: Indiana University Press, 1999), 17, for a list of authors who note this.

6. Phyllis Bird as quoted in *Eve and Adam*, 17.

Second, it pains me how often women are compared with Eve as sexual seducers. I have heard some Christian men sympathetically argue that prostitution should be legalized because it would protect the women in the "oldest business" in the world. These men seem to think that a woman simply decides to become a prostitute because she likes it – after all, she takes after Eve! – just as a man might choose any other profession. While we may think that women always have other options, women in the sex trade are groomed by society and indoctrinated to believe that the only thing they are good for is sex. Prostitutes are in constant danger of serious injury or death. Reuters research conducted in Boston shows that one-half to two-thirds of the men who buy sex behave like criminals and have no respect for the women they buy, because they consider them to be a different "type" of woman.[7] Legalized prostitution is no solution for women. If we want to see change within our society, we must teach and empower women towards other options. However, the dangers for women do not stop in red-light districts.

The third area of wounding from church teaching and practice is that, almost universally, women's gifts are neglected in the church. Women in the church are often valued beneath children in terms of how much support they get from church treasuries. Some churches do not allow women to pray publicly or out loud. In other churches, women can only pray after the men have prayed. In some Christian environments in the East, women are prohibited from going to church when menstruating or after childbirth. In some contexts, women are even prohibited from taking the communion. In other churches, women and men sit strictly segregated, and families cannot sit together for worship. I have seen all of this.

I recently witnessed an exposition where a Christian man claimed publicly that God may give gifts to women, but his church would *not* recognize them. He argued that women should be beautiful and avoid engaging in the dirty business of every day leadership. From an early age, women have been treated with this kind of arrogance and disdain in the church. This kind of teaching takes away women's dignity, strips them of their God-given gifts, and pushes them to the fringes of the church – and eventually over the edge.

Fourth, when Christian women are compared to Eve, the point being made is usually not about their equality in creation and their equality in sin. Rather, since the early church, women (following Eve) have been identified

---

7. R. Krasny, "Men Who Buy Sex Tend to Commit More Crimes, Study Says," *Boston Reuters* (19 July 2011); online https://www.reuters.com/article/us-prostitution-survey/men-who-buy-sex-tend-to-commit-more-crimes-study-says-idUSTRE76I73F20110719.

as the exclusive sinners and seducers. Though Adam sinned, his sin was Eve's fault. Most of us have a solid respect for these early church teachers because we feel that they were much closer to the incipient apostolic church than we are today. Yet correspondingly, one may claim that the church has not changed since the Reformation, and we know the mind of Martin Luther!

Though there are traces of medieval doctrines still visible in traditional churches, the theology and practice of the church have generally moved forward. How could the Cappadocian fathers have had a better view on the matter? They still had a solid historical distance from the apostles, even though it was smaller. Also, the influence of their own Hellenist pagan environment should not be underestimated. Hellenism blamed women for everything, including for prolonging the misery of men by constantly incarnating their souls, which would otherwise be free in their divine spirituality.[8] In the same way, Eve was blamed for the misery of the world under sin.

Teaching about the equality of men and women in sin is just as important as teaching about their equality in creation. Adam sinned, and males are not merely seduced sinners that would be okay if God had not created women. Though Adam makes this excuse in his response to God, the Bible is clear: men and women are equally guilty of sin, and they should not be differentiated on account of it.

Fifth, the church needs to emphasize that Christ's sacrifice saved both women and men equally. If the church does not hold sin against a Christian man in order to deny him from leadership and teaching, it cannot hold sin against a Christian woman either. The Bible is full of male characters who sinned substantially, but we still think that men are capable of leadership positions. Cain was a crook. Should all men be doubted as disguised killers? Ahab led Israel astray. Should churches prevent other men from leadership because they may lead churches astray?

But this is exactly the kind of illogical reasoning that is used to prevent women from teaching or leading within the church! Because Eve sinned first, women cannot teach men. Jesus died for women too, and he sealed them with his Spirit. Because Christian women are redeemed, they should never be compared to Eve's transgression. Rather, they should be looked upon from the perspective of paradise – having been restored. Women can be resourceful

---

8. This is an outcome of Aristotle's reasoning. See P. Allen, *The Concept of Woman: The Aristotelian Revolution, 750 BC–AD 1250, vol. 1* (Grand Rapids: Eerdmans, 1997), 83–103, particularly the chart, 84.

and strong partners in the task of caring for a hurting world. This, as Jesus pointed out, is the mission of God in the world, and it is a huge task that requires all hands.

Sixth, the church often fails to be a caring environment of the kingdom of God for women, because they have experienced so much contempt and violence within it. Sometimes, this happens because of a lack of awareness. For instance, a church may insist that a twenty-six-year-old woman needs a male co-leader to chaperone her, because she might otherwise fall prey to male students. Yet male leaders don't have female leaders for the same supervision, because the women with whom they work might seduce them!

This points to the importance of carefully picking teachers within the church, because those who have not been called or equipped can pass on harsh and unjust instruction to the next generation. To give an example from my country, after World War I, many people migrated to the United States, and somewhere between the Ford factory and the churches (mostly Baptists and other evangelicals) that welcomed these migrants, many came to know the Lord. My great uncle ended up studying at Northern Seminary and stayed in the US to serve as a pastor, but many people returned to small villages in the old homeland with loads of enthusiasm, but not much training in their new faith. Their knowledge of the faith and the Bible sufficed for the villagers they served, who were predominantly illiterate. Whatever they had learned in Bible studies in the US kept the church going for the years between the two World Wars. Many learned to read in order to read the Bible themselves.

But as faith grew and people moved from the villages to the city, the cultural village mentality became the focus of the religion rather than the word of God. The new generation of teachers, who had been taught by those returning pioneers, were suddenly confronted with more difficult intellectual questions. From the 1960s through the 1990s, Croatian Baptists stagnated because there were not enough skilled teachers. Though the decline is often blamed on the Communists, the truth is that evangelizing, preaching, and teaching were, for the most part, inadequate in the new circumstances. Teachers could not minister to the new generation, which was more educated and was facing violent repression.

I grew up in this environment, and in my experience, women stuck out as the teachers. Some stayed single because they believed that the Bible only restricted married women from teaching. These women, such as Rut Lehotsky and Marija Andriček, did not shy away from learning and so bridged the gap. My own generation of leaders (male and female alike) were trained and supported in their ministries almost exclusively by these women.⁹ Rut Lehotsky was eventually recognized and honoured with a Doctor of Divinity at McMaster University in Canada, though she did not receive much formal or public recognition in her own country.¹⁰ In what was Yugoslavia at the time, women worked on the fringes, caring for the old and ill, taking care of the children and youth, basically picking up the pieces that men did not recognize. Like many women I have seen in the global church, they were also very careful not to disturb the hierarchies of men who were preaching and teaching.

The history of Baptists in Europe – both in the east and the west – should declare these amazing women as Baptist saints. Mary Raber points out that,

> Throughout a history that dates back to the mid-nineteenth century, women have served ably (and often at great personal cost) as sisters of mercy, literature colporteurs, administrators, traveling evangelists, editors, Sunday school teachers, cross-cultural missionaries, authors, choir directors, deaconesses, preachers, and radio broadcasters. During times of deep crisis, while male leaders were imprisoned, exiled, or killed, women held churches together and actively interceded on behalf of prisoners of conscience, both male and female.¹¹

A woman leader, who worked in Russia before the 1980s, complained to me that after "liberation," a new generation of young men suddenly came back from their studies in the West (at some evangelical schools) and began to wage war on women's ministry in the church. She evaluated that, unlike most women in the *East West Church and Ministry Report*, it is much harder for women to have a ministry now.

---

9. There is a great need to research these women, since outside of sporadic mentions in periodicals, hardly any academic work has been published on their accomplishments.

10. There are no public records of this available on the internet. McMaster's website mentions a document, where she is mentioned as the recipient of this award in 1998; https://www.mcmaster.ca/, search for "Rut Lehotsky."

11. "Before and After: Baptist Women in Post-Soviet Ukraine," *East West Church and Ministry Report*, 24, no. 4 (2016): 7; online: https://www.academia.edu/32983138/Women_in_Evangelical_Churches_in_the_Former_Soviet_Union_A_Response_to_an_Interview_of_Pastor_Shiranai_Dosova, quoting the book by N. Beliakova and M. Dobson, *Zhenshchiny v evangel'skikh obshchinakh poslevoennogo SSSR, 1940–1980 gg.* [Women in Evangelical Congregations of the Postwar USSR, 1940–1980] (Moscow: Indrik, 2015). Yugoslavian Baptist women were strongly influenced by the missionary efforts of the Russian Baptist women, and they had already organized their work in 1936. D. Peterlin, "'Tabitha': The First Baptist Women's Association in Zagreb," *Kairos* 2 (2007): 247–272, file:///C:/Users/Korisnik/Downloads/6_Peterlin_Tabitha%20(1).pdf.

It is sad when women who have their minds set on Christ have their gifts ignored, doubted, and debated. Women who can endure this ordeal become strong leaders, but they are usually banned to the fringes and feared for their exceptional strength. Women who do not survive the ordeal of constant doubt become a paradigm of losers, for they could have survived anything if they had truly been called! Yet as Jesus warns: "woe to the one by whom the stumbling block comes!" (Matt 18:7).

We need to accept each other as brothers and sisters who are equally created, equally prone to sin, equally saved by Christ, and equally gifted for service. Working together towards God's redeemed community, we become one body of Christ as we testify that love, peace, and cooperation are the signs of the kingdom of God. If we cannot love, our actions speak louder than all our verbal evangelism. If the power of God cannot bring peace to the church, how can it bring peace to the world? If we oppress women within the church, women in the world will assume that the Christian faith has nothing to offer them. If we ignore and marginalize women, the church will only run on half of its potential. How are we going to account for that before God?

If we can behold women in the church freely, we will see the hidden picture of God's kingdom already forming within the women in the Old Testament. God's promise to the woman in Genesis 3 is that she and her offspring will stand up to the serpent – and the Bible has many testimonies about strong women who have opposed evil!

Leadership in the Old Testament: Deborah

In my long life in the church, I have never heard a sermon on Deborah. This is a pity, since the story about Deborah and Barak in Judges 4 offers an important biblical paradigm for male-female relationships in a fallen world. First, Deborah is counted among the major judges in Israel, and several chapters in the Bible are devoted to her. She is a charismatic leader, a woman who hears the word of the Lord and trusts it. In fact, she is such a good leader that people recognize her as one even in the midst of her thoroughly patriarchal society. Tikva Frymer-Kensky, a Jewish scholar, suggests that Deborah's identification in Judges 4:4 as *eshet lapidot* can mean the wife of Lapidot (a man), or a woman from Lapidot (a place), or even a "fiery women."[12] Each of these possible translations can be interesting in their own right, but it is significant that a

---

12. T. Frymer-Kensky, "Deborah: Bible," in *Jewish Women's Archive's Encyclopedia*, online: https://jwa.org/encyclopedia/article/deborah-bible.

woman made it onto the plaque of fame among those who were leading Israel during the time where there were no kings.

One needs strong leaders in times of trouble, and Deborah is trusted to make good decisions. She is not afraid to make executive decisions, for she listens to God and then calls Barak to lead Israel's armies against a strong enemy. She is a creative thinker and a strategist, for she orders the unusual plan to trap Sisera, the experienced warlord of the Canaanite king. The waters that turn the plain into mud turn Sisera's advantage of nine hundred fearsome chariots of iron into a ridiculous, fleeing mess.

Barak was God's obvious choice for this battle, and although he is a capable military man (for no army would follow him otherwise), he insists that he cannot do the job without Deborah's presence on the battlefield. He does not care about his own fame (Judg 4:8–10) or personal profit. In the end, Sisera is defeated by two women, who are evidently brave enough to look the enemy in the eye – Deborah and Jael. Of course, we could moralize anachronistically about Jael's method, but we are in the Old Testament setting in a situation of war. Wars are always about outsmarting the enemy, and it is hypocritical to call out Jael as a blood-thirsty woman.

Barak is strong enough to put Israel's cause before his own ego. This is unusual, and he insists on it, even after Deborah warns him that he will remain "fameless" (4:9). In any church situation, the benefit for the people should be more important than one's personal ego. After all, the glory of the kingdom of God and the salvation of humankind is at stake! There are many political games in churches that are played to determine who will get the fame. Often, women are allowed to do anything as long as the glory from the project stays with the head male, even if he does not invest much effort. Women are always welcome to do a job, but they should not expect to be paid as much as men for it.

I was recently at a special event that was held in a place that ordains women as pastors, and yet not one woman spoke or was publicly recognized, though a river of male pastors flowed up onto the stage. The women pastors were all backstage, setting up hours before the festivities started, and they remained there afterwards to tidy up. Recognizing women is an important part in the battle against the enemy. Imagine the impact it would have had if someone had called the anonymous women pastors from that event up front in order to honour them for their work? True equality should be reflected through equal representation in our public presentations.

I long for men like Barak in our churches, men who will be strong enough leaders to say, "if you are not going with me, I am not going" (4:8). We need men who don't need to fish for constant public affirmation because they know who they are in God, and so they can acknowledge women and encourage them to be who they are and to do what they are called to do.

Yet men like Barak are pitifully lacking in churches. My theological studies eventually helped me to understand that not everything in the Bible is God-ordained. Violence is never God's will, although vengeance is always his, and it will find the violent perpetrators (Rom 12:19). People still often interpret their violent acts as the will of God. When reading the Old Testament, we must be aware that the people who described God to the listeners/readers had not yet experienced God's love and mercy in Jesus, and so their evaluation of God is based on their experience of the pedagogian (to borrow Paul's language in Galatians), the law, and the framework of their ruthless social environment. It is easier to understand God's "wrath" from the perspective of justice: in order for justice to be achieved for the victim, the perpetrator needs to be stopped (i.e. punished).

It is important to make the distinction between the Old and the New Testament, where now the Spirit is given to all who believe. Being like Daniel is not the primary purpose of the passage on Daniel. We are not called to imitate Old Testament men, but to get to know the God of Daniel. This is why men with shortcomings, such as David, can be described as being after God's own heart (1 Sam 13:14; Acts 13:22). The moral in these stories is about God's heart – not Daniel's devotion or David's status or supposed perfection. Humans cannot earn God's favour. God gives it to us freely, even when we are sinners!

The Radical Inclusion of Jesus

I recently witnessed a discussion with a young man in my country, who wanted to know exactly when God had changed his mind about men having to live monogamously, while people who were "after God's own heart" (like David) had lived happily with many women – and even with some to whom they were not married! I was startled by the question at first, not believing that I had heard correctly, but I was even more shocked by the inability of the presiding professor of theology to answer him. Evidently, he kept going around with this question that no one could answer. But God never changed his mind about what is good and pure! He created one man and one woman to belong together. Anything else is an expression of human sin – and yet, he loves the sinner!

When Jesus comments on Moses's permission to divorce one's wife (Mark 10:1–12), he clearly states that this concession was made "because of your hardness of heart" (10:5), since "from the beginning" (10:6), God made male and female, and the two should be one flesh (10:7–8). From what we have seen so far in this book, the hardening of men's hearts has come through their desire to exercise power over others. Jesus's word is, "Not so among you" (10:43) and not so "from the beginning" (10:6).

Like the Old Testament, the New Testament features men who have many wives, because this is the state in which these people encountered Christ. Yet it is quite clear that this is not a biblical norm, but an unfortunate state of affairs. In social circumstances of antiquity, the new believer with many wives had to choose from two options – either having one wife and forsaking the others to destruction, since on their own, they could not gain a living; or else, continuing to care for all their wives, knowing that this was not what God had in mind "from the beginning" (10:6).

Jesus's equal treatment of women is also expressed in the way he welcomes them as his followers by teaching them and affirming their discipleship, as he did with Mary of Bethany. Against the accusations of her own sister, Jesus affirms that she "has chosen the better part, which will not be taken away from her" (Luke 10:42).

Growing up, I can vividly remember the confusion my church preachers had with this as they tried to explain that both Martha's and Mary's callings were good and profitable and that Jesus was not really saying that Mary's calling was better. Interestingly, the Gospel writers, who probably did not think much of women in general since they were the sons of their own patriarchal culture, did not try to conceal Jesus's different attitudes concerning women. Jesus cast so much light on them that they took the trouble to describe how he had changed the status of women.

Though Jesus had twelve male apostles, their function was to represent Israel's twelve sons in God's new salvation plan.[13] Jesus had other true disciples, and these women stood by his cross, were present at his grave, and were the first to see him alive again. The first apostle to the "nations" was a Samaritan woman (John 4), who believed and understood what Nicodemus, a learned, know-it-all rabbi (John 3), could not comprehend or accept. Jesus's ministry was carried out and supported by his female disciples (Luke 8:2–3).

We have already mentioned Jesus's countercultural thoughts about motherhood when a woman in the crowd wants to bless his mother for having such a great son (Luke 11:27). While the environment wholeheartedly agrees with her, Jesus is not impressed. In one sentence, he remodels the common and holy tradition: "Blessed, rather are those who hear the word of God and

---

13. A. Besançon Spencer, "If Jesus Were Really Counter-Cultural in His Treatment of Women, Why Didn't He Choose Any Women to Be His Apostles?" *Mutuality* (Winter 2009): 18, online: https://www.cbeinternational.org/sites/default/files/tough_spencer.pdf.

obey it!" (11:28). Jesus subjects everything to true discipleship. Christians are, first and foremost, Christ followers. Jesus does not devalue motherhood, but he places it where it belongs.

This leads to an important point, which is that women are not saved by their children, nor through them, though some try to argue for this because of 1 Timothy 2:15: "Yet she will be saved through childbearing." Whatever the author of this passage meant, he does not mean that bearing children is the path of salvation for women. This text needs to be read and understood within the social circumstances of Ephesus in the first century, which were threatened by false gnostic teaching. The text is offering a practical solution for a particular situation. If motherhood did not work for Jesus's mother, because any disciple of Jesus is more blessed than her, it will certainly not offer salvation for other mothers.[14]

If Jesus thought that women were valuable disciples, followers, and missionaries, why do we have so much difficulty with this today? Unpacking the traditions about the roles of women in both society and the church is like opening Pandora's box of the structures of sin! So many issues come to the forefront. If women are going to be able to speak up in church, we will need to have much more discernment about using our best gifts for the community. In many places, the only criterion for ministry is being a male. When we begin to ask deeper questions about qualifications for ministry, we will inevitably step on some entitled male toes.

For instance, if we stand up against human trafficking, we will end up featuring the issue of demand in our churches, which is primarily a male issue. If we teach equality in marriage, we will have to deal with the ugly sins of adultery and violence, which so many women have silently endured because they have been taught that the "head" is entitled to privacy about his

---

14. In a short commentary on 1 Timothy, D. Guthrie, *New Bible Commentary*, ed. D. A. Carson et al. (Downers Grove: InterVarsity Press, 1953; repr. 1994), 1294–1304, esp. 1298, shows the whole range of frustrations that many commentators have with this passage. My own reading of the pastoral epistles was greatly shaped by the lectures of Gordon Fee, which were held at the Evangelical Theological Seminary in Osijek in 1988, where he deliberated on the false teaching in the pastorals and the women's part in it. In G. Fee, *1 & 2 Timothy, Titus* (Grand Rapids: Baker, 1988), 76, he writes, "Thus, as with the instruction on the proper objects of prayer (all people), so with the proper demeanor in prayer (men without arguments, while women's place in the worshipping community is to be a quiet one), the reason for these particular instructions is best understood as a response to the activities and teachings of the wayward elders." R. C. Clark Kroeger and C. Clark Kroeger, *I Suffer Not a Woman: Rethinking 1 Timothy 2:11–15 in the Light of Ancient Evidence* (Grand Rapids: Baker, 1992), argue from a similar platform, which is that this text is an affirmation of femininity against gnostic ideas presented in the Gospel of Thomas or The Gospel of Mary that propagate the idea that women need to become male in order to be "worthy of life" (173).

sin. Many ugly scenarios may be revealed that we have chosen not to see and have surrounded with taboos.

We may discover that the demon of disregard for women can only be driven out by a total change of the hierarchical systems, which will require a lot of tedious work, particularly if we do not believe in revolutions. We may even need to challenge structures that seem to be healthy on the surface. Sin has many ways to conceal itself. Sometimes, it looks like light. For instance, Sweden must be admired for their leading role in combatting prostitution and human trafficking. It looks great when we look at it in isolation from the rest of the world. However, Sweden (along with most Western countries) has a large number of men who explore sex tourism, thereby supporting the sex trade market in other, poorer places in the world.[15] As we address equality for women, we will have to keep our eyes open to the new ways that sin tries to adapt to and pollute our best intentions.

We need to tackle this sin in the church, and men are the primary ones who need to tackle it. Sexual drives need to be discussed and examined so that people can be confronted with what they are doing when they "play" with women. Women were not created to be abused for men's pleasure – whether to raise his children, make him feel good, serve him, be subjected to his violence, or be the stepping stone for his own promotion. This is not what Jesus taught, and we should stop pretending that it is by pointing to sporadic, complicated Scriptures that seem to support it. Let us think deeper. Women are saved by Christ, and this belief must be revealed in the church.

Marginalizing Women in the Early Church
Jesus's acceptance of women and their amazing involvement in the earliest church should be our starting point for understanding the difficult passages from Paul's letters. If Jesus established the principle of equal discipleship for men and women, Paul's theology must be understood as an attempt to enculturate it – or to adapt it to churches that were still living within the structures of sin. Thus a biblical word to men is not complete without a comment about the difficult passages by the Apostle Paul, the so-called "misogynist."

A ton of material has been written on this issue, but it is often not consulted by church leadership, because women's issues are either not recognized or they

---

15. J. Medin, *Welcome to Sin City: Swedish Male Sex Tourists in Prostitution Abroad*, a report from Sweden's Fair Travel Network (October 2018), online: https://schystresande.se/media/filer/087ab2/welcome-sin-city.pdf. I even wonder about this report. For instance, I do not understand why the explicit story about "Karl" had to be placed as an introduction to a report that is apparently combatting sex tourists.

are marginalized as unimportant. And yet, Paul often addresses the subject because he realizes how important male-female issues are, both for the family and for the functioning of the church. How can we talk about accepting the "small" while bashing women? How can we preach peace while accepting violence in Christian homes? How can we talk about freedom while keeping women captive?

God has been good in every generation, and there are many men and women who have sought to investigate this issue thoroughly so that women will not be excluded from the mercy of God and their rightful place in Christ's church. In our generation, Elisabeth Schüssler Fiorenza's *In Memory of Her* puts biblical women back on the maps of theology. When it was first published, the ground of biblical theology shook. Suddenly, women were everywhere in the New Testament, assuming all kinds of leadership positions, including being apostles (e.g. Rom 16:1–16).

Paul's Affirmation of Women Who Minister the Gospel

To understand Paul's "hard passages" about women, we should first place them within the broader context of his ministry. This gives us an amazing picture that is incomparable with anything else we know of the ancient world and its attitude towards women. The social stratum was not as unified, as we are made to believe by some books, and there were probably always women who would not comply with the traditional roles – even in antiquity.[16] But did women impinge on the incipient church – and if so, how? Did women give a boost to the growing church by incorporating their potential within a setting that breathed equality in Jesus, the Messiah?

Romans 16 is such a wonderful testimony to the involvement of women in the gospel. But in order to appreciate it, Christians have to free themselves from their own medieval cultural burdens. The list in Romans 16:1–16 is comprised of twenty-eight names of people whom Paul praises for their valuable contributions to the ministry of the gospel in the world. Nine are women, which is about a third. Even more impressive, Paul renders titles to some of these women.

Phoebe is a *diakonos* (note Paul deliberately uses a masculine word) of the church in Cenchrea, which is the western harbour of Corinth (Rom 16:1). Paul sometimes uses the word *diakonos* to denote his own status (1 Cor 3:5), so in this church, Phoebe holds the official position of "minister." Phoebe is designated as a *prostatis* of many, which is a term used to describe her position

---

16. We saw this already in Bruce Winter's featuring of "new women" in the Roman empire.

as a "benefactor," something that was highly regarded in her society. Phoebe is using her status, wealth, and faith to minister to her church, and she is recognized for her service by her church and also by Paul.[17] Her travel to Rome probably occasioned Paul's letter to the Romans, since she could be trusted to carry it and read it in Paul's stead, as was the custom.[18] From the word choice and the situation, it is impossible to interpret Phoebe's position as a common woman who cooked for Paul on occasion or did his laundry, according to some traditional ideas about women's roles.[19]

---

17. Dunn, *Romans 9–16* (Nashville: Thomas Nelson, 1988), 886–889, points out several striking details. First, Paul calls Phoebe "sister." The feminine form of the well-attested male *adelphos* for members of religious associations is an exception, although women in particular were active in religious associations. Its popularity in Christianity must be understood as a sign of equality. Second, Phoebe is a "minister" rather than a "servant" or deaconess (against the NIV). Third, her influence is "universal." Fourth, she is described as "worthy" of the Roman's hospitality. Fifth, she is a *prostatis*, about which Dunn comments: "The unwillingness of commentators to give 'prostatis' its most natural and obvious sense of 'patron' is most striking" (888). This would describe Phoebe as "patron, protector," even "leader or ruler."

18. A. Chapple describes the process and importance of the letter bearer in the Roman world in "Getting Romans to the Right Romans: Phoebe and the Delivery of Paul's Letter," *Tyndale Bulletin* 62, no. 2 (2011): 195–214. "It was not uncommon . . . for letters not to arrive at their destination" (197). This article is particularly interesting as it uncovers the many hardships and hazards this task entailed, which are usually not taken into account: Phoebe had to figure out a route that would bring her to Rome before Paul arrived in Jerusalem so that the Romans could pray for him; she had to make sure that a substantial scroll did not get wet or damaged on the way; she had to determine which churches would get the letter first, as there were evidently several communities, and they were not necessarily on speaking terms, but Paul trusts Phoebe to "convene a gathering" (208) to deliver the letter to all the individuals mentioned in the greetings. Or, Paul might have been expecting the letter to be copied for all these house groups, which would have been an expensive undertaking. Lastly, by bringing the letter, Phoebe would have been expected to read it in church, performing it publicly in front of a mixed audience: "the hearers could safely assume that the reader, as bearer of the letter had been coached by the sender in how to read it" (213).

19. In an online sermon, J. MacArthur, https://www.gty.org/library/sermons-library/45-119/love-for-the-saints-part-1X, describes Phoebe as follows:

> This dear lady, Phoebe, no doubt had some particular role of service that she rendered in this congregation. Now note that the word "servant" is the word *diakonon*, from which we get our familiar word deacon. Now that word knows no gender. It is neither a masculine word nor is it a feminine one. *Diakonon* defies that kind of gender distinction. Thus it refers in very general terms to one who serves, to one who serves, be he male or she female. And its use in the New Testament is very broad and very general. I try to point this out in a little book I've written called *Deacons*, what the Bible teaches about deacons. It is a very broad and general term. Now frankly it doesn't necessarily mean anything official. There are many, many uses of that word which originally meant *to serve a table, to wait on a table and came to mean any kind of simple, humble service or any kind of ministry in general*" (emphasis mine).

Although some might want to contort Paul's words by assuming that he is merely praising women who cook and bake for church potlucks, serve in church kitchens, and do all kinds of practical things, this text shows Paul commending these Christian women for working hard for the gospel and caring for the church in many different capacities by using their extraordinary gifts. Only one person on the list is commended as a "mother," and the way Paul relates this, it seems that Rufus's mother (Rom 16:13) has been like a mother to Paul, a woman of faith who made her home a welcoming and relaxing place for travelling preachers. This means that she understood the work and appreciated those who were ministering by making it her business to anticipate their hardships and offer them temporary rest.

Interestingly, in naming the married couple, Prisca and Aquilla, Paul lists the wife's name before the husband's, a practice that is unusual even today (16:3). Prisca was most likely named first because she was more prominent in the gospel ministry.[20] She is also identified as the teacher of Apollos (Acts 18:24). Together, Prisca and Aquilla helped Paul establish two large churches in Asia minor: one in Corinth and one in Ephesus (Acts 18:18–20).

Those who would like to impose traditional roles on women in the church have particular difficulty with Junia, whom Paul recognizes as an apostle, along with her husband, Andronicus (16:7). This is the only case where a couple is described as being "apostles," and they were apostles before Paul. This places their work within the church in the 30s, only a few years after Jesus's resurrection. There is a wide consensus among scholars today that Junia refers to a woman,[21] since Junias is not a documented male name, but Junia is a well-documented women's name. Junia's giftedness to the global church was recognized by her own church, who sent her out along with her husband. This couple's ministry was relevant enough for Paul to mention them both, and so they must be considered as more than local ministers or teachers. Like Paul, they probably engaged in reaching out to new areas. Paul described his

---

He does not identify the accusative masculinum in *diakonon*, which derives clearly from a noun in masculinum, as affirmed in J. MacArthur, *MacArthurs Commentary on Romans 9–16* (Chicago: Moody, 1996), 359–360, where he says, "Servant translates *diaconos*, the term from which we get *deacon*. The Greek word here is neuter . . ."

20. Dunn, *Romans 9–16*, 892.

21. In considering the automatic assumption that Junia is a man, against all historical data, Dunn, *Romans 9–16*, 894, notes that it is a "striking presumption of male presumption regarding the character and structure of earliest Christianity" (894). See also P. Lampe, "Junia/Junias: Sklavenherkunft im Kreise der vorpaulinischen Apostel (Röm 16,7)," *ZNW* 76 (1985): 132–134, and *Die stadtrömischen Christen in den ersten beiden Jahrhunderten: Untersuchungen zur Sozialgeschichte* (Tübingen: Mohr / Siebeck, 1989), 124–153.

apostleship as follows: "I make it my ambition to proclaim the good news, not where Christ has already been named, so that I do not build on someone else's foundation" (Rom 15:20).

Returning to the occasion for the letter to the Romans, Paul is hoping that this list of people can help bring about reconciliation in their local communities, which seem disunited. By doing so, they will also create a favourable soil for Paul's impending ministry in the West.[22] Paul counts on both the prominent women and men in the church to work together. Many of these people have worked with him on other occasions, and Paul knows what they can do. Paul's western mission is at stake, as he plans to leave Asia Minor and Illyricum and move on to Spain (Rom 15:22–29) to bring the gospel into new territories. Because Phoebe is bearing Paul's letter, he includes her name as a natural connection to the groups there. Thus her first mission is to bring these people together to consider this important issue for the gospel.

Understanding the Role of Women in Philippi

It is important to understand the situation of the Philippian church, which Paul founded on his second missionary journey. The situation here is somewhat comical. God is revealing his will to Paul by closing the usual missionary doors (Acts 16:6–8). Finally, Paul has a vision of a Macedonian *man* who urges him to come and help in Macedonia. When they cross over into Philippi and seek a place of prayer, they encounter a bunch of *women* and no official synagogue (Acts 16:13). Is it possible that God did not trust Paul to take his intentions for the gospel seriously if a group of women called him, and so a man came in the vision instead?

Today, when Christians tread through the ruins of Philippi and find the gushing creek outside the northern old city walls, they also find beautiful peace in the shade of the old trees and a small and simple Orthodox chapel, which was erected in memory of the women leaders of Philippi's church. The memory of these amazing women that ministered the gospel with passion and dedication is kept alive there. Frescos depict some men as well, including Luke, who served with these women – and possibly also "under" them. One fresco features Lydia, strikingly tall above the man and woman at her sides.

Reading the Scriptures with our eyes open for glimpses of women will give us a lively picture of the ministry of women to the church – though not one of moral perfection, since no human endeavours are perfect. No wonder the gospel spread like wildfire in those early days, for both men and women equally

---

22. I have elaborated on this in Magda, "Unity."

and counterculturally shouldered the task together. Even great apostles, such as Paul, depended on this cooperation. We can only venture into reading the more difficult passages in Paul by starting with this basic affirmation. If they seem to contradict female involvement, a particular cultural issue is at stake that needs to be identified.

Understanding the Role of Women in Corinth

Antoinette Wire believes that in Corinth, Paul's problem is with the women in particular.[23] This is an interesting take on a bunch of historical reconstructions and shows a careful reading of a biblical text that is usually skimmed over. For instance, if the argument about factions in Corinth is followed, one recognizes immediately that "Peter's" and "Christ's" factions (1 Cor 1:12) are more or less rhetorical and that Paul's issue with Apollos resurfaces in several other places. In 1:12, four factions are mentioned, with Apollos's being the second. In 3:4, Peter and Christ are omitted, and Apollos is the only rival. In 3:5-6, the following rhetorical question is raised: What (not "who" in the Greek) is Apollos in the larger scale of events? Because the Corinthians belong to God and God gives the growth, Paul maintains that both he and Apollos, along with everything else, belong to them, just as the Corinthians belong to Christ (3:22). Thus everything else – especially having human favourites – is "foolishness" (3:19) and "futile" (3:20). The conclusion in 4:6 again features only Apollos and Paul: Paul has "applied all this to Apollos and" himself for their "benefit . . . so that none of you will be puffed up in favor of one against another." The final revelation comes in 16:12: "Now concerning our brother Apollos, I strongly urged him to visit you with the other brothers, but he was not at all willing to come now."

It seems that Wire is right to suggest that – rhetorically – the Corinthians and Paul both know that the actual problem in Corinth is this Alexandrian philosopher, whose eloquence is stealing the show in Greek Corinth against Paul, an apostle who is not a rhetor. Apollos is unwilling to yield to Paul's wishes and accept Paul's apostolic precedence in Corinth, and he seems to have enough backing to push this refusal through. While this reconstruction is persuasive, Wire continues with her reconstruction by connecting Apollos's eloquence with Priscilla's instruction (Acts 18:1) and adding the common prejudice that the women are talkative.[24] As the main part of 1 Corinthians

---

23. A. Wire, *Corinthian Women Prophets: A Reconstruction Through Paul's Rhetoric* (Minneapolis: Fortress, 1990).

24. Comp. Wire, *Corinthian Prophets*, 37, 50-51, 209-211.

features problems with speech gifts in the church, Wire concludes that Paul's problem are the women, who have decided that Apollos is their (new) apostle.

Wire's main argument hangs on 1 Corinthians 14:34–35, where Paul retracts his statement from Galatians 3:28–29, which is that women and men are equal in Christ and have equal gifts to contribute. He probably taught this in Corinth as well. Now, for some reason, he takes it back. Wire believes that he is insisting on his divine ordination. He is revoking his prior teaching while the women (and their new eloquent apostle) are insisting on it.[25] This kind of reasoning is difficult, as it presupposes a substantial change in Paul's mind regarding the ministry of women within only a few years. Wire would also have to argue away Romans 16, which was written from Corinth after 1 Corinthians.

Yet the bigger problem with her claim is that Paul abandons his own teaching in 1 Corinthians 14:34–35. This passage does not read as a Pauline text, and some manuscripts append these verses at the end of the chapter. Their insertion ruins the natural flow of the instruction on prophesying. In Fee's commentary on 1 Corinthians, he suggests that this passage was a side note written in the margin by some later scribe, reflecting his own problem with women in the church.[26] If these verses are not Pauline, Wire's argument that Paul is renouncing his own teaching on equality to force women into submission is seriously flawed.

Without these verses, Paul asks for order in public worship because that contributes to the gospel ministry. The women (prophets) in Corinth must have had an outstanding role, and so Paul confronts them with some misconceptions. There are historical reasons to believe that prophetesses could have been leaving their husbands for their newly found freedom and calling in Christ. Kroeger and Kroeger reconstruct this situation in Ephesus, but it may just as well apply to the Corinthian women. If women had the prophesying Spirit of God within them, they would not have been available for sexual intercourse with their husbands because, culturally speaking, this is how their prior religions had worked. The body and the spirit needed to be kept separate. With the permanent presence of God in them, they understood that they no longer needed to uphold traditional marital roles.[27]

This interpretation would have been supported by Paul's counsel that, in view of the Christian mission, it is better for people not to marry (1 Cor

---

25. Wire, *Corinthian Prophets*, 152–158.

26. Fee, *First Corinthians*, 699–708, 699. P. B. Payne, "Ms. 88 as Evidence for a Text without I Cor 14.34–5," *NTS* 44 (1998): 154, seems to confirm Fee's suspicions.

27. Kroeger and Kroeger, *I Suffer Not*, 197–202.

7:7–8), which he may have taught before, and he still held when he wrote 1 Corinthians. In particular, this would help clarify 1 Corinthians 7:10 about why women should not divorce their husbands. People do not need to marry, but if they do, then they need to live with it. Being a Christian and having a spiritual experience or being a prophetess in the church is in line with the other duties of being a wife and mother.

It is possible that all the passages concerning women in 1 Corinthians are contextual (aside from 14:34–35, which has textual problems, as discussed above). All these passages should be read against the background of both Jewish and Hellenist religious tradition, which taught that prophecy was mediated by angels.[28] Angels were many things, including mediators between prophets and God's throne. In explaining 1 Corinthians 11:10, Fee's main concern about the "authority on/over her head because of the angels" is the fact that the text sounds like a concession to women – an exception that frees them from male authority. He writes: "Paul seems to be affirming the 'freedom' of women over their heads, but what that means remains a mystery."[29]

However, if angels are not negative forces from which men should protect women,[30] but rather mediators of the word of God, then we have a meaning that is consistent with whatever else Paul has to say about marriage relationships and freedom in Christ elsewhere. Everywhere, including Corinth, women should stay within their status. If they are married, they should not seek to divorce their husbands for the sake of some spirituality. Spirituality is compatible with human life in marriage, including sexual relationships. The only concession given to a married woman is the freedom to respond to the word of God herself. She is given full freedom of religion and authority over her own head concerning her standing before God.

In 1 Corinthians 11, when Paul discusses head coverings, we may have a related problem. It is generally accepted that priestesses in pagan temples did not cover their heads, but wives did. Paul addresses issues of culture here, but he uses a simile about heads. The parallelism between men shaming their head (Christ) if they prophecy with their heads covered and women shaming their heads (their husbands) if their heads are uncovered is a distorted parallelism.[31]

---

28. For instance, A. Evans, "Hellenistic Connections to Jewish Beliefs about Angels," *Scriptura* 112 (2011): 1–12.

29. Fee, *First Corinthians*, 521.

30. The traditional connection, as Fee points out, are "the male angels, who on seeing the women unveiled, lusted after them after the manner of the 'sons of God' in Gen. 6:2," *First Corinthians*, 521.

31. Fee, *First Corinthians*, 514.

It is even more complicated if we consider that Jews generally pray with their heads covered. Paul tries to argue from hierarchy in the Godhead, but it does not sound convincing or clear even to him. It is clear that Paul's instruction is not about men and their relationship to Christ in prayer or Christ's relationship to God.

Rather, Paul is concerned about the public prayer and speech of women who have broken away from the conventions of their environment. It is also clear that Paul's instruction is for women to place themselves under the authority of their husbands because breaking away from this convention is detracting from their testimony in the city. Prompted by new freedom in Christ, Paul tries to argue that there still needs to be order, as in all the churches of the saints (1 Cor 14:33), because people who come to church should not be confused by the chaos created by loud, chaotic speakers in tongues and prophecies.

I have often observed that when women are suddenly freed from a long yoke of traditional abuse that has silenced them, the pendulum swings in the other direction, and women become unbearably loud. In Corinth, through the experience of Christ amidst a wealth of spiritual miracles and gifts, these women seem to be seeking to live out their freedom to the fullest. Having been socially repressed by their background, confused by the teachings of an affirming philosopher such as Apollos, married away at a young age to much older men, living a secluded life with children, their freedom was a new experience, and they sailed with it.

When Paul calls them back to duty, taking back what he already taught them about freedom (Gal 3:28–29), he is not welcome. It is hard for them to hear Paul telling them, "All things are lawful, but not all things are beneficial. All things are lawful, but not all things build up" (1 Cor 10:23). Though what the women are doing may be "lawful," it is not beneficial for their families or the witness of the gospel. Though what the women are doing may be "lawful," it is not building up the church. We should not read hierarchies into this text, but see it as Paul's attempt to explain the concept of submission within the freedom of God.

Paul finishes his argument with a discussion of the equality of men and women. He says: "Nevertheless, in the Lord woman is not independent of man or man independent of woman. For just as woman came from man, so man comes through woman; but all things come from God" (1 Cor 11:11). The emphatic summons to regard what is "proper" (11:13) regarding women's outfits in prayer does not sound like a theological issue, but a sociological issue, with an impact on gospel outreach in Corinth. Within the social environment of Corinth, it is improper for women to walk about with their hair cut short or without a veil. The Corinthian women prophetesses most probably removed their veils as a way of proclaiming their independence, which shamed their husbands. Yet they did not cut their hair, which meant that they did not identify themselves as prostitutes. But Paul warns them that abandoning the veil (and abandoning their husbands through formal divorce) is not unlike becoming a prostitute. It seems sufficiently clear from the text that the Corinthian women did not want to be identified in that way.

Managing norms of society regarding marriage and balancing these norms with freedom in Christ and his calling has never been easy. Although my husband has a recognized and international role and ministry of his own, my ministry as a leader in the church has sometimes been used to downplay his role and authority. Our decision to negotiate our ministry with each other and to speak openly when we feel that one of us has overstepped has caused some people to call him a "henpecked husband." At the same time, we have been told by others that our marriage has helped them find hope for their own relationships. So even though Paul does not uphold an immediately understandable model for us, he certainly hits on an important issue.

There are many men who still believe that their wives are their property (even if they do not say so) and feel entitled to all their time and care. This makes it difficult to free women for their callings and to acknowledge their gifts. Therefore, Christian men need to consider how they can find a way that, together and as partners, both men and women can serve the Lord, who is above them both.

Understanding Paul's Teaching about Household Codes

This question leads us to the next subject in Pauline studies, which has often been short-circuited in order to subdue women: the household codes and related texts about regulating a Christian marriage and family life, including one from 1 Peter (Eph 5:21–6:9; Col 3:18–4:1; 1 Pet 2:18–3:7).

Household codes are social conventions. While some authors look for theological reasons to enforce these codes, centuries of theological debates show that this is difficult to support. In the ancient world, it was expected behaviour for wives to be subordinate to the authority of their husbands. A "charismatic chaos" in relationships would prevent people from joining Christian communities. Interestingly, both Peter's and Paul's instructions to husbands and wives are set within a broader context of instruction about right Christian behaviour. Male-female relationships are at the core of the transformation of communities, and new life is best seen in this intimate realm, where all masks fall away, and we are who we are.

The instructions in Ephesians and Colossians bear similarities and are probably dependent on each other. Again, the emphasis in both is that Christian conduct must be "wise" and attractive to people "outside" (4:5). I will explore here the longer version from Ephesians.

> The relationship between the so-called prison letters is complicated, and so is the relationship between the Ephesian and Colossian household codes. While Philippians and Philemon are easily settled within the circumstances of Paul's Roman imprisonment, scholars find that Colossians and Ephesians are different, up to a point, where some doubt Pauline authorship because of differences in vocabulary, style, Christology, church governance, and even gnostic teaching.[32] However, there are good reasons to maintain Pauline authorship, primarily since Colossians has been considered Pauline and that arguments about language and style can be interpreted both ways in an occasional theology – in other words, Paul is a missional theologian, and he addresses issues that concern a particular situation.[33] Addressing this interpretation adequately may require a new take and also "new" words. Colossians shares many themes and words with Ephesians. For Belz and others, this means that the author of Ephesians may have corrected the theology of Colossians to make it more Pauline.[34] In this case, the Ephesian household codes would be the "correct" ones with which to engage. The main stumbling block to Paul's authorship of these letters is the kind of church organization that shows an early church hierarchy ("incipient Catholicism"), which is perceived to go against Paul's claim of equality. Yet our own discussions have shown that, for Paul, the outward structures do not go against freedom in Christ. In my own theology, I will follow the early church tradition in accepting both letters as Pauline. Consequently, Paul may have elaborated in Ephesians what he first drafted in Colossians.

The household codes in Ephesians do not start – as some translations suggest – by beginning a new paragraph and adding a new heading in Ephesians 5:22. In the Greek, 5:22 has no verb, because the verb from 5:21,

---

32. E.g. see L. M. Belz, *The Rhetoric of Gender in the Household of God: Ephesians 5:21–33 and Its Place in Pauline Tradition*, doctoral thesis (Chicago: Loyola University, 2013), 39–42.

33. E.g. see H. Marshall, S. Travis, and I. Paul, *Exploring the New Testament 2* (London: SPCK, 2002), 159–160.

34. E.g. Belz, *Rhetoric of Gender*, 39–42.

"*being subject* to one another out of reverence for Christ," is carried over into the next verse. Even in 5:21, it is not a full verb, but a participle, which is normally dependent on a full verb. The full verb on which the participle, "being subject," is dependent is found in 5:15: literally, "pay attention at how you live/walk." A number of participles describe this "wise" Christlike walk: by making the best of your time (5:16), by not being a drunkard (5:18), by speaking in psalms and living with thankfulness (5:19–20). The last participle then says: "Walk wisely by subjecting yourself to each other out of reverence for Christ." In this verse, "each other" means everyone in a church setting, both men and women. This means, for instance, that everyone will know when to stop pushing their ideas in a meeting, because Christ is more important than the colour of the church carpet or the food at a conference. Submission because of Christ concerns all realms of life, and first of all, the most intimate realm of marriage relationships.

We must understand the apostolic request to the Ephesians within the framework of mutual submission in the faith in Christ and the utter dedication to his glory in our earthly life. An ancient home was extremely hierarchical and subject to the *pater familias*. Everyone in the home was the father's property, and he could kill them without having many questions asked. The idea of the family being a "man's castle" is a leftover from this ancient concept and reveals why crimes have been committed in a place that was meant to be a safe haven.

Thus when Paul argues for submission, he has two verses for wives and nine for husbands. Women knew their place and "being subject" to the husband was not anything new. They may have experimented with freedom in Christ, as we see with Corinthian women prophets, but in 1 Corinthians, they are called back into submission because the husbands are their "heads."

As we have already discussed, married women did not have many opportunities to provide for themselves, and they were dependent on their fathers, husbands, or sometimes even sons for their living. If a woman went solo, but still expected to be supported by the man of the house, it would be a source of constant tension in the relationship and transferred, as frustration usually is, to the wider community. Then Christ would be blamed rather than praised because of the new religion. Thus Paul calls the women back and enforces the cultural expectations of their environment. He reminds them that there are two reasons for subjection. The first is practical: the man is her head – the source of her livelihood and income, for which she should be thankful. The second is for the glory of Christ so that Christ's name will not be blasphemed. We also see this in 1 Peter.

Peter's exposition is interesting, as it turns Paul's order upside down, starting from the slaves and masters and calling women to subject themselves to their own husbands (NRSV has "accept their husband's authority") so that the unbelievers among them "may be won over without a word by their wives' conduct" (1 Pet 3:1). But the reason for voluntary submission from the wives in this case is, once again, evangelism: to win over the unbelieving husband and, as the author of 1 Timothy puts it, "so that the name of God and the teaching may not be blasphemed" (1 Tim 6:1).

Today, families in many places are structured differently. Many women are educated and financially independent. They do not need to be subject to the men in their lives as a source of livelihood or as "saviours." Yet Ephesians 5:21 still applies because submission is required of *all* "out of reverence for Christ." In the ancient community, it may have been easy to determine that "submission" for wives basically meant obedience to their husband's decisions. In our current circumstances, "submission" is much more complicated, particularly since the biblical text requires reciprocity: "Be subject to one another!" (5:21). Submission becomes interesting in a context that doesn't have any outward coercion. Why would I choose to submit when I could just do my own thing?

Mutual submission is even more interesting. Neither a husband nor a wife can apply the imperative on the other. It does not say, "Husbands, make your wives submissive because of Christ." Thus husbands may not force their wives into submission. Rather, Paul says, "Husbands, love your wives" (5:25). In antiquity, people rarely married for love because marriage was about survival. So Paul is not talking about romantic love here. In talking about love, Paul could have used a whole range of words, but he uses *agape*, which is the love of God for an undeserving sinner. If husbands want to understand this imperative of love, they should consult 1 Corinthians 13. But to make sure that husbands understand the nature of this agape love, the apostle adds that husbands should love their wives "just as Christ loved the church and gave himself up for her" (Eph 5:25). In Paul's concept of marital relationships, husbands cannot claim anything for themselves. They can only give, just as Christ gave up everything for the church. Submitting to this kind of love becomes easy.

Theologians have differing opinions about whether or not love is submission,[35] but it seems that giving oneself up for another requires utter submission. Evidently, Paul expects a massive resistance to this concept from

---

35. O'Brien, *Ephesians*, 418, is very dogmatic against Snodgrass, *Ephesians* (Grand Rapids: Zondervan, 1996), 269, writing, "This does not mean, as Snodgrass claims, that: 'In the final analysis submission and agape love are synonymous.'"

the men.³⁶ Therefore, metaphorically speaking, he has to bring in heavy artillery to make his point. Yet in writing these words, Paul had no idea how they would be misunderstood in the generations to come.

In this case, Paul calls the husbands to love and give themselves up for their wives, just as Christ gave himself up for the church. But since the wives are to submit to the husbands because of Christ, some husbands think that Paul is comparing husbands to Christ. This identification turns Paul's argument upside down! For through this interpretation, husbands have maintained that because Christ (as God) has authority over the church, husbands have authority over their wives, and so wives better worship husbands, just as the church worships Christ. Though this may exaggerate the point, since most Christian men would never express this verbally (as that would be blasphemy), many husbands, nevertheless, behave as if they are the gods of their households.

Yet Paul argues the other way around. He tells the women to be subject to their husbands, but then he tells the men to mimic Christ's love by putting their wives' needs before their own. The church did not deserve love and mercy, yet Christ gave up his divine status to offer himself for the church. This is how Christ cleansed his church and made her beautiful. Love makes people worthy of love, not the other way around. We do not show our worthiness by submission and then receive the love of Christ! A Christian husband must not expect, let alone demand, worship, for that belongs to God alone. A Christian husband is called to imitate Christ by offering self-sacrificial love to his wife. This process begins when he leaves his mother and father and becomes one with his wife.

Because I come from a patriarchal setting, I do not know how Paul thought this would work, since when men are put in charge, they often rule through threats and violence. Paul says that the relationship between Christ and the church is a mystery, but it has worked because of love.

Does this mean that men need to become more feminized? If they are called to sacrifice themselves for their wives and never demand respect, will women go crazy with demands and ruin men? Aren't men supposed to be "wild at heart"? Haven't the feminist movements domesticated them? These questions are confusing, because we are no longer hunters and gatherers. Old ideas have been abandoned because they were inefficient and did not work towards the

---

36. O'Brien remarks, "Exhortations to husbands to love their wives occur only infrequently outside of the New Testament," quoting Lincoln, *Paradise Now and Not Yet: Studies in the Role of the Heavenly Dimension in Paul's Thought with Special Reference to Eschatology* (Cambridge: CUP, 1981), 374, and W. Schrage, "Zur Ethik der neutestamentlichen Haustafeln," *NTS* 21 (1974–1975): 1–22; 12–13.

needs of the new world. However, mutual love and submission are not warm and fuzzy. Was Jesus a wimp when he took up his cross and walked to Calvary? Was he feeble when he stood by the women of his time, with an army of mighty men looking down on him? Even today, standing by women requires a spine, because it opposes a world that is focused on power and position. Loving by sacrificing oneself without expecting anything in return requires a strong faith in a God who can bring about change and even resurrect the dead.

A relationship of mutual trust and submission in love and respect models a Christian marriage in any circumstances, particularly in our contemporary world. Love says to the world that lasting relationships between opposites are possible, that we are all from "earth" rather than from different planets, and that we are here to care for each other and to find happiness in this relationship. Love and understanding begin in the home, with husbands and wives submitting to each other because of Christ. Such marriages reflect God's glory in the church and society.

Expanding Paul's Teaching to Women in Ministry

Having affirmed submission as a Christian trait that is required of both men and women in order to display Christ's glory in the world, we need to broaden the discussion to men and women in church ministry. Does the Bible really say that all women have to be submissive to all the men in the church? Does it really require women to be quiet at all times? While this is a very common belief around the world, we have to understand that the male-female issues described in the Bible almost exclusively relate to marital relationships. This should not surprise us, for in the old world, the husband (or father or son) was his wife's (or daughter's or mother's) boss, and so nobody else could have any say about how he treated her or what she could do.

The conventions regarding women have changed substantially in our day, and our world no longer expects women to sit at home. There is a general opinion in many parts of the world that both girls and boys should be academically trained and have a profession. Yet the structures of sin continue to obstruct change, and so there are still vast areas of the world where girls are not educated, both for practical reasons and for a lack of immediate models. In such places, it is often considered biblical for women to stay at home and bring up the children, while the men go out and bring home the proverbial bacon (or, in a contemporary adaptation, soy turkey strips). While this may reflect how society worked in the past – and the Bible did not invoke a revolution to change it – God's instructions do not differentiate between tasks for men and women. There were no "pink" gifts for women and "blue" gifts for men. On the contrary, contemporary life experience shows how women have proven themselves in all areas of human life as equal with men, and yet they are often not considered fit for leadership roles in the church.

There has been a tendency to interpret the texts we have already looked at anachronistically by teaching that women are ontologically inferior. Yet if the verses are read in their context and immediate church situation, we see a different principle at work, which requests male-female equality and mutual submission.

The Bible verse that has been responsible for wreaking the most havoc in male-female relationships in the church is 1 Timothy 2:12: "I permit no woman to teach or to have authority over a man." If the other verses are ambiguous, this one seems to be very apodictic. Yet to understand this verse, we must apply a very careful reading.

First, we must consider its literary context. After the author of the text affirms emphatically that he is the "appointed herald and messenger" (1 Tim 2:7) of the truth that "there is one God; there is also one mediator between God and humankind, Christ Jesus, himself human, who gave himself a ransom for all" (1 Tim 2:5), he suddenly decides that women should be put in their place. Mirror reading is forbidden in theological research, yet it is interesting to ask why the author's concern about the conduct of women is connected with the larger issue of the one and only mediator between God and humans – "Christ Jesus, himself human" (1 Tim 2:5).

This discussion seems to be framed by overtones of the pagan religious system and also communication between the heavens and the earth in Greek cosmology. Put in this context, women who lack biblical knowledge are loudly insisting that their new freedom in Christ means freedom from their husbands because of the spirit of prophecy that now lives in them.[37] It could be that these new women in Christ feel that they no longer need husbands, or that, as prophetesses, they can now teach their husbands, even though they lack proper training in the Scriptures and include all sorts of gnostic myths in their understanding, many of which include sexual manipulation.

Second, for reasons displayed earlier, this text is only addressing wives rather than woman in general. These wives are not only dependent on their

---

37. Kroeger and Kroeger, *I Suffer Not*, chs. 12–14, in particular, give substantial evidence about how Christian women might have misinterpreted their new standing in Christ in the light of the myths of both Hellenism and Judaism. Gnosticism, as a kind of syncretistic and arbitrary pulling together of diverse religious (and/or philosophical) traditions, makes it difficult to pinpoint exactly what kind of combination triggered this passage, since "no two Gnostics agreed on an issue" (Ireneus, *Against Heresies*, I.11.1).

husbands, but they also lack instruction and knowledge, which makes them unaware of their indecent behaviour in the public space. In Corinth, they were loud. Here, in Ephesus, it seems that they are being loud, bossy, and flaring, showing off their newest jewellery, dress, and hairdos.

This continued to be a problem in the medieval church, for John Chrysostom criticizes husbands for buying their wives jewellery in order to show off their status rather than teaching them proper piety.[38] Thus what is supposed to be a "holy" prayer to God has become a fashion show, with some undesirable spin-offs of female hysteria arising from unorthodox ideas about spirituality. In the case of Chrysostom, rather than correcting the wives for their extravagance, the husbands are encouraging it to display their high status. In conclusion, it can be said that this is a public issue that has its core in the home. The issue also reveals a lack of female instruction, which may be more than a private matter. This is of particular concern today, and so churches must take care to ensure that their teachers (of both men and women) have appropriate knowledge and experience.

Third, to interpret this text in 1 Timothy 2:12, we need to understand the meaning of the word that is translated in the NRSV as "having authority over." To do this, we must set aside our own church setting and try to understand what the author means by women "teaching" men in his context (2:12). Education has changed so thoroughly since the first church, and so we cannot think about how we teach in our churches today. To begin, the early church did not have a Bible or any other books as we have available today. The other problem is that the word *authentein* (which is translated as "having authority over") is only used here in 1 Timothy and nowhere else in the Bible or any other ancient Greek document. Thus we cannot really know what this word means, particularly since the context is beyond clear understanding.

The little that can be understood is that the women in Ephesus lack true knowledge about their faith, their conduct is inadequate, and they are abusing their Christian freedom to "teach" their husbands. The context seems to be marriage, which impacts the church by changing the whole worship environment. We learn that men are no longer lifting up holy hands in prayer (1 Tim 2:8). Why are they angry? What are they arguing about? Is the conduct of the uneducated women a matter of dispute? Paul's argument from Genesis and the account of human sin (Gen 2:13–15) connects with this situation,

---

38. John Chrysosthom, *Homily on Ephesians*, 13, at New Advent online: https://www.newadvent.org/fathers/2301.htm.

where the women seem to have been seduced first and are now expanding their false influence within the church.

Pulling these considerations together, it is evident that the author of 1 Timothy is addressing a particular Ephesian problem in antiquity. Thus this situation can hardly be compared with a situation in a contemporary Baptist church, where both men and women have been instructed in all sorts of knowledge, including a fundamental knowledge of the Bible and theology. It is particularly inappropriate to apply this passage to women who have completed formal higher education or studied the Bible and theology in seminaries – sometimes with more zeal than men! Prohibiting their teaching because of the situation in 1 Timothy would be wrong.

Equally Created to Do Good Works in Christ
To conclude, a church can have women in all positions of leadership as long as they have been recognized as gifted, have submitted to the teaching process, and are supported by their husbands, especially if their husbands are not believers. And yet, all these criteria should be the same for men who are ministering in the church! Both Christian husbands and Christian wives should make space for one another to exercise their gifts and callings for the benefit of the kingdom of God, for both are called to submit to each other (and to their families) out of reverence for Christ. There is no space for a one-size-fits-all model. Rather, marriage partners need to consider their ministries prayerfully as it pertains to the home, church, and society so that both can contribute to what is good and beneficial for the glory of God in the world.

When we live as partners in marriage and submit to one another, we revere Christ, and this will open up many opportunities for ministry. At times, mutual submission will mean that we will need to make space to prioritize the family for one or both partners. Nobody outside of the marriage can tell us when this needs to happen, nor who is supposed to devote more attention to the children. Whenever two people come together, each partnership will be unique, and the decisions they make together in Christ will need to accommodate both according to their gifts. Sometimes, this is difficult to achieve, particularly in settings with heavy traditional baggage or a lot of interference from immediate relatives or church structures and traditions.

Nevertheless, the God who created and gifted us, both male and female, also created "good works, which God prepared in advance for [us] to do," because we are all "God's handiwork created in Christ Jesus" (Eph 2:10).

A Biblical Word to Women

The Scripture passages that we have already discussed are as important for women as they are for men. We have seen that "submission" is a method of living together in marriage, but also in the kingdom of God and the church here on earth. Submission happens through love as we all work to benefit one another and to seek God's glory rather than our own. When women look to please their husbands and to put them and their children first in their lives, it may appear to be submissive, but it is not. Rather, women try to get a free ride, so to speak, on the coattails of men's success. If a wife acknowledges her husband as the head, but sees herself as the neck that turns the head where she wants it to go, what does this reveal about male-female relationships?

In the last section, we examined male "headship" and discovered that "boss" is not what the Bible had in mind. Rather, the man in the marriage relationship should initiate love first and give himself up for his wife first, just as Christ loved his church and gave up his earthly life for her. Paul calls men to a more hands-on role in the love relationship, which was countercultural to the ancient society of early Christianity.

Genesis tells us that a man needs to let go of his mother, his primary life-giver, which means that he has to move away from his first role as the "recipient" of the life and care of his mother. When Paul calls husbands to love sacrificially, he is telling them that they should not wait for their wives to submit, nor should they expect their wives to meet their needs or care for them like their mothers. This means that men not only have to learn how to be independent from their mothers, but they also have to be capable of loving others, not just themselves. Biblically, men are not heads to be manipulated by women. Rather, they are to take responsibility for the world by first loving their wives and families.

Yet these Scriptures also require women to scrutinize their intentions thoroughly and to seek a path of change. Are women truly manipulative monsters, or the "devil's gateway,"[39] as some men claim? Or are they, as research reveals, the victims of abusive relationships, abandonment, trafficking, poverty, and pain?

As I have worked with women and tried to empower and encourage them, I have come to see that women are often victims, but they can also be willing victims. Moreover, victimhood is a pattern of behaviour that can be learned by both men and women, but it is often required as a way of life for women by

---

39. Tertullian, *On the Apparel of Women*, I.1.

some religious traditions.[40] Thus it could be said that women are groomed to accept victimhood, and it can sometimes have the face of heroism.

My own life is telling. From many angles, I have grown up privileged. I went to a good school and was never told directly that there were things that did not apply to me, or that I could not do something because I was a girl. But my life was not easy, because my parents went to work in Germany when my brother was eight and I was ten, and we ended up with some of their friends, which meant changing schools and our way of life. Later, my brother and I were moved to Germany, and so we had to learn a new language, which my father thought we could do on our own from a grammar book and some LPs. That year, my sister was born, and my mother was unwell, so I became a mother at age eleven. That role continued with my two brothers, who were born over the next seven years. I was cooking, cleaning, caring for babies and toddlers, doing laundry and dishes, while also fighting to learn at a German Gymnasium.

This was during the 1970s, when the feminist movement was just beginning, and I lived some thirty kilometres away from the university city of Tübingen. As high school students, we had a blast envisioning our future study days in that beautiful, old university city, and so we read like crazy towards that goal. At fourteen, I ended up teaching Sunday school to twelve or so children in our small church because there was nobody else to do it. I also co-led a German and a Croatian youth group at the churches we attended. It felt normal for me to stand in front of an audience and let my voice be heard, and my pastor thought this was acceptable, and I certainly never imagined it could be wrong. Early on, I learned to trust God. Through all these years, I was fascinated with Scripture, reading it, examining it, and testing its truths against my life circumstances.

I was handling life, because it needed to be handled, and I knew I could handle it – whether I was learning a new language in two months, caring for a new baby at age eleven, cooking an elaborate meal, or working towards a high school diploma. Early on, I discovered books, which helped me along the

---

40. I have not come across research on this particular issue of women being "willing victims," but I base it on my experience and observation for the past twenty-five years of working with women. Also, research in other areas – such as the undisputed role of religion in furthering many aspects of discrimination in women – presupposes that women will accept victimization. UN Women launched the Global Platform on Gender Equality and Religion in 2017, recognizing that "Building on the growing recognition that the role of faith-based organizations in addressing the needs of women and girls is critical," online: https://www.unwomen.org/en/news/stories/2017/3/news-global-platform-on-gender-equality-and-religion-launched.

way. When my church called me to be a Sunday school teacher, I remember sitting for hours in the library of the school, reading up on pedagogy theory.

Many years later, I sought a therapist because of my tendency to be a control freak, and she helped me to see that I was not so much accomplished as I was an abandoned kid who had to stay alive. "You have to imagine this situation," she said. "It is like a kid that gets lost in a supermarket. The child has two options: to sit down and cry or to get up and figure out a way to solve the situation." I was definitely the second type. I was not accepting that I was a victim of harsh decisions that had been made for me in my younger years. But I learned when I was eight (and even before that) that I had to handle life, keep it under control, put a handle on it, and never let it be untended, because things tended to fall apart. This has made me an achiever. People look at my life and ask, "How did you do all of this?" Truly, it has come about because of a good portion of psychological imbalance, and my kids have suffered because of their "know-it-all" and "keep-it-all-under-control" mom. But we all survived, which is God's grace!

When I look back on my life, I understand how I became a woman that fights a direct battle. I hate manipulation and political games. I do not believe that any of this has a place in Christian relationships. I still come across as too blunt and direct. However, when you are left in chaos, the best thing to do is to solve it by meeting it head-on, right?

The five years I served with the BWA have taught me a few things that have enabled me to give a more politically balanced answer to this question. I have learned to accept that people work in different ways because their experience of the world is different, and not many people, especially women, can manage a head-on approach. I have also learned that men do not appreciate the head-on approach from women. I also understand that my primary response to the structures of sin is the head-on approach of a "dragon woman." My life has equipped and trained me not to be a victim, but a winner. I consider riding on the coattails of anyone as unworthy for everyone. I never imitate the ways of others. This has been a hard and painful path – not just for me, but also for the people that have worked with me. While it is true that we may not have done much work otherwise, that is not an excuse.

Yet the worst outcome of this approach to life has been that, most of the time, I have felt abandoned, rejected, and alone. The intimacy that I craved since I was eight years old seemed to slip through my fingers. Though many people loved me, I was not able to feel their love, because my eyes were always fixed on the chaos that needed attention and control.

Thankfully, God leads, intervenes, and helps us grow out of our frustrations. I am still an achiever. I am still blunt and direct. I am still task-oriented, but I have discovered another side of me, and it is growing as I let it grow. This side is best revealed in my marriage with my husband. While I used to try to "handle" my husband, feeling responsible for his feelings and achievements, we have become partners these days. I do not offer advice without being asked, nor do I expect it to be taken when I offer it. Most times, I do not feel threatened and abandoned when my thoughts are not immediately accepted. This has helped him to step up and discover some of his skills, which have sat dormant in the dark places of his heart. As we celebrate the thirty-eighth anniversary of our marriage, we would both say that it has been a good way, and we have both become so much better individually through this process.

As I have travelled the world and met people in many different cultures, I am fully aware that the life paths of women differ, along with their approaches to marriage and life. There are so many interrelated influences that create unique responses in each person. Yet I have also observed that, by and large, women tend to assume one of three general approaches to life. This book would not be complete without challenging women to examine their approach to life and marriage and how that impinges on her marriage, family, and Christ's church.

What Is Your Primary Response to the Structures of Sin?

This question has been hanging in the air since chapter 1. So far, I can imagine that I have stepped on many women's toes, and I expect that some women will be more frustrated with this book than men. Women who have swallowed the bait that the world is throwing at them tend to keep living within the structures of sin, at their own and the world's expense. Though the bait might look good on the outside, it is attached to a hook.

In this next section, I will look more closely at the baits and hooks so that we can consider other options. God's love calls us to grow so that we not only receive his mercy, but also bear witness to it by becoming his arms and feet in the world that he loves. This may be a difficult process, but it is one that will be beneficial for everyone involved – although, as with all change, not everyone will be thrilled at first. We will always face substantial opposition to change. We have to remember that when we become who we are in God, we challenge the hierarchies of sin and death, and they will fight back – from both within and without.

Goddesses: Embrace More than Your Physical Beauty

Becoming a goddess is an old occupation, but it has recently developed innumerable industries – makeup, hair treatment, skin treatment, manicures, pedicures, cosmetic salons, and fashion. There are pills and vitamins for any kind of condition and even treatments to prevent ageing. Being a goddess requires solid effort and investment.

In my work with students, I see so many young women who put hours upon hours into their looks – training, hairdos, makeup, shopping tours. If they invested only a portion of that time in reading class materials, they could be rocket scientists! But they do not want to become rocket scientists. They want to become the girlfriends of men who will become rocket scientists. In my time as a professor, I have met girls who try hard to look stupid just because being smart does not fit the description of a goddess. Sadly, our culture enforces this kind of approach on young girls by setting up beauty standards that follow them everywhere, almost like the presence of God. If you cannot compare, you will never be someone's goddess. You have to become someone's goddess by the age of . . . (in some places, it is as young as twelve!), or you will end up as a spinster and an old maid, which must be avoided at all costs.

Tradition plays into the goddess culture from a young age. Many people call their little girls a "princess" and then set out to do everything for this little princess, keeping her safe and promising to take the stars from heaven for her. She becomes the centre of the universe for her dad, and her mom's project is to get her married. Jane Austen's humorous description of Mrs. Bennett, the mother of five daughters, depicts the craze with which mothers of her time tried to marry off their daughters. The grooming of goddesses starts as a romantic expression of parental love, but as a paradigm, it becomes very dangerous. Goddesses have courts that attend to their needs, and so they don't have to do anything for themselves, but are pampered to look beautiful as the world falls at their feet. Some prince charming will come one day soon, and the goddess will become his princess, and he will care for her like a beautiful young child who will never have to grow up. He will take care of her happily ever after.

If you listen to such traditions in your teen years, it will be a recipe for disaster. Your hormones drive you, your mother teaches and directs you, your father treats you like a princess, and the culture tells you that you are born a goddess, and you are entitled to find someone who will worship the dirt your feet walk on and will continue to care for all your needs. When you find this one, you assume it's fate, and you ask no questions. Your mother and father assure you that he will provide for your every need, and you abandon your education and cling to your man. You give him your all, including your potential and your body.

Yet once you have given your all, you are abandoned, because goddesses are difficult and expensive to maintain. They have irrational wish lists and are hard to please. They believe that others are responsible for all their needs and for how they feel. So as younger and more beautiful models appear on the horizon, your worshipper looks for another and ends his relationship with you, either formally by divorce or informally by adultery.

For women, the goddess approach is a fast track to the top of the hierarchies of the world. Yet the only requirements to achieve this status are physical beauty and wealth. Thus goddesses go through life without growing up or using their potential. As their beauty fades, their later years are usually miserable. Their real dreams for a good life remain unfulfilled, because they have to compete constantly with the influx of new goddesses, but they are bound to fail. An empty woman whom no one can satisfy or please is not attractive to anyone.

On lower social levels, the goddess approach is even more dangerous, because the only asset these goddesses have is their fading beauty, and the princes that once stood in line turn into common johns. They transform goddesses into prostitutes that can be bought for a small amount of money. The story of the Samaritan woman is paradigmatic, for women who are not taught about their worth or potential beyond their physical attraction to men risk becoming prostitutes. They live by finding yet another man after their prince has abandoned them. The tradition that teaches girls to be goddesses turns girls into commodities, and they become easy prey for human traffickers. Selling yourself to the highest bidder may feel like an easy way out of the slums and poverty, but this shortcut to happiness is a tragedy that dehumanizes girls before they have even learned about life.

Women who find themselves in this category have been seduced to believe a fairy tale about a happily ever after, but what do they do when they find themselves ridden by poverty and violence, without respect or the means to support themselves, without a family or a future? What can they do when they realize that their best years are gone and they are left with nothing and nobody? Like the Samaritan woman who was seeking living water (John 4:1–42), the good news is that Jesus meets these women to give them new life. The biblical promises of God can encourage women to stop looking for life from men, because God has already equipped and strengthened them, and so they are capable of change.

Last spring, I met an African woman who came to me after I gave a talk on the Samaritan woman's fight with tradition and how Jesus changed that and made her a missionary to her people. She told me that she finally understood what had happened to her. She felt like she could move on and stop looking for men to give her life. I admired her faith and courage as she promised that, from now on, she would step out in faith and help other women so that they could have a better life with Jesus.

Interestingly, only a few months later, I spoke to a woman in my own town who had the exact same story to tell. "I cannot believe that I have been so blind for so many years, while God has given me all these gifts," she told me as she resolved to make her story known to women. Now she is organizing Christian women in the city to make this truth known. These stories not only highlight the amazing change in these two women and how their thirst was finally quenched by God's living water, but they also reveal the amazing power of gushing water springs that started flowing from them into the deserts of the world, transforming them into living spaces where many more people – not just women – can find refuge and strength.

Naturally, this kind of change is demanding, and support is vital. Young women need mature Christian women to stand by them when the world is trying to persuade them that they better find themselves a man. This reveals the importance of women's ministry as a place of support within churches. We are called to hold each other accountable and champion each other's change. Women who have already gone before us can help model the changing power of God. When women support one another and help one another process their pain, amazing things can be accomplished out of the ashes of lost years.

In the US, the Christian Women's Job Corps was initiated by the Women's Missionary Union, and it helps women finish their educations and find jobs. It also offers spiritual guidance and mentorship as well as hands-on suggestions about how to respond to the practicalities of life from women who have already been there. In South Africa, a project called Hidden Treasure started a chain of charity stores to provide necessities for women as well as the wider church. The emphasis is not on business, but on giving women whose lives are falling apart an opportunity for change. Many projects and task forces have sought to help victims of human trafficking find new life – from starting coffee places in Nagaland to outreaches in Prague and Amsterdam. In all of these programs, women support women as they seek to honour the life Christ has given them.

God has prepared good works for his people (Eph 2:10). As Calvin says, "When he says, that 'we are the work of God,' this does not refer to ordinary creation, by which we are made men. We are declared to be new creatures, because, not by our own power, but by the Spirit of Christ, we have been formed to righteousness. This applies to none but believers."[41] God has gifted women believers, too, and is leading them to redeem the horrible experiences that they have had within the structures of sin as a liberating testimony to others, for these experiences become their redeemed potential for good in the hands of God. But this process starts with God challenging women to let go of the idea that in order to live a good life, you need a man. A husband and a family may be part of a God-willed good for many women, but God has the priority in worship, which no man can take from a woman.

When women come to understand that they have authority over their own heads with regards to worshipping God and being obedient to him, they will challenge their "deadly bodies" by stepping out in faith to do the good works that God has prepared for them. Yet doing so will challenge the structures of sin in their marriage, family, church, and society as they stand up to their victim mentality, stand up to perpetrators of violence in their home, and look evil in the eye as they confront their abusers – even when they know the structures of sin will support them (as is often the case within the church). There are so many structures that need confrontation, including those that question education for women. Challenging these structures will lead women to live an intensely engaged life that will move them far beyond a single-minded concern for a man's love.

God's "good deeds" have often been defined superficially as merely bringing food to the sick neighbour or giving money to the poor. Women's good deeds will be standing up to violence and injustice, even when they think that nothing can be done. While it may be tempting to accept the injustice and violence quietly or to teach your little girl to yield to tradition by telling her that this is what life is like for women, this is not the way of God, who wants to set the captives free.

God will stand by women of faith as they make the transformation from goddesses for men to God's warriors and builders (Isa 61). They will lavish the world with a beauty that by far surpasses their outer selves, and they "will be called oaks of righteousness, the planting of the Lord, to display his glory" (61:3). They "shall build up the ancient ruins"; they "shall raise up the former devastations"; they "shall repair the ruined cities, the devastations of many

---

41. Calvin, *John Calvin's Commentary*, Christian Classics Ethereal Library: Ephesians 2:8–10, online on *Bible Hub*, https://biblehub.com/commentaries/calvin/ephesians/2.htm. I do not handle the theological question about predestination here, as Calvin claims. This text is not a philosophical deliberation about who enacts salvation or whether humans have a free will. Rather, Paul speaks to people who are Christians, affirming their new selves as being capable to do the good works of God in the world, a discussion similar to that of Rom 8:11 above.

generations" (Isa 61:4). They will become a vital, active part of God's beautiful regeneration in this world.

Holy Mothers: Stop Being a Victim

Sin often enters what was initially created as "very good" by God and, little by little, turns it into something bad. For this reason, it is easy to buy into the tradition of holy motherhood. There is nothing more beautiful in life than becoming a mother. It feels divine, because giving life truly is divine.

Being a mother has long been valued in the biblical tradition, but it has also been an important step of self-preservation. For many centuries, having children was the best and safest retirement investment. Yet raising children today is expensive,[42] and some calculations suggest that a mother does enough work to add up to a solid college teacher salary in the US.[43] No wonder so much care is invested in cultures around the world to prepare girls for marriage and childbearing!

This decisive global economic factor has changed in the West with the millennials, who tend not to invest in children, but in themselves and their careers. However, evangelical (and many Baptist) environments in the West have also embarked on a "back to tradition" train. In light of the challenges of globalization, "traditional" values have been proposed as an overall strategy to make the world a better place. So even in the West, we have a growing number of people, including women, who believe that assuming the traditional role of a mother is "biblical."

"Holy mothers" are similar to "goddesses," since some goddesses eventually become more stable when they become mothers. This model sounds viable and even scriptural, as it legalizes male-female relationships and gives women more permanent security. On the other hand, it coincides with the biblical interpretation that women will be saved through childbearing (1 Tim 2:15). Such a reading also presupposes that a woman without a man is a headless creature who is incapable of living and fulfilling her purpose in life.

---

42. Globally, it costs between $160,000 to $233,610 (not including college education in the US) to raise them. In my country, raising a child or building a house is equally expensive. According to UNICEF, you need roughly $9,000 to raise a child for a year in the developing world; but for the US in 2015, it was calculated to cost $233,610 to raise one child to the age of eighteen.

43. According to a calculator issued by *Quarts at Work*, online: https://qz.com/work/1083411/this-calculator-makes-the-unpaid-work-women-do-visible/, my average work hours in the household with four children would have cost about $1,400 per week if it had been paid. This amounts to a whopping $67,000 a year.

Along with this, there is the practicality of having children as insurance for old age. Thus "holy motherhood" is pushed by many traditions. The households that used to be supported by agriculture depended on all the hands that could be found for the many chores around the house and fields. While this may no longer be an immediate need in the contemporary household, it is still true of modern societies in general. Our own pensions will substantially depend on the next working population, but as the pension system crumbles in Europe, we may become dependent on the children we have raised, who we trust will be loyal to us out of love and respect.

A woman recently told me how her father had left her family when she was only seven years old. She was the oldest of four, and one of her siblings was mentally disabled. When her mother started working a full-time job, all household chores and the organization of the home became her responsibility. Her education was unimportant, so she dropped out of high school. Yet she is full of potential, because all her life, starting at age seven, she managed the complex tasks of running a home with three other children and a mother who could not forget the ruin of her marriage. Though she was taken in as her mother's confidant, she was also often a punching bag for her mother's frustration. "On the outside, we looked like a functional family," she told me. "On the inside, I see now, I was dying."

On another occasion at a theological conference in Prague, I learned that there are Baptist families in India who sell their daughters to human traffickers. The logic of this is hardly understandable to white middle-class Europeans, but the math is simple. Selling one child will provide for the others. Most often, the traffickers make it easy by telling parents stories about the perfect life their little girl will have in the home of some rich Westerners. Whatever we want to think of it, and even when we feel our children are a burden to us, all children are assets. The structures of sin will try to persuade us to the contrary, but that is a lie, for children are full of potential and may become artisans, scientists, or world leaders. But when we keep children existing just above the point of starvation, we harvest all of their potential. In hierarchical systems, such "harvesting" is what makes production immensely less expensive and profits immensely bigger.

Thus the concept of "holy motherhood" is not a Christian invention, since wanting to become a mother is natural for women and is also a divine provision. There is certainly nothing wrong with being a mother or wishing to become one, but this reality makes it difficult to see the problem with venerating motherhood.

As we have seen before, Jesus objects to the woman who praises his mother, because the "womb that bore him and the breasts that nursed him" are secondary to listening to and believing his words (Luke 11:27–28). Just as the "goddess approach" focuses on a woman's beauty, "holy motherhood" reduces women to their reproductive organs. We may offer lip service to the beauty of motherhood and elevate mothers for their sacrificial love, but when we degrade them to birthing machines, we relegate their value to the sons they bear.

A mother's position may be more stable and preferable than the position of a goddess, because the children she bears will require more of her services. However, motherhood as its own goal is socially dangerous, because it neglects women's potential and encourages them to develop in ways that benefit the structures of sin.

Many women buy into the package of "holy motherhood," especially in Christian environments, because the self-sacrificial life sounds so spiritual. It is God-ordained, because God created her with certain reproductive organs. It is spiritual, because she is fulfilling her place in the divine hierarchy of God, husband, and her and the children. Her "cross" is to give herself up for her children and family, knowing that her great sacrifice will bring about greater good. Holy mothers feel their children's pain and need without being told. They respond to all the unspoken wishes of their family. What exceeding love!

While there is some truth to this romantic picture, the deeper truth is that everyone needs to give selflessly and love abundantly. There is also something substantially wrong with this picture, which Jesus addresses when he corrects the woman who praises his mother. A small child requires a mother's intuition and sacrifice for its well-being. When a mother first has a little one, she often experiences frustration because she doesn't know why her baby is having crying tantrums. Later, she learns to anticipate and respond to what her baby is feeling. She is becoming one with this little bundle, and it is a glorious feeling! Except, when the baby grows out of it, if the mother's only experience of intimacy is feeling one with her baby, she will want to hang onto her children forever.

But this is pathological, because it transfers the mother's own feelings and needs onto the child or young adult, and the so-called great sacrifice is revealed as great selfishness. Years ago, she lost herself, and the only option for her now is to live as a codependent, someone who insists that the other people in her life are actually herself. For instance, if her husband gets a promotion, she thinks, as the saying goes: "Behind every great man there is a great woman who holds the proverbial three corners of the house." When her children graduate, it is her accomplishment, and the children have to stay with her eternally. These mothers like to hear: "Blessed is the womb that bore you and the breasts that nursed you" (Luke 11:27).

But Jesus objected to this. A little pride in the achievements of our children is acceptable, as long as we know that they are their achievements and not ours. But when a mother insists that her grown-up daughter or daughter-in-law cannot care for her own babies, because she feels this new baby is actually also hers, she is wreaking havoc in the family. I have heard a mother threaten that she would call social services on her daughter just because the new parents had different ideas about parenting. Codependence is seen in constant interference into adult children's lives by phone calls and visits.

While there is nothing wrong with extended family meals, in our part of the world, it is an unwritten rule that adult children (sons in particular) must come "home" to meals regularly if they ever managed to leave the parents in the first place. Naturally, it is difficult to let go of your children, and being alone again may be frightening. But living through your children and having no life outside of them is a sign of worshipping "holy motherhood." Because of the mother's sacrifice, the husband and children are expected to repay that debt daily through routines that resemble worship. If they do not, they run the danger of upsetting the deity.

Furious goddesses get upset when things are not as they wish them to be, but such a response is neither godly nor Christian. Moreover, goddesses make it difficult for their husbands and children to worship God. Similarly, the all-controlling holy mother makes it difficult for her adult family to maintain a relationship with her. Their visits become rare or consist of pure duty, which is never fulfilling. Motherhood does not entitle mothers to expect payment in the form of eternal servitude. Thankfulness and respect cannot be ordered. Our children did not ask to be born, nor to receive our care. Their existence is our decision.

The commandment for children to respect their parents is their own. If their parents choke them, they will try to escape. If parents insist, or if they have raised weaklings, their behaviour will only break up the new family. "Holy mothers" must beware how damaging their so-called "love" is to the women their sons grow to love. Motherhood requests much sacrifice, but motherhood never makes the mother disappear completely as a person. So mothers need to forget the sacrifices of motherhood as their children grow. Mothers have been blessed with so much, and the blessings far transcend any sacrifices.

In most cases, a mother's life continues long after her children leave the home. As we have seen, roughly two-thirds of a woman's life will be spent on something other than motherhood. Mothers need to discover and nurture that something else during motherhood – rather than abandoning their life while they are still living it. Christian mothers, in particular, learn so many lessons as they raise their children within the structures of sin, and so it is their responsibility to find God's life for them outside of motherhood by paying attention to the gifts and opportunities on their doorsteps. Doing this will make life easier for their adult children, but it will also help mothers with small children.

Most of all, children need a mother who is more than a mother. This is a life lesson that cannot be learned any other way. What "finding yourself and keeping in touch with yourself" means in any given moment of your life is between God, the mother, and her family. I had the privilege to translate for Jill Briscoe, a renowned Christian minister and author, who led a group of women on a vision trip for World Relief during the Croatian War in the 1990s. She delivered this paradigm changing message at the women's conference we organized: "Women have got it wrong when they try to live by this popular rule: 'God is first, my family second and the church third on my list of priorities.' For Christian women, God is first. If God is first, he will handle all other priorities. Depending on what is happening, sometimes, the family comes first, sometimes the church, etc." This was great advice for me as a mom of four small children, and it is still great advice for me as a mom of adult children, who live around the world while I juggle multiple responsibilities and embark on new tasks.

Every new family has to find their own way in a world that is changing drastically, and which the old generation cannot keep up with any more. Asking new families to maintain allegiances to the old regimes is an additional burden to an already difficult task. Being a grandmother carries a different responsibility than a mother has to her child. Mothers and grandmothers will naturally come into conflict if there is nothing in their lives other than motherhood, especially if the grandmothers insist on eternal and holy motherhood.

This may be the place to call on Proverbs 31. If you are not called to be a mother for your life, what could you be doing? My travel has shown me that in some parts of the world, this is an impossible question to ask women. The list in Proverbs 31:10–31 is not exhaustive, especially in our contemporary setting, but what can it suggest when motherhood stops being a primary occupation? Interestingly, Proverbs 31 seems to come as advice from a mother to her influential son.[44] Against all tradition, this wise woman suggests that a wise man will not want a *tabula rasa* for his wife. As attractive as this may be in the beginning of a relationship, husbands do not want a clinger, a needy wife, who always needs instruction and attention. They need women of character and initiative, wise and compassionate women whose focus will be much broader than their own families. Wise women pay attention to the poor, the world and its business, and the future. This is wise advice for sons even today.

As scary as strong women may be for young, insecure men, those who want to prosper do not want weak women. Their focus should be on growing up to become strong men worthy of strong women, because strong women make the best partners for mission in the world. Women who practice and develop the gifts that God gave them for the benefit of the family and the world will strengthen their own families, and this will include helping their husbands grow up to assume the purposes of God in their life. Women who stay blank and needy soon become a nuisance to themselves, their families, and society. They are also, as is evident from the pastoral letters, a nuisance to the church, because their frustration is played out in envy, gossip, and the perpetuation of wrong teaching, since learning is not their first priority. They like to be spoon-fed with ready-to-swallow formula.

Many women's groups in the church have become places where women who have failed to live a "God first" life vent the frustrations of their godless lives. While this may be emotionally beneficial and even cathartic, it does not go further than a short-lived feeling. Such women's groups often reject

---

44. T. Longman III, "Book of Proverbs I" in *Dictionary of the Old Testament: Wisdom, Poetry, and Writings* (Downers Grove: IVP Academic, 2008), 539–552, 549–550, points to the hermeneutical lens of Prov 31 as a reference and description of the "Woman Wisdom" in Prov 1–9, who calls the young man – the probable reader of the text – to the right path. A. Barnes, *Notes on the Bible* from 1834, from Internet Sacred Texts Archive, online: https://biblehub.com/commentaries/barnes/proverbs/31.htm, writes: "If we refer the chapter to Israelite authorship, we may remember the honor paid to the wisdom of Miriam, Deborah, and Huldah." In line with this, King Lemuel's mother would be equally honoured for her wisdom. Not much is known about this king or his mother, as the name is mentioned twice in the Bible and only in Prov 31. Also, there is more than one way that theologians understand this text. Some see the introductory Wisdom chapters (1–9) and this concluding chapter on the wise woman as a type or allegory of the initial "Woman Wisdom." Others see this chapter as being modelled on a real, wise Israelite woman, such as Ruth or Deborah. See T. Hildebrandt, "Genre of Proverbs," in *DOTWPW* (Downers Grove: IVP Academic, 2008), 536. However this is understood, it is striking that the wisdom the son puts forward in the book (or oral utterance) is attributed to his mother. Lemuel would qualify as a "wise child," according to Proverbs 10:1, who was not his mother's "grief." The connection between the first and last part of the section is also discussed, but for us, it is more important to note that the source of this wisdom does not change. Either these are the words of his mother, or it is the outcome of his own observations on account of the words of his mother in the first part.

any thorough theology as difficult and unnecessary, sometimes because they shun confrontation, but mostly because they believe that theology is not for women. Therefore, women's ministry in the church is driven by emotion and "applied theology," where the theology is absent and what is "applied" is a watered-down, quasi-Christian teaching. Today, it often comes from dubious YouTube channels.

Unfortunately, church leadership rarely pays attention to this, or they send men to preach at women's meetings. But generally, church leaders are happy as long as women do not rock their hierarchies. They do not realise that unhappy women have a wide range of subtle ways to rock the boat of the church and its future – and most of them are unconscious and indirect reactions to the structures of sin, such as concealed anger and frustration. Excluding women in order to keep their negative energy out of the worship space is similar to removing kids who disturb the service. In both instances, churches are giving up on potential life now and in the future.

Yet women's work is desperately needed in the church, because amazing goals for the kingdom of God can be achieved when women find and exercise their gifts and support each other. This is extremely important because we are still living within the structures of sin. The Spirit of God is at work, and women are finding their gifts and applying them in ministry against all odds – against bad theology and bad experiences in the church. But if these ministries are not attractive to a new generation of women, they have probably been infected with the (un)holy motherhood syndrome, and they need to be overhauled so that new ministries can develop.

When God is put first, immense learning takes place – not only from past experience, but also from the knowledge of the new world that is emerging as we continue learning and developing. The process requires listening and flexibility, because the changes are taking place so rapidly. But when we are willing to change, the glory of God will be revealed anew through a new generation of women.

Dragon Women: Challenge Ungodly Structures

At the beginning of this chapter, I identified myself with this third female response to the hierarchies of sin. I realize that I share this with many women who are in positions in church leadership. We take on the fight for our place in the hierarchies head-on. This is a fair response, as we seek to compete, just as men do, for positions in the world or the church. We know our gifts and want them incorporated, and we don't try to manipulate others behind the scenes. After so much has been said about the manipulative ways of women who want to come to positions vicariously through their husbands and children, this sounds like *the* Christian way. No hidden motives. No necks that turn heads. And yet, this approach hangs, naturally, on the basic human sin of trying to climb up the hierarchies.

When I turn to this final section, I can approach it only as a sinner who has bought into this kind of sin. While there is something intrinsically good about taking up the fight openly and head-on, it does not mean that this fight is righteous. The fight needs to be seen for what it is – a struggle to prove oneself within the structures of sin. This is where it also needs to be criticized, and this criticism can benefit both women and men and also the church in general.

The first problem with this approach is the fact that some women have bought into it by segregating "women in ministry" as a special rank of women who are set apart and not to be confused with ordinary "women's ministries." This establishes a hierarchy that creates strife between women and their "ministries." We saw similar strife when the "other disciples" heard about John's and James's ambition to secure positions of honour in Jesus's kingdom (Mark 10:34–44). In the end, putting down "ordinary" women is just another way to gain privilege in male hierarchies.

In my global ministry, I have seen these fights in many contexts. In some places, the structures have accepted the "dragon women" who made up the structures. After all, the structures do anything to make people think they are good. These dragon women serve as the *ikebanas* of the male structures, women who balance the quota and shut down the discussion, without any real integration into the structures. Therefore, we are still discussing if it is biblical to have women in ministry. What exactly can women do in church? What is inappropriate?

While women "in ministry" may think that their problems are different than regular church women, who seem to be satisfied to ride on a man's coattails, it becomes evident that these problems are the same. Though women "in ministry" may have a higher position, they are still marginalized, either by not having a place, or by being given a more or less fictitious place among the men. Often, hierarchical dragon women help the hierarchical structures fight women in general, because dragon women are set apart as an example of the type of woman that cannot be included. This way is difficult and filled with rejection and pain as well as personal sacrifice, and so many women cannot easily identify with dragon women. At the same time, dragon women actively play the part of achievers who cannot be copied. They intentionally set themselves apart from "other" women and even despise them.

When these dragon women finally create space for women in the hierarchies, they often draw in men so that their achievements will not benefit other women. They have learned the ways of men, and so they identify with men rather than women. They treat women as men do. Sometimes, dragon women are said to be even worse than men, though they are only replicating the way men treat women and other men within hierarchical structures. Yet conventions do not expect women to behave this way, and there have not been enough women in these structures to model different behaviours.

The question of "women in ministry" also exposes another pragmatic problem in Baptist life and teaching. By definition, Baptists are not hierarchical. They believe in the priesthood of all saints and that women should be included on all levels.[45] Leadership roles may give people more visibility, but, in a Baptist setting, they do not come with power over others. Therefore, just as Jesus taught, leaders must be servants first. From a human perspective, and especially from the way in which social, economic, and political structures work in the world, it is felt that there is something wrong with this concept when it hits practice. How does one lead without having power over the people he leads? How can one lead without a recognized status within the church? If someone carries the responsibility for a ministry or the church (especially if money is involved), shouldn't he be able to make decisions on other people's behalf? Shouldn't they submit to his decisions?

While the world enforces such hierarchical considerations on the church, if Baptists buy into this thinking, they will lose the decisive landmark of their origin. It may seem that the Baptist insistence on the priesthood of all saints

---

45. I. M. Randall, *Communities of Conviction,* 65. Randall maintains that there were fears among the Baptists "that having trained ministers would lead to a new clerical caste" in commenting on Johann Gerhard Oncken's moto, "every member a missionary." A "forerunner confession" by Balthazar Hübmaier, an Anabaptist, in 1524 clearly states the issue that separatists had with the mainline church. Among them, article 8 refers to the equality of all believers that have been baptized. "Since every Christian believes for himself and is baptized for himself, everyone must see and judge by the Scripture whether he is being properly nourished by his pastor." Quoted in W. L. Lumpkin, *Baptist Confessions of Faith* (Valley Forge: Judson Press, 1959), 21. The *Declaration of Faith of English People* from 1611, article 11, which was published in Amsterdam, suggests that even in the absence of officers – "as yet they have no Officers, or that their Officers should be in Prison, sick, or by anie other means hindered from the church" – the people still have a right to convene as a church, and perform all the ordinances. Article 20 also mentions women and men as deacons, which is one of two supervisory offices recognized from Scripture (Lumpkin, *Baptist Confessions,* 120–122). Although for obvious reasons within the still strongly patriarchal context, women are rarely discussed outside of "believers" and baptized "men," they were almost equally present in conversion stories, and it would be valuable to investigate their active role in the churches. Almost everywhere in the account of Baptist beginnings, couples are mentioned, who accepted faith and were baptized.

is an ideal that is impossible to maintain or implement – in this world, at least. But if we allow those in the top positions to have power over others, it will necessarily spread downwards, creating strife everywhere. Moreover, it will necessarily discriminate against the weak – the poor and the "other race," or women.

This import of the standards of the world is why some Baptists still insist on headship in Baptist churches. After all, it is practical, at least when there are irreconcilable differences of opinion, for someone to make an executive decision and bring us forward. The same goes for legal liability. We give the power and right to the person who has made it up the ladder and proven himself worthy of that position. As logical as it all feels, it is still a system to which Jesus said clearly, "not so among you!" (Mark 10:43).

Investigating what it means to be Baptist in a hierarchical world is important – and not only for Baptists or Baptist women in particular. An appropriate response to this tension may open alternative models and ways to be proactive in a world that is at the ends of its wits and is losing hope in the future. "Bottom up" leadership has become highly appreciated, since it brings about progress by engaging many, particularly those on the margins. Baptists stood on this as they learned it from Jesus. Leadership is about serving others, like Jesus. It may sometimes lead to a death that someone else deserves, but it also leads toward the hope of resurrection.

So women "in ministry" are those who are already on the road toward greatness in the kingdom of God, but they need to realize that what they have suffered is the course of things within the structures of sin. They also need to realize that they cannot push for their own status within the church. As Jesus warned John and James, recognition must be left in the hands of God. Our work is to serve. This does not mean that the question about the status of women in the church should not be raised. Nor does it mean that church structures should not be criticized for failing to recognize the women who serve in their communities. On the contrary, all workers deserve recognition and even pay from their congregations. Injustices need to be brought forward and discussed. But women in ministry are also living within the structures of sin that befall the church, and we will all have to drink from Jesus's cup of suffering.

Being a strong woman is demanding and difficult, but it is tough to fight the hierarchies of sin directly in society – and even harder in the church. The world presupposes hierarchical wars and trains people for it, but the church preaches acceptance and support, and you expect everyone to be working for the same cause, giving their best rather than stabbing you in the back to gain easy points and more visibility. You expect to be recognized because of your sacrificial work, but instead, women in ministry are often dealt the whole spectre of male insecurity. Leaders who lack knowledge also tend to feature proportionally big egos. Women who run into such egos may first try to improve themselves, because women tend to assume that they are being rejected by church leaders because of their own inadequacies. They are simply not good enough. In all cultures, women are taught about their inadequacies and intrinsic sinfulness in many small and concealed ways. People may pretend they have not heard you and continue a conversation as if your contribution did not mean anything. Some behave as if you are not even in the room.

To give an example, while I was reading for my PhD about Paul's missionary strategy, I was sitting on an (all male) board that was organizing a national event on missions. A discussion started about the speakers, and someone suggested a woman, but there was a swift and decisive conclusion that there were no women who could contribute anything "on that level." Needless to say, my expertise in the matter was demonstratively higher than any of the men who ended up teaching at the event. Experiences like this make women doubt themselves. It took me years to realize that I was considered a threat to many male leaders in my region. I felt this and thought I needed to work on myself, train more, and do more to prove that I was capable and worthy. But all of my training only enforced their animosity and neglect. It was not my lack of capability and calling that made them neglect me. Rather, it was my calling and expertise that challenged their structures.

Eventually, every woman in ministry recognizes that she will never be good enough, because she will always be a woman. The heavy artillery of sporadic Scriptures will be drawn out, and when you start to defend your position, the last argument will be that it is your word against the word of a recognized Bible teacher. The list of disappointments and abuse goes on and on. It is easy for strong women to become resentful, angry, and cynical. You not only become cynical of the leaders and their leadership, but you also get angry with the many women who seem to play dumb and play games with the men. They work against you by enforcing the system you are fighting and hold down your feet like iron casts. You are always compared with these women.

When everything is added up, it would be easy to leave the church altogether – and many of us have contemplated that thought on occasion. It is truly sad that some of our best people must walk this painful path in a church that pays lip service to love and inclusion but acts the opposite. It is with great sorrow that some of the most gifted women feel they can no longer stay. They leave their church as they fight for their sanity. One can only take so much abuse and neglect. I have spoken to many capable women recently who have felt this way. We need support systems to live through this.

Thankfully, God has given me a husband who has not grown weary of listening to the frustration and who has continued to challenge me to consider the way of Christ. Thankfully, also, God has given me sisters who have modelled and championed the sweetness of Christ in the arena of global leadership in Baptist churches and beyond. This is another important reason that we need local and global organizations that respond to the suffering and pain of women and advocate for their rights.

I have learned two lessons in this. First, the church needs to make it a priority to consider how it treats women. This is a question of life and death for the contemporary church, and therefore it should be a top priority. Has your church developed ways to listen to your strong women – the executives, professors, and women in ministry? How have you treated them as the church? Do you just ignore them because it would require too much change to accommodate their gifts and ideas? Do you put it all away because most women seem happy with how things are? Do you adequately recognize the workers within your church? Are there paid positions for both men and women? Are women only accepted in times of crises and then forgotten when things go back to normal, and men take over? Such questions need to be raised, addressed, and continually asked.

Second, this is difficult to admit because I am a strong woman. But when life squeezes us, regardless of where the pressure comes from, it reveals our substance. Sometimes, the pressure reveals a nasty surprise. The suffering of the present time for strong women often comes from the structures of sin that are still at work in the body of Christ. This is very painful and difficult to handle. For a long time, this suffering made me bitter and disappointed. I cannot say I have fully overcome this bitterness and become sweet, because I know how easily I revert to the dragon when someone pushes the right buttons.

Nevertheless, I have learned to try to trust the will of God and to pass whatever has been done to me unfairly onto him. I have learned that even though there are people who will slam the door in my face and try to cut me off from this and that, from God's perspective, they are just closing a path where my gifts cannot be used to their full potential. God has a better place for me. Whenever I am suffering and can let go of the pain and observe what God is doing, I am always surprised by his amazing wisdom and the options that he opens up for me so that my enemies cannot "triumph over me" (Ps 25:2).

So far, I have only mentioned women "in ministry." A word is in order for all the warriors of Christ in the hierarchies and arenas of the world. These women are in a place that is full of opportunities for the kingdom of God, although it seems like they are abandoned and left alone, or they may feel like the whole world is on their shoulders as they handle both work and often also a family.

They must recognize for themselves where they are dancing with the devil and playing the hierarchy of sin game. A good start is to ask, why. Why am I doing all this? Who am I without my work and "all the things" under my control? Am I on a mission to prove myself to someone? Life has made us strong, but sometimes, the harshness of life has made us doubt that we are worthy of love, and so we are trying to earn it and buy it by hard work. God is not this harsh "master," but wants us to relax in the faith that he loves us. We should do the work we do out of love, not because we feel that the world will collapse if we stop to breathe.

The next question to ask is, what needs to change in the structures to make them fit *your* needs rather than the other way around (how you need to fix yourself in order to fit into the structures, which are too narrow to allow for women's needs)? Women who are strong enough to stand up to abusive structures and make them fit their needs must also work for the women who are not strong enough to fight the structures directly. Our world needs strong women who will ask tough questions, find solutions, and implement them in order to challenge the structures of sin and change them with the love of God. Regardless of what made these women strong, God places them where they are so they can become his agents of change. Women who stick their necks out for the benefit of all need prayer and fellowship. If they cannot find them in their own places, there is always the opportunity to look more broadly! This is why we need international women's work so that we can find support, experience, and the best practices. In this way, we become a factor of change in the world.

Strong Christian women in the hierarchies of the world are game changers. This does not mean that they are better than men, nor that they will create God's kingdom on earth, nor that they should even attempt to do this. Rather, it means that by being Christlike, they will be able to challenge the structures of sin on behalf of those who cannot do it themselves. This will show the captives that a different life is possible. God's glory becomes visible as we hope against all hope – and God will always have the last word.

Epilogue

Next Steps

There are many little ways that Christians can become agents of change in the world, but they all start with challenging the structures of sin by standing on the "testimony of Jesus," as John of the Revelation sometimes calls it. From what we have seen, standing on Jesus's testimony means that we intentionally and willingly stop treating ourselves and others as commodities of the gods of this world. This process of buying (manipulating) and selling people for one's own promotion on the hierarchies of sinful power promotes death in the world. All people are created by God, and so we belong to and have the right to be sustained by the earth. Whether identified as women or refugees, Roma, or untouchables, all people are born as God's handiworks. If certain people are refused sustenance – a place to live, food, air, clothing, water, even work – then someone else has unlawfully taken what is warranted by God to be rightfully theirs. The created world belongs to God and has been entrusted to us to care for, not exploit. Christians must model this kind of responsibility. Exploiting the earth is the primary trigger for human trafficking, slavery, and many other forms of abuse. Regardless of what we think concerning the threats of global warming, Christians owe it to God to treat what is his with utter respect. As Psalm 24:1 puts it, "The earth is the LORD's and all that is in it." This biblical, non-economic view of humanity will only reveal itself when we live responsibly towards the whole creation and show regard for the sanctity of all life – not just protect the interests of (some) humans.

Combatting Slavery and Human Trafficking

What has been proposed in this book can help Christians combat human trafficking, slavery, and other forms of abuse in the global world. Christians will be challenged by the difficult environments that they will engage as they fight for trafficked victims in the slums of prostitution, on the one hand, and fight against their pimps and traffickers in the criminal scene, on the other.

This work is not for the faint-hearted, as it may plunge us into the pig slop of the world, where we might find ourselves grabbing the devil by his horns, so to speak. We will need to have courage and faith.

But when we look at human trafficking, slavery, and abuse from the perspective of the structures of sin, we can see that they are not so much an anomaly, but are actually thriving on the structures of sin. To stand up to human trafficking, slavery, and abuse properly and comprehensively, we will need to understand their dynamics within the hierarchies of sin. From this perspective, the "pig stall" is the outcome, the place of death that is the end result of treating people like commodities, but the process started when men began to exclude others in order to gain godlike status and to seek to rule over them. Women are first on the list of outcasts, so men have marginalized them and tried to keep them away from the hierarchies of power. But whenever women play into this war for power and become easy victims or sell themselves to the highest bidder, they perpetuate human trafficking by believing that their life and future is in men rather than God.

This dynamic unveils the church's mission. Rather than trying to grab the devil by the horns only to get tossed around in the pig's slop, Christians need to unmask the hidden structures of sin by opposing their logic of godlessness – first in their own midst and then as they reach out to the world.

The first step in responding to human trafficking is to recognize how women are marginalized by men within the church. Though many Christians seem blind to this dynamic in the church, it is visible when we compare the number of women with men who are paid to minister in our churches. It is audible when we proclaim our oppressive theologies about the place of women in the church. It is felt through all the unwritten rules and prejudices that seek to exclude and belittle women in the church. Yet it continues to be buried whenever marital and family problems are encountered – and then concealed – in church counselling. If a church learns to see, hear, address, and challenge the hidden hierarchies of sin working within her own ranks, it will become a lamppost of hope, bearing revelatory light into the structures of sin in the world.

For instance, although the concept of freedom has become important in our modern global society, the truth about the enslavement that is happening in the world is often covered up. "Escort girls" and "immigrant workers" are euphemisms for "prostitutes" and "slaves." To fight human trafficking, we need to name what is happening: the selling of human souls. R. Bauckham rightfully dedicated a whole chapter in *The Climax of Prophecy* to listing the goods that were sold at the markets of the Roman Empire. The list in Revelation 18 ends with "slaves and human souls." Yet this chapter easily disappears from triumphant premillennial readings as spoiled Western Christians attempt to flee – as Apostle Paul put it – the "sufferings of this present time" (Rom 8:18). So far, Christians haven't been very interested in the implications of Revelation 18 for those who are profiting from and mourning for Babylon. The triumphalist reading – *"It serves them right! It will be destroyed anyway!"* – blinds the church to the depth and relevance of this Scripture for us today. We need to stay with this text long enough to perceive how our churches can be identified as one of the three groups of those who are mourning for the loss of Babylon because they profited greatly by doing business with her and taking part in her luxury (Rev 18:9). In *The Moral Vision of the New Testament*, Richard Hays concludes that Revelation is not being read correctly if it does not unsettle those who are entitled within a system and comfort those who are oppressed by the system.[1] The book of Revelation is a critique of the church – not the Roman Empire. It is the story of the church in the global society at the end of the first century CE, which has many parallels with our global society today.

Although we now have better knowledge about the geography of this planet and know that Roman Empire was not truly "global," Revelation presents a vision of the universal structures of sin to which our modern world easily subscribes. The inhabitants of the Roman Empire were living very differently from the people before them. They travelled the Mediterranean in only a week or two. They learned about other people's religions and ways of life and brought home souvenirs and recipes.[2] It is easy to imagine how this new lifestyle appealed to those who were rich enough to be able to indulge in it. It is also easy to imagine how the vast majority, who could not travel and just lived their lives in the shadows of the rich, would have tried to find ways to experience at least some of this glamour on their own. By describing the Mediterranean in the first century context, we can see its similarities with our global world today. What was ship travel back then is air travel now. Though not everyone travels, and not everyone is thrilled about multiculturalism or exploring vast lands, having the option to connect changes both those who stay at home and

---

1. R. Hays, *The Moral Vision of the New Testament* (Edinburgh: T & T Clark, 1996), 169–187. He writes: "Revelation can be read rightly only by those who are actively struggling against injustice," and, "Something very strange happens when this text is appropriated by readers in a comfortable, powerful, majority community: it becomes a gold mine for paranoid fantasies and for those who want to preach revenge and destruction" (183–184).

2. L. Casson, *Travel in the Ancient Rome* (London: George Allen & Unwin), 1974, 115–137. Comp. Strabo, *Geography* 15.1.2; from Loeb Classical Library. Online: https://archive.org/stream/Strabo08Geography17AndIndex/Strabo%2007%20Geography%2015-16#page/n15/mode/2up.

those who travel. As everyone tries to cope with the overflow of information, the ongoing fluidity and movement creates opportunities for people to leave the relatively secure nets of home. As a result, some inevitably become victims of trafficking. In a global society, this usually happens far enough away that it can be rationalized or negated.

For example, a group of Western students who came to the UN Consultation on the Status of Women (CSW) were confounded to learn that 57,000 people are trafficked each year in the US, including American citizens. Human trafficking in a global society is a huge business, and we should not be surprised that the "kings of this world" have a part in it, nor that it is everywhere. The world is driven by economics, and selling humans, drugs, and arms are the most lucrative businesses in the world.

As our contemporary global society connects, banks, and entertains itself via the Internet, human trafficking has grown immensely. Multitudes enforce it and create the demand for it without even being aware of their complicity as they live comfortable lives in the pursuit of luxuries. One look at the global poverty calculator reveals our distorted ideas about poverty.[3] I come from a country where most people will immediately admit that they are poor. However, most people have a roof over their heads (often in a single-dwelling house), a regular income of some sort (even if it is their parents' retirement money), a car, a TV, furniture, and a lot of stuff they do not need or even use. They buy clothes and shoes as needed and eat at least three meals a day. Many buy snacks on the way to work or go out for coffee (Croatia has a thriving outdoor coffee culture). People organize barbeques and celebrate birthdays, christenings, and many other occasions together. But when people measure themselves against TV programs and advertisements, they feel that they are doing poorly. In our churches, we need to take a reality check at least once a year to remind ourselves what we really need for life and to be convicted about our surplus.

Revelation 18 uncovers this problem for us, revealing that our surplus is depriving other people of the space and sustenance that God gifted to them as well, but which has landed disproportionately with us. Our surplus is creating slaves and second-class people on the other side of the world. Globalisation has blinded us to the unjust treatment of workers who make the luxury goods

---

3. For instance, in *Pew Research Centre*, online: https://www.pewresearch.org/fact-tank/2015/07/16/are-you-in-the-global-middle-class-find-out-with-our-income-calculator/. Or the world poverty clock, online, https://worldpoverty.io/headline.

to which we think we are entitled. The evil Babylon speaks the language of entitlement:

> I rule as a queen;
> I am no widow,
> and I will never see grief. (Rev 18:7)

Christians often recite this with an aura of spirituality. After all, we are "sons and daughters of the King," and so we are entitled to a good life, one that will never see grief. But entitlement precedes the great fall. As the church, we must take this lesson seriously. The seer of Revelation hears a heavenly voice, calling on God's people:

> Come out of her, my people,
> so that you do not take part in her sins,
> and so that you do not share in her plagues;
> for her sins are heaped high as heaven,
> and God has remembered her iniquities. (Rev 18:4–5)

Coming "out of her" starts with the recognition that we are not poor, but rich – a message that Christ has for the church in Smyrna (Rev 2:9). "Coming out of her" is a spiritual and physical distancing that is preceded by spiritual insight and faith in God, where we recognize that we need much less than "Babylon" requires through her constant demand-expanding commercials. The definition of "poor" in a culture that is pursuing luxuries is misleading, and Christians need to take a long and hard look at their own lives and life narratives. Have we swallowed the bait? Is it time to give God what is already his?

Revelation 18 promises that "Babylon" is coming down, and it features three groups of people who will come down with her and mourn her destruction. First, there are the kings of the world who "fornicate" with the "great prostitute" (Rev 18:9–10). The language is harsh, but it is no different from the ramblings we hear about politicians in pubs, especially during elections. Those at the top of the hierarchies of power buy and sell others to stay in the game, with Babylon as the super-power who impersonates God. Paradoxically, without the cooperation of those who are being bought and sold, Babylon could never become so powerful. Second, there are the "shipmasters and seafarers, sailors and all whose trade is on the sea" (18:17). Babylon needs these workers for easy communication, so that the goods and money can be transported. These people are the in-between men who connect power with the economy. Third, there are the merchants, who do the selling and the buying of luxury goods (18:11–17): the "cargo of gold, silver, jewels and pearls, fine linen, purple, silk and scarlet, all kinds of scented wood, all articles of ivory, all articles of costly wood, bronze, iron, and marble, cinnamon, spice, incense, myrrh, frankincense, wine, olive oil, choice flour and wheat, cattle and sheep, horses and chariots, *slaves – that is, human lives*" (18:12–13).

According to the End Child Labour in Tobacco Industry Foundation (ECLT), there are over 40 million slaves on all continents today. Women comprise 71 percent, and one in four is a child.[4] These people may be sex workers as a result of human trafficking or forced labourers (particularly in agriculture and fishing industries, but also in textile and computer production), producing luxuries that drive our culture of indulgence. The entire world makes an estimated 150 billion USD profit from slavery each year, and developed economies alone earn 47 billion.[5]

All this underlines the fact that laws, as important as they are, cannot accomplish much. Laws are reactive. They are activated after a criminal act has already been committed, and, in many places, the system is extremely slow. Human traffickers and modern-day slave holders work the system to their benefit. While many people try to raise awareness, advocate for, and get involved in humanitarian action to help victims of human trafficking, there are few results. In a session at the CSW of the UN, I learned to see how rescuing one woman out of forced prostitution only frees the space for another woman to be trafficked to fill the vacancy.

While saving even a single victim is important, real change only comes from a humble and compassionate heart, which voluntarily gives up luxury because it hurts people – even on the other side of the world. When you do this, economically speaking, you are eliminating demand and making a huge impact.

In combatting human trafficking, eliminating demand should be the rule. This means that churches need to name and oppose the male drive to rule over others, including over women. As we have seen, this is Jesus's own command. Whenever we do otherwise, we submit to the lords of this world and do as they do. This includes sexual behaviour. Prostitution and human trafficking can end only if those who buy women stop this demand. Churches need to uncover the sin that is hidden in the myth that a home is a man's castle. It is not

---

4. Online: https://www.eclt.org/en/news-and-insights/facts-on-modern-slavery-a-global-problem.

5. International Labour Office, *Profits and Poverty: The Economics of Forced Labour*. Online: https://www.ilo.org/wcmsp5/groups/public/---ed_norm/---declaration/documents/publication/wcms_243391.pdf, 13.

enough to relegate sexual education in the church to sporadic general decrees from the pulpit, such as, "You shall not commit adultery!" There needs to be clear instruction about why people are prone to commit adultery and how they can escape. Adultery is common in the church – and not only for a few sporadic people. We need to help one another admit to our struggles and ask for forgiveness if we are going to recover a path of freedom. Unfortunately, even though we live in a highly sexualized global society, and the Bible has a lot to say about sex, these topics are so embarrassing to church leadership that they hardly ever hit the pulpit. If the church misses this topic, Christians will be instructed about sexuality and power from other sources: film, porn, the Internet, and advertisements. These sources will perpetuate the culture of sin and death in the church. If the instruction of Christians about sexuality comes from Hollywood, glossy magazines, and a blooming porn industry that is easily accessible from our homes online, we should not be surprised by all the sexual sin in the church. "I have a right to have my sexual needs fulfilled," a philandering married woman who called herself Christian insisted. Though she is born as a sexual being and has that "right," her right stops when it hurts other people.

We not only have a church that is blind to this issue, we also have a church that hurts the victims. I have talked to Christian women whose Christian husbands have been unfaithful to them for years, and the only council they got from the church was to accept their cross and keep the secret for the sake of their family. When these women finally drew a boundary and threatened to leave their husbands, the church blamed the women for splitting up the family. Churches rarely blame philandering husbands or their acts as the root of evil – even though adultery is biblically defined as "divorce" (Matt 5:31–32). Rather, women are blamed for not forgiving their husbands as would Jesus do. The undertone of this is that women somehow *make* their husbands seek other women.

Ugly sins such as human trafficking have many faces and deep roots. Christians must uncover and address them in their own midst first and then, as a testimony of new life, in the wider society. Though the complexities of human trafficking and modern-day slavery seem overwhelmingly complicated, the Bible has a simple rule of thumb: do to others what you would like them to do to you. We need to stop creating demand in the church now. We need to teach women and men to live in unity as equal children of God. If only the hundreds of millions of Baptists in the world took this seriously and started living as equals in their homes, churches, and neighbourhoods, they could generate a global tipping point towards change.

This reasoning has wide consequences for church strategies and church rhetoric. Take, for instance, the word "evangelism." Evangelism should not mean only "to speak the word of salvation," but, in this case, "to speak the word of how Jesus saves you from your sinful sexual desires and how that has saved your family." Or it could be "to speak the word about how Jesus saves you by giving you a faith in a future during your times of despair, so that you do not need to throw yourself on a man for security." This is biblical language and not some new social invention. God's gospel did not come in general terms, but "in word" that is confirmed by deed and by the power of the Spirit of God (Rom 15:18–19). If this re-definition scares us, we should ask ourselves when our gospel became only a general teaching, a philosophy that needs no material proof of a changed life. We may discover that this happened when the church abandoned its countercultural existence in the world and began to accept leaders whose hearts were still bound and obedient to the structures of sin.

For all these reasons and for many more, God's boundaries about sex make a lot of sense because they identify the intricate structures of sin and how they are marketed in the church. The church must teach and proclaim God's standards and power within our hyper-sexualized culture. The church must offer proper counsel and care for the victims and also challenge the perpetrators in order to bring God's shalom to all. The church must tackle difficult discussions and address issues that have been hidden under the carpet for many generations, creating trans-generational havoc in relationships and hurting the testimony of the church. The church must re-evaluate traditions and structures that govern her life, such as the superficially pragmatic definition of sin as an arbitrary sinful deed. Ungodly practices originate from the top by those who hold the power. This has been revealed by both historical and recent revelations about sexual abuses and sexual misconduct within many Christian denominations – including Baptists. Uncovering the works of evil always presents an opportunity to confront deeper issues and move forward as a church. The structures of sin will resist all these efforts, because repentance interferes with the economy of trafficking. Those who are free cannot be commodities, and they are also poor customers.

Addressing human trafficking is a complicated issue that requires the whole church to confront the sinful structures of the world. We will need to let go of our "holy ignorance" and indignation. We will have to admit that evil things can – and do – happen in the church. We will need to tackle our own sinful bodies and renounce the structures of sin that we have created. Only when we oppose sin can we become a countercultural force, a visible presence of the good news that will bear light and hope into the darkness of the world.

Women's Ministries in the Church

A biblical theology about mending male-female relationships in the church must include a word about women's ministries. Globally, there is discussion about whether we need women's ministries, especially among younger women. Accordingly, this once thriving work is now speedily declining in many places. For many years, I had my own doubts about the need for this ministry even though I was involved in it. As women get older, they can become truly tedious in their need to (s)mother everyone. They seem to lose their grip on the world and live in the past. That said, I now believe that the church cannot become a witness in the world if it is not fuelled by a vibrant local and vocal women's ministry. Following are three reasons that women's ministry is deeply important to the work of the church in the world.

Challenging Hierarchical Church Structures

First, the hierarchies of sin must be challenged. They cannot be challenged effectively by the gods (entitled people) from within, because the truth is that privilege does not like to share. Women, as we have seen, experience the death of the world more immediately than men because they tend to be confined to the lowest rungs of the hierarchical structures. Girls experience inequality in their homes from a young age, and they grow up learning the language of captives, which is unknown to the lords at the top of hierarchies. "I am blind to the issue of women," a brother in the church told me. "I never differentiate. It is always the best that get the job." Indeed, he was blind, for even after this confrontation, he could not see what might be wrong with his all-male leadership team. The darkness and death of the world hits women much earlier than men, and they do not have the luxury to be blind to it.

People are generally blind to sin and death. When God threatened Adam with death if he ate from the "tree of knowledge of good and evil" and warned him that on "that day" he "shall die" (Gen 2:17), Adam didn't seem to die, for he continued to live for another eight hundred years (Gen 5:4). But death became evident to Eve when she had to mourn the death of her son, Abel, at the hands of her other son, Cain, and only the birth of Seth brought her some comfort (Gen 4:25), for with Seth, "people began to invoke the name of the LORD" (*Yahweh*, Gen 4:26).

The discussions about the historicity of these primeval accounts are a hot topic in some Christian circles, but that is not the point here. Adam died eventually, but death as a result of sin entered the world immediately. Adam was created for eternity, and yet he died by his own choice. Today, the structures of sin that Adam introduced seem to be running the world toward its deadly end. The Germans recently announced that we are using up the earth's resources much faster every year.[6] In 2019, a single year's allowance of the earth's resources was used up by July 29; the year before it was not used up until October. As the world population explodes, the resources are squandered away by the so-called civilized nations, and large regions of the world are futilely trying to catch up with consumption rather than slow it down. Around the world, women are feeling the pain as they cannot feed their children even one proper meal a day.[7] These women need to speak up and challenge the world about this and other issues, such as violence and abuse of all forms, including disrespect, belittlement, discrimination, and exploitation.

Women's ministries in the church need to amplify abused and marginalized women's voices around the world regarding the pain and suffering that they are experiencing. Women need to join their voices together and shout so that the church can hear them and seek to respond to the victims and challenge the perpetrators as well as the structures of sin and death that abuse women. When this happens, the blindness within churches will be healed, and Christians will become much more sensitive about other forms of discrimination, injustice, and slavery.

Incarnating the Good News in the World

Second, women have an important role to play in helping to sustain mission work around the world through their incarnational (i.e. practical, hands-on) involvement. At the beginning of this millennium, the Women's Missionary Union (WMU) helped me to see the amazing impact that women have had on the church.[8] To give one example, the Women's Department of the Baptist Union in South Africa have helped make South Africa a better place through

---

6. Ch. Elsner, "Von heute an leben wir auf Pump" in *ZDF Heute*, July 29, 2019. Online: https://www.zdf.de/nachrichten/heute/welt-ueberlastungstag-2019-von-heute-an-leben-wir-auf-pump-100.html.

7. According to Food Aid, a British Foundation, 1 out of 7 people in the world are hungry while 1/3 of food produced perishes unused. Their statistics also show that "Poor nutrition causes nearly half (45%) of deaths in children under five – 3.1 million children each year." Online: https://www.foodaidfoundation.org/world-hunger-statistics.html.

8. WMU work and vision can be observed online: http://www.wmu.com/. Their headquarters are in Birmingham, Alabama.

work opportunities, retreats, and other projects.⁹ In my own region, the gospel was carried forward by women in the church. Women tackled alcoholism, taught children, brought the poorest children to summer camps, connected our region to the larger community of Baptist women, and supported the work of the church financially, helping to keep it alive and thriving, particularly during times of crisis. As I have already mentioned, almost everyone in church leadership in our country – both male and female – has been trained in one way or another by women.

Women's organizations mobilize resources to give a concrete face to the gospel. They also challenge the church and confront the darkness of the world – even when the church is deaf to their voices. Lottie Moon,[10] the founder of the WMU, was rejected as a missionary because she was a woman, but she transformed her fate by making missionary outreach possible for anyone who felt called. The WMU supports global mission by training the next generation of girls in the US and abroad. Women's ministries have shown how we can change the world by living the word rather than just preaching it.

Seeking to incarnate the gospel is not the same as seeking to inaugurate the kingdom of God on our own. Historically, some Christians have thought that they could inaugurate the kingdom of God in the world if those at the top of the hierarchies professed Christianity – a thought that often comes to Christians when they evaluate their political leaders. During the fourth century, the Roman Emperor, Constantine, deemed Christianity as the only state religion after the church endured three centuries of systemic tribulations.[11] However

---

9. Some of the work of the Women's Department of the Baptist Union, South Africa, which is only the tip of the iceberg, can be traced in their official blog online, http://baptwomen.blogspot.com/, along with the official page of the BU, https://www.baptistunion.org.za/index.php/fi/departments/baptist-woman. Neither website gives a full picture of their involvement, which is a common problem with women's work, which hardly has the visibility it should have in many places.

10. C. Parker, "Lottie Moon," in *New Georgia Encyclopaedia: Religion*, online: https://www.georgiaencyclopedia.org/articles/arts-culture/lottie-moon-1840-1912; also C. B. Allen, *The New Lottie Moon Story* (Nashville: Broadman Press, 1980).

11. There is substantial discussion among scholars whether this "Constantinian Shift" was an important and disturbing development which should be a warning sign for today (a theory conceived in Anabaptism of the 16th century but widely publicized more recently by J. H. Yoder, "Is There Such a Thing as Being Ready for Another Millennium," in M. Volf et al. eds, *The Future of Theology: Essays in Honour of Jürgen Moltmann* [Grand Rapids: Eerdmans, 1996], 65), or ambiguous for the future of the church (P. Leithart, *Defending Constantine: The Twilight of an Empire and the Dawn of Christendom* [Downers Grove: InterVarsity Press, 2010]; for instance, he points out that while Constantine may have introduced Christianity, it was for pragmatic reasons e.g. quoting A. Momigliano – that Christians discovered how to make barbarians members of the church, because 'the ordinary barbarian was . . . a nightmare' to the Romans. Therefore what seems a defence of the church in the East is in fact a defence of

we evaluate this historically, the first church history written by Eusebius of Caesarea identifies the triumphalism that became evident in the church after this event.[12] Today, many still mark it as the beginning of the "darkness" of the middle ages, when the church became married to politics. Though the Bible calls us to action in the world, God has a great grand finale for the earth that is dependent on his own will. However, biblically speaking, our behaviour and the earth both have a part to play in this eschatological event, because we can create patches of hope and new life amidst the darkness and death of the world.

In nineteenth-century England, the pandemonium of the industrial revolution brought the majority of people up to the edge of their existence. Marx and Engels had gloomy predictions, but then factory workers and industrialists encountered the gospel, and the climate changed. The anticipated bloody revolution failed to materialize[13] as many people began to live and even thrive because of the gospel. Globalization needs to be shaped by a truly human face, and women's ministries in Christian churches are a natural starting point because women tend to feel the pain of the structures of sin first. Thus they often know what is needed to bring about change. The Spirit of God within them urges them to care instead of curse, to respond instead of complain about the darkness. As Christian men accept the challenge from women, change direction, and join this mission, they will help dismantle the hierarchies of sin. As we trust together that God cares for us while we care for others and the world, our faith will grow. Communities will find their strength and potential

---

the Empire, 292). See a fuller discussion in J. D. Roth, *Constantine Revisited* (Eugene: Wipf & Stock, 2013).

12. Eusebius in his *Vita Constantinae* writes from the enthusiastic vision that finally heaven dawned on Earth when the Roman Emperor Constantine conquered Rome (1:91: "All the nations, too, as far as the limit of the western ocean, being set free from the calamities which had heretofore beset them, and gladdened by joyous festivals, ceased not to praise him as the victorious, the pious, the common benefactor: all, indeed, with one voice and one mouth, declared that Constantine had appeared by the grace of God as a general blessing to mankind." Also: II.19); supported the Christian church by lavishing on them many material blessings (e.g. I:92), including sponsoring (and some say, influencing) the world council in Nicaea (I:94). See also an extensive exposition on Eusebius and his relationship to Emperor Constantine in A. C. McGiffert, *The Church History of Eusebius* (Cincinnati: Lane Theological Seminary, 1890), 21–22.

13. Ch. Armstrong, "About God's Business," *Christian History* 110 (214). Online: https://christianhistoryinstitute.org/magazine/article/about-gods-business, evaluates Elie Halévy's thoughts published in *England in 1815* (New York: Barnes & Noble, 1961); *The Birth of Methodism* (Chicago: Chicago University Press, 1971); *The Liberal Awakening 1815–1830* (New York: Barnes & Noble, 1961). Halévy attributed England's success to handle the pandemonium of the English industrial revolution to "the silent influence exercised over the nation by these independent churches of the lower middle class . . . These free churches created an atmosphere in which the two mighty watchwords, revolution and reaction, were emptied of their significance," vi.

from the small people who are brave enough to hope in God and take action. The net of darkness no longer seems intricate or scary when even a small light is turned on.

Coming Together in Solidarity, Equality, and Unity

Third, women's ministry nurtures Christian solidarity, because whenever we stand together, we bear light into the darkness of the world. Women are natural connectors, because they have had to learn to help one another in order to survive. Because women have not been indoctrinated by the titans at the top of the structures of sin, they tend not to use inculturation in their "outreach," a method that has been heavily critiqued because its goal is to adapt another culture to our own because we think ours is superior and we have the "right" theology. Women understand that mission must be "from everywhere to everywhere,"[14] and so they exchange experiences, resources, and best practices to further the cause of God as they live out his vision for love, justice, and peace in the world.

To give an example of women working together, a bunch of women in Nepal decided that they needed to stand together against their abusive alcoholic husbands, who were squandering the family's money on alcohol and then beating their wives and children. There was never any money for education or the needs of daily life, and so the women decided that they would all come to the rescue of anyone whose husband came home drunk. They came together and told their husbands that their salaries had to be invested in the household rather than alcohol. If any husband became violent, all the women stood with the woman who was being attacked. The men were intimidated by having to face so many women at once, and so they gave in slowly. They stopped drinking, and then the abuse stopped. They started working regular jobs, which brought in regular income, which improved conditions for the children. Rather than being abused, traumatized, and hungry, roaming the streets to beg or work, the children started going to school and concentrating on learning. Family life at home became much happier for everyone – including the men. They stopped feeling powerless and became proud of their achievements as well as the achievements of their children, who began to graduate from school.

As we have already seen in Corinthians, Paul describes a wealth of problems that also apply to our modern-day church. Even the Apostle Paul's church

---

14. Comp. P. Borthwick, *Western Christians in Global Mission: What's the Role of the North American Church?* (Downers Grove: InterVarsity Press, 2012), 39.

is imperfect, for in his Eucharist requirements, he criticises the Corinthians for "humiliating the poor." This requirement reveals the darkness that the structures of sin create. In my global work with women, I have seen such humiliation of the poor, and I have also seen contempt for the poor from the rich. However, most affluent Christians are blind to this dynamic because they live their lives without being aware of other people's struggles.

To give one example, the BWA has thought a lot about how to host Baptist global meetings, since most participants cannot afford four- or five-star hotels. While these larger, high-class hotels in more expensive countries can accommodate conferences for many people and provide food and space for breakout sessions, the poor can only come on scholarships, and so they enjoy the fellowship as second-class citizens. They have to stay in a different hotel, eat takeout sandwiches between meetings, get up much earlier to arrive for the meetings, and return to their beds much later. When they are gracefully invited to a local restaurant by someone who can afford it (which happens often), they become painfully aware of their poverty, experiencing pleasure (because it is an experience they cannot afford themselves), shame (because the manners of the place may be beyond their clothes), and defeat (because they know that at home, they could live for a month on what was squandered for one meal). This makes the experience extremely difficult, even if it is offered with the best intentions and love. This is just one of many examples that can help us ponder the question, *how can we come together as equals in Christ?*

We need to enforce the premise of equality and being one in Christ. Solo Christianity (including mono-culturalism) is causing the church to malfunction and die. Paul's suggestion to rich Corinthians to "eat at home" and to enjoy their privileges in the privacy of their own social environments is neither a blessing of their wealth nor a licence to neglect the poor. Rather, when Christ followers come together at the Lord's table, they should wait for one another before they begin eating so that they can experience equality, albeit for a short moment, which is different from their segregated places in the hierarchies of the world. Paul urges the Corinthians to declutter their life from social and cultural agendas so that the Lord's table can be exclusively about Christ and equality.

For this to happen, Christians will need to examine their souls regarding their individual sins and ask for forgiveness. But the equality of the Lord's table beckons them to a much deeper examination, one that moves beyond legalistic preoccupations with their personal souls towards a deepening awareness about how their actions affect the body of Christ and its witness in the world. The Lord's table (or any meeting where Christians gather because of the Lord) must be equally open to all. As unusual as Paul's advice sounds at first, it is in harmony with his other claims that social change and freedom can only emerge within those who are reconciled to God; they cannot be ordered through external regulations and laws.

Imagine the exercise of coming together as equals once a week (or even once a month), where Christians intentionally forget their social differences and behave as equals, where no culture is allowed to overpower another because of social status, rank, colour, title, or money, where there is no culture of false humility trying to manipulate the rich to share what they have. As people come to the Lord's table to partake in this mercy, they also draw closer to each other. Christians cannot draw nearer to the Lord without drawing nearer to others at the table. When we refuse to draw near to brothers and sisters in Christ, we refuse to come closer to the Lord. Paul believes that closeness in the presence of the Lord facilitates change. Spiritual proximity helps people come to know and cherish each other as they share their lives with one another. As people share life together, it becomes difficult to return home to social distinctions and feelings of entitlement and pride. *If my brothers and sisters have so little, how come I have so much? If what I have is God's mercy and not earned by my two hands, then how can I share with others just as God has shared heaven with me? What are the resources that God has given me to share?* When we recognize the body of Christ in this way, we become powerful tools for evangelism in a world of unbridgeable differences. When we learn to see the other parts of Christ's body and respond to their needs, the blood (Christ) finally begins to circulate through the whole body, bringing oxygen and nutrients to each part, nourishing and empowering the body to work together to bear good news into the world. If the blood doesn't circulate in this way, the body will stagnate and die.

From what we have seen, women who have endured pain within the structures of sin tend to understand the need to work together in this way much better. For this reason, empowering the community is more often seen in women's work. Also, women around the world need the reassuring presence of their sisters in Christ, because they so often grow up with extreme self-doubt, and so they are insecure about their abilities and gifts. I have seen doubt in highly educated women in the West as well as the majority world. Coming together as Christian sisters in a global community helps us verbalize our problems, model ways of overcoming oppression, and encourage one another toward action. It also makes us aware of the prejudices and traditions that hold us back even as the Spirit of God spurs us to bring about change within our own lives and the life of our communities.

When the Bible speaks of shalom – peace – I think of this kind of exchange of resources, this kind of functioning, where everyone participates, shares, and receives one another's resources "in order that there may be a fair balance" (2 Cor 8:14). The "fair balance" is not just about the money. Riches come in many packages – such as wisdom, intuition, experience, intelligence, a wide perspective, resilience, local knowledge, scientific understanding, artistic expression, a gift for figures or bookkeeping, the gift of writing . . . The list is endless and continues to expand as the world develops. I see this exchange as a sort of *perichoresis* (i.e. circumincession),[15] where we remain who we are while all we have fills the space and is equally accessible to all in order to enable everyone to function in the best possible way.

It is an awful waste when these resources remain trapped within marginalized people because the structures of sin discriminate against them or tradition diminishes them. The structures of sin and death seek to trap and lock up potential so that sin can continue to produce more sin and death without being disturbed. Women's work unleashes the resources and unlocks the potential that can help transform churches into places of God's shalom. Though bringing about such changes may feel like chaos or even suffering, it is necessary and good, for Paul reminds us that our suffering now is nothing compared with the resurrection glory that will eventually be revealed in God's children for the whole creation to enjoy.

Though the focus of this book so far has been the call to the church "to come out of Babylon," blessing the curse has a wonderful flip side in the final chapters of Revelation. Three more passages follow after the call to "come out of her" in Revelation 18:4 and they conclude the vision with a heavenly city descending to the world. God has been building it and polishing it through the hardships of tribulation. The pain and struggles were not in vain.

These last passages in Revelation are more difficult to interpret than the rest of the book. They are governed by the conjunction "and" which creates the feeling that John is just collecting random items from his vision of eternity and does not know how to put them together. There were scholars who suggested

---

15. Alister MacGrath, *Christian Theology: An Introduction* (London: Blackwell, 2011), 242, explains that *perichoresis* allows us "to think of the Godhead as a community of 'being' in which all is shared, united and mutuality exchanged." There are excellent thoughts on how this is relevant for the church in F. S. Fiddes, *Participating in God: A Pastoral Doctrine of the Trinity* (London: Darton, Longman & Todd, 2000), 15, who points readers to the "vigorous and perceptive" work of the Orthodox scholar J. Zizioulas. For me, *perichoresis* became more than a doctrine through pondering over the necessary boundaries in human relationships and how a community can be built with the necessary and healthy delineation of persons in a counselling setting.

that the original author never managed to sort out this part of revelation, because he had died, or was otherwise prevented. So his disciples or an editor just pulled together the loose items into some kind of arbitrary order.[16] This editor had a difficult task, because there were more questions than answers in those visions. Why would a millennial kingdom need to precede the final scenario? Why would there be a need for healing leaves of the trees in New Jerusalem? Why would there need to be a warning that "nothing unclean will enter it, nor anyone who practices abomination or falsehood, but only those who are written in the Lamb's book of life" (Rev 21:27)?

Yet, these questions only emerge if we look at Revelation as futuristic, a prediction of circumstances remote from those of the readers. But if Revelation is read as an epistle, that is, as a letter occasioned by the circumstances in the church, and by a vision of the church's[17] possible fate and future, things fall in place. We realize that the author brings everything back to the initial challenge to a church. It may on its way now go through the "sufferings of the present times" (to borrow the language from Paul's Rom 8:18) and John sees this even intensifying to the extreme soon. But there is a purpose in all of it. It is a process of purification. The churches John addressed he sees as lamp posts and stars in the night of this world right now. They must not lose their light and their position. If they do, if they succumb to the ways of the world they will become darkness as well. They will have no part in the perfect divine city; they will not be the bride of Christ. The warning of Revelation 18:4–5 is then echoed as the concluding warning in 21:27: "But nothing unclean will enter it, nor anyone who practices abomination or falsehood, but only those who are written in the Lamb's book of life." Only those holding on to Jesus during the hard times will be ready to participate in the vision.

The vision of the future is combined with epistolary instruction to the church to present a goal worth pursuing. It comes with the promise, not of a paradise regained, but of a new and improved divine reality. It is out of the scope of my book to elaborate on the exegetical options of this picture – but

---

16. E.g. R. H. Charles, *A Critical and Exegetical Commentary on the Revelation of St. John*, vol. 2 (Edinburgh: T & T Clark, 1920), 144–154.

17. There is substantial agreement among the scholars that the seven churches of Asia Minor in Revelation 1–3 were meant to represent the church in John's time, or at least, all the churches which he knew in Asia Minor. C. A. Coates seems to think that there is a general agreement among his contemporaries in 1923 that "These assemblies are viewed as representing all the assemblies, seven being a number suggestive of completeness," in *An Outline of the Revelation* (London: Stow Hill Bible and Tract Depot, 1923), 5; comp. W. Ramsay, *The Letters to the Seven Churches* (Whitefish: Kessinger, 2004), 50–51; also A. Pohl, *Offenbarung des Johannes, Teil 1* (Wuppertal: Brockhaus, 1973), 65–67.

as a conclusion to this book, I will point us to some features which should sound very familiar:

The same angel that brought the downfall of Babylon, shows John the new heavenly city (as the bride of Christ it can be identified as the church; Rev 21:9). It is completely divinely polished – it is no longer a mere lamp post or a lone star in the darkness of the universe; it can be measured by angelic measures and found perfect (21:15–16). It is so perfect that God and the Lamb dwell in it without the need to separate in a temple: Do they dwell in and through their inhabitants in a perfect *perichoresis*, maybe (21:22)? The new Jerusalem is an inclusive place for all the nations and all bring in the best of what they have got, all their glory (21:26). Everything is accepted. It is a place where all the nations finally find healing and sustenance because of the wonderful river of life and in the trees around it. There will be no tears, no sickness and no death (7:17). But most interestingly, "there will be no curse" (from the Greek: 22:2)! And finally, only one will be worshipped in the New Jerusalem and he will be among his people.

This is the agenda and goal to which the children of God have been called and to which they must aspire here and now already – as it is their preparation time for eternity. There is a promise that by uncovering and tackling the night of the curse in the church we embark on the work of God towards a glorious church and a new world.

Bibliography

Abramsohn, J. "Chancellor Angela Merkel and Her Quiet Rise to Power." In *Deutsche Welle*, no date. Online: https://www.dw.com/en/chancellor-angela-merkel-and-her-quiet-rise-to-power/a-1600411.

Achtemeier, P. J. *Romans*. Atlanta: J. Knox, 1985.

Adams, E. *Constructing the World: A Study in Paul's Cosmological Language*. Edinburgh: T & T Clark, 2000.

Adebayo, B. "A Kenyan Doctor Is Seeking to Legalize Female Genital Mutilation." *CNN*, 25 Oct 2019. Online: https://edition.cnn.com/2019/10/25/africa/kenya-doctor-fgm-petition-intl/index.html.

Aijazuddin, A. "Rethinking Geography in the Postmodern World." In *Space, Society, and Geography*, edited by S. Banerjee-Guha. Jaipur; Delhi: Rawat Publications, 2002.

Allan, R. *Missionary Methods: St. Paul's or Ours?* Cambridge: Lutterworth Press, 2006.

Allen, C. B. *The New Lottie Moon Story*. Nashville: Broadman Press, 1980.

Allen, P. *The Concept of Woman: The Aristotelian Revolution, 750 BC–AD 1250*, vol. 1. Grand Rapids: Eerdmans, 1997.

Ambrose. *On Paradise*. Online: http://www2.iath.virginia.edu/anderson/commentaries/Amb.html.

Anić, R. *Kako razumjeti rod? Povijest rasprave i različta razumijevanja u Crkvi*. Zagreb: Institut društvenih znanosti Ivo Pilar, 2011.

Armstrong, C. "About God's Business." *Christian History* 110 (2014). Online: https://christianhistoryinstitute.org/magazine/article/about-gods-business.

Augustine, Aurelius. *Confessions*. Translated by A. C. Outler. Dallas: Southern Methodist University, 1955. Online: https://www.ling.upenn.edu/courses/hum100/augustinconf.pdf.

Aune, D. E. *The New Testament and Its Literary Environment*. Philadelphia: Westminster, 1987.

Bach, A., ed. *Women in the Hebrew Bible: A Reader*. New York; London: Routledge, 1999.

Bacon, B. W. "Pharisees and Herodians in Mark." *SBL* 39 (1920): 102–112.

Barnes, Albert. "Genesis." In *Notes on the Bible*, accessed online through *Bible Hub*: https://biblehub.com/commentaries/barnes/genesis/1.htm.

Barnes, E. *Coming Together: A History of the Women's Department, Baptist World Alliance*. Falls Church: BWA Women's Department, 2010.

Barrett, C. K. *A Commentary on the Epistle to the Romans*. London: Adam & Charles Black, 1959.

———. *The First Epistle to the Corinthians*. London: Adam & Charles Black, 1968.

Barth, K. *Kurze Erklärung des Römerbriefs*. München: Chr. Kaiser Verlag, 1964.

———. *The Epistle to the Romans*. Oxford: Oxford University Press, 1968.
Barth, M., and H. Blanke. *Colossians*. New York: Doubleday, 1994.
Bartholomew, C., ed. *A Royal Priesthood*. Carlisle: Paternoster, 2002.
Bartholomew, C., and F. Hughes, eds. *Explorations in a Christian Theology of Pilgrimage*. Aldershot: Ashgate, 2004.
Bassler, J. *Divine Impartiality: Paul and a Theological Axiom*. Chico: Scholars Press, 1982.
Batha, E. "US Woman Says Strict Christian Parents Subjected Her to FGM." *Reuters*, 1 April 2019. Online: https://www.reuters.com/article/us-usa-religion-fgm/us-woman-says-strict-christian-parents-subjected-her-to-fgm-idUSKCN1RD2LI.
Bauckham, R. *Climax of Prophecy*. London: T & T Clark, 1993.
Baumert, Norbert. *Antifeminismus bei Paulus*. Würzburg: Echter Verlag, 1992.
Baur, F. C. "Über Zweck und Veranlassung des Römerbriefs und die damit zusammenhängenden Verhältnisse der römischen Gemeinde." *Tübinger Zeitschrift für Theologie* 3 (1836): 59–178.
Becker, J. *Die Auferstehung der Toten im Urchristentum*. Stuttgart: KBW, 1976.
———. "Erwägungen zur ezechielischen Frage." In *Künder des Wortes. Beiträge zur Theologie der Propheten*, edited by L. Ruppert et al., 137–149. Würzburg: Schreiner, 1982.
Becker, S. O., A. Fernandez, and D. Weichselbaumer. "Discrimination in Hiring Based on Potential and Realized Fertility: Evidence from a Large-Scale Field Experiment." *Labour Economics* 19 (2019): 139–152. Online: https://rm.coe.int/168046031c.
Beker, J. C. *Paul the Apostle: The Triumph of God in Life and Thought*. Philadelphia: Fortress, 1980.
Beliakova, N., and M. Dobson. *Zhenshchiny v evangel'skikh obshchinakh poslevoennogo SSSR, 1940–1980 gg.* [Women in Evangelical Congregations of the Postwar USSR, 1940–1980]. Moscow: Indrik, 2015.
Belz, L. M. *The Rhetoric of Gender in the Household of God: Ephesians 5:21–33 and Its Place in Pauline Tradition*. Doctoral thesis. Chicago: Loyola University, 2013.
Berger, P., and Th. Luckmann. *The Social Construction of Reality: A Treatise in the Sociology of Knowledge*. London: Penguin, 1976.
Bernstein, A., and K. M. Jones. "The Economic Effects of Contraceptive Access: A Review of the Evidence." Online at *Institute for Women's Policy Research*, https://iwpr.org/publications/economic-contraceptive-access-review/.
Besançon, S. A. "If Jesus Were Really Counter-Cultural in His Treatment of Women, Why Didn't He Choose Any Women to Be His Apostles?" *Mutuality* (2009) 18. Online: https://www.cbeinternational.org/sites/default/files/tough_spencer.pdf.
Betts, T. J. *Ezekiel the Priest: A Custodian of the Tora*. New York: Peter Lang, 2005.
Block, D. I. *The Book of Ezekiel, Chapters 25–28*. Grand Rapids: Eerdmans, 1998.
Blomberg, C. *Neither Poverty nor Riches: A Biblical Theology of Possessions*. Downers Grove: InterVarsity Press, 1999.
Blount, B. K. *Revelation: A Commentary*. Louisville: Westminster John Knox, 2009.

Böckle, F. "Geschlechterbeziehungen und Liebesfähigkeit." In *Christlicher Glaube in moderner Gesellschaft*. Freiburg: Herder, 1981.

Boff, L. *Jesus Christus der Befreier*. Freiburg: Herder, 1989.

———. *Zukunft für die Mutter Erde: Warum wir als Krone abdanken müssen*. München: Claudius, 2012.

Bornkamm, G. *Paulus*. Stuttgart: Kohlhammer, 1979.

Borthwick, P. *Western Christians in Global Mission: What's the Role of the North American Church?* Downers Grove: InterVarsity Press, 2012.

Bowers, W. P. *Studies in Paul's Understanding of His Mission*. PhD Thesis, Cambridge University, 1976.

Boyarin, D. *Radical Jew: Paul and the Politics of Identity*. Berkley: University of California Press, 1994.

Božinović, N. "Istorija ženskog pokreta." Beograd: Autonomni ženski centar, 2006. Online: https://www.womenngo.org.rs/zenski-pokret/istorija-zenskog-pokreta/219-nekoliko-osnovnih-podataka-o-zenskom-pokretu-u-jugoslaviji-izmedu-dva-rata.

Brandenburg, H. *Der Brief des Paulus an die Galater*. Wuppertal: Brockhaus, 1961.

Brandenburger, E. *Adam und Christus: Exegetisch-religionsgeschichtliche Untersuchung zu Römer 5, 1–21 (1 Kor 15)*. Neukirchen: Neukirchner Verlag, 1962.

Braun, P. *Die Keuschheit der Engel: Sexuelle Entsagung, Askese und Körperlichkeit am Anfang des Christentums*. München: Hauser, 1991.

Breeze, M. "Imposter Syndrome as a Public Feeling." In *Feeling Academic in Neoliberal University: Feminist Flights, Fights, and Failures*, edited by V. Taylor and K. Lahad. London: Palgrave Macmillan, 2018.

Breuer, J., and S. Freud. *Studien über Hysterie*. Leipzig; Vienna: Deuticke, 1895.

Brown, P. *The Body and Society: Men, Women, and Sexual Renunciation in Early Christianity*. New York: Columbia University, 1988.

Bruce, F. F. *The Book of Acts*. Grand Rapids: Eerdmans, 1976.

———. *The Letter of Paul to the Romans: An Introduction and Commentary*. Leicester: Inter-Varsity Press, 1985.

Bultmann, R. "Die Eschatologie des Johannes-Evangeliums." In *Glauben und Verstehen 1*, 134–152. Tübingen: Mohr Siebeck, 1966.

Butler, D. "Church Decision Whether Women Have Souls: Results." Online: https://groups.google.com/forum/#!topic/net.women/PtEmp8kJC4A.

Caferkey, J. "Making More Sustainable LEDs with Reusable Materials." In *Green Tech Media*, 2017. Online: https://www.greentechmedia.com/articles/read/sustainable-led-reusable-materials.

Caldwell, C. "Ten Bogus Ideas My White Culture Taught Me Growing Up." *Baptist News Global* (20 January 2019). Online: https://baptistnews.com/article/10-bogus-ideas-my-white-culture-taught-me-growing-up/#.XbkOBuhKhPY.

Calvin, J. *John Calvin's Commentaries*. Christian Classics Ethereal Library. Online: https://biblehub.com/commentaries/calvin/romans/8.htm.

Cassidy, R. J. *Paul in Chains: Roman Imprisonment and the Letters of St. Paul*. New York: Crossroad, 2001.

Casson, L. *Everyday Life in Ancient Rome*. Revised edition. Baltimore: Johns Hopkins, 1998.

———. *Travel in the Ancient Rome*. London: George Allen & Unwin, 1974.

Cerfaux, L. *The Christian in the Theology of St. Paul*. New York: Herder & Herder, 1967.

Chapple, A. "Getting Romans to the Right Romans: Phoebe and the Delivery of Paul's Letter." *Tyndale Bulletin* 62, no. 2 (2011): 195–214.

Charles, R. H. *A Critical and Exegetical Commentary on the Revelation of St. John*, vol. 2. Edinburgh: T & T Clark, 1920.

Chinnici, R. *Can Women Reimage the Church?* New York: Paulist Press, 1992.

Chira, S. "The Universal Phenomenon of Men Interrupting Women." *New York Times*, 14 June 2017. Online: https://www.nytimes.com/2017/06/14/business/women-sexism-work-huffington-kamala-harris.html.

Chrysostom, J. *Homilies on Ephesians* 13. Online: https://www.newadvent.org/fathers/2301.htm.

———. *Homilies on Genesis*. Online: http://www2.iath.virginia.edu/anderson/commentaries/ChrGen.html.

Cifrak, M. *Ta u vjeri, ne u gledanju: Egzegetski doprinos moralnoj poruci Novog zavjeta*. Zagreb: KS, 2013.

Clark Kroeger, R., and C. Clark Kroeger. *I Suffer Not a Woman: Rethinking 1 Timothy 2:11–15 in the Light of Ancient Evidence*. Grand Rapids: Baker, 1992.

Clark Kroeger, C., and N. Nason-Clark. *No Place for Abuse*. Downers Grove: InterVarsity Press, 2001.

Cloud, H., and J. Townsend. *Boundaries: When to Say Yes, How to Say No to Take Control of Your Life*. Grand Rapids: Zondervan, 1992.

Coates, C. A. *An Outline of the Revelation*. London: Stow Hill Bible and Tract Depot, 1923.

Collins, T. *The Mantle of Elijah: The Reduction Criticism of the Prophetic Books*. Sheffield: Sheffield Academic Press, 1993.

Conzelmann, H. *Acts of the Apostles: A Commentary*. Minneapolis: Fortress, 1987.

———. *Die Apostelgeschichte: Handbuch zum NT 7*. Tübingen: Mohr Siebeck, 1972.

———. *First Corinthians*. Philadelphia: Fortress, 1975.

Cotter, W. "Women's Authority Roles in Paul's Churches: Countercultural or Conventional?" *Novum Testamentum* 36, no. 4 (1994).

Cranfield, C. E. B. *The Epistle to the Romans*. Edinburgh: T & T Clark, 1979.

———. *Romans 1–8*. London: T & T Clark, 2011.

Crossan, J. D., and J. L. Reid. *In Search of Paul: How Jesus' Apostle Opposed Rome's Empire with God's Kingdom*. London: SPCK, 2005.

Cullmann, O. *Die Königsherrschaft Christi und Kirche im Neuen Testament*. Zürich: Evangelischer Verlag, 1945.

———. "Le caractère eschatologique du devoir missionaire et de la conscience apostolique de S. Paul. Étude sur le κατέχον(ων) de II Thess 2.6–7." *RHPR* 16 (1936): 210–245.
Dahl, N. *Studies in Paul: Theology for the Early Christian Mission*. Minneapolis: Augsburg, 1977.
Davis, E. "Swallowing the Scroll: Textuality and the Dynamics of Discourse in Ezekiel's Prophecy." In *Signs and Wonders: Biblical Texts in Literary Focus*, edited by J. C. Exum. Atlanta: Scholars Press, 1989.
Dawkins, R. *The Blind Watchmaker*. London: Penguin, 1986.
Demaine, A. L., and M. A. Báez-Váscez. "Bio Fuels of the Present and the Future." In *New and Future Developments in Catalysis: Catalytic Biomass Conversion*, edited by S. L. Stuib, 325–370. Amsterdam: Elsevier, 2013.
Descartes, R. *Philosophy and Theology: A Discourse on Method*. London; New York: Dent & Son; E. P. Ditton & Co., 1912.
"Domestic Abuse Is a Gendered Crime." In *Women's Aid*. Online: https://www.womensaid.org.uk/information-support/what-is-domestic-abuse/domestic-abuse-is-a-gendered-crime/.
Donaldson, T. *Paul and the Nations*. Minneapolis: Fortress, 1997.
Donavan, V. J. *The Church in the Midst of Creation*. Maryknoll: SCM, 1989.
Donfried, K. "A Short Note on Romans 16." In *The Romans Debate*, edited by K. Donfried, 44–53. Edinburgh: T & T Clark, 1991.
———. *The Romans Debate*. Edinburgh: T & T Clark, 1991.
Douglas, J. D., et al. *New Bible Dictionary*, 2nd edition. Leicester: Inter-Varsity Press, 1985.
Downs, D. J. *The Offering of the Gentiles*. Tübingen: Mohr Siebeck, 2008.
Dragutinović, P. *Interpretation of Scripture in the Orthodox Church: Engaging Contextual Hermeneutics in Orthodox Biblical Studies*. Belgrade: Christian Cultural Centre "Radovan Bigović" and Biblical Institute of the Faculty of Orthodox Theology, 2018.
Duchrow, U., and F. J. Hinkelammert. *Property for People, Not for Profit: Alternatives to the Global Tyranny of Capital*. New York: Palgrave Macmillan, 2012.
Dunch, R. "Beyond Cultural Imperialism: Cultural Theory, Christian Missions, and Global Modernity." *History and Theory* 41, no. 3 (2002): 301–325.
Dunn, J., ed. *Paul and the Mosaic Law*. Tübingen: Mohr Siebeck, 1996.
———, ed. "Romans, The Letter to." In *Dictionary of Paul and His Letter*, edited by G. F. Hawthorne and R. P. Martin, 835–850. Downers Grove: InterVarsity Press, 1993.
———. *Romans 1–8*. Nashville: Thomas Nelson, 1988.
———. *Romans 9–16*. Nashville: Thomas Nelson, 1988.
East West Church. "Before and After: Baptist Women in Post-Soviet Ukraine." *East West Church and Ministry Report* 24, no. 4 (2016): 7–9. Online: https://www.academia.edu/32983138/Women_in_Evangelical_Churches_in_the_Former_Soviet_Union_A_Response_to_an_Interview_of_Pastor_Shiranai_Dosova.

Eggenberger, C. "Der Sinn der Argumentation in Römer 13, 2–5." *Kirchenblatt für die reformierte Schweiz* 100 (1944): 243.

Eicholz, G. *Die Theologie des Paulus im Umriss*. Neukirchen-Vluyn: Neukirchner, 1985.

Eliot L. "Neurosexism: The Myth That Men and Women Have Different Brains." In *Nature*, 27 February 2019. Online: https://www.nature.com/articles/d41586-019-00677-x.

Elliot, N. *The Rhetoric of Romans: Argumentative Constraint and Strategy and Paul's Dialogue with Judaism*. Sheffield: Sheffield Academic Press, 1990.

Elsner, C. "Von heute an leben wir auf Pump." In *ZDF Heute*, July 29, 2019. Online: https://www.zdf.de/nachrichten/heute/welt-ueberlastungstag-2019-von-heute-an-leben-wir-auf-pump-100.html.

End Child Labour in Tobacco Industry Foundation (ECLT). "Facts on Global Slavery: A Global Problem." Online: https://www.eclt.org/en/news-and-insights/facts-on-modern-slavery-a-global-problem.

Eusebius. *Vita Constantinae*. Online: https://www.newadvent.org/fathers/2502.htm.

Evans, A. "Hellenistic Connections to Jewish Beliefs about Angels." *Scriptura* 112 (2011): 1–12.

Exum, J. C. *Signs and Wonders: Biblical Texts in Literary Focus*. Atlanta: Scholars Press, 1989.

Fausto-Sterling, A. *Sex/Gender: Biology in a Social World*. New York: Routledge, 2012.

Fee, G. *1&2 Timothy, Titus*. Grand Rapids: Baker, 1988.

———. *The First Epistle to the Corinthians*. Grand Rapids: Eerdmans, 1987.

———. *How to Read the Bible for All Its Worth*. Grand Rapids: Zondervan, 1982.

"Female Genital Cutting." *VoA*. 28 March 2013. https://www.youtube.com/watch?v=tEyaxw4bR2k.

Feuerbach, L. A. *The Essence of Christianity*. 1841. Online: https://www.marxists.org/reference/archive/feuerbach/works/essence/.

Fiddes, P. S. *Participating in God: A Pastoral Doctrine of the Trinity*. London: Darton, Longman & Todd, 2000.

———. "Review of Moltmann's God in Creation." *Journal of Theological Studies* 38, no. 1 (1987): 262–265.

Fitzmyer, J. A. *Romans: A New Translation with Introduction and Commentary*. London: Doubleday, 1993.

Fitzpatrick, J. "Original Sin or Original Sinfulness." *New Blackfriars* 90 (2009): 458–473.

Flacius, M. *How to Understand the Sacred Scriptures*. Translated by W. R. Johnston. Saginaw: Magdeburg Press, 2011.

Flanagan, N. "Did Paul Put Down Women in 1 Cor 14:34–36?" *Biblical Theology Bulletin* 11 (1981): 10–12.

Focus on the Family. "Submission of Wives to Husbands." Q & A, Online: https://www.focusonthefamily.com/family-qa/submission-of-wives-to-husbands.

Food Aid. "Poor Nutrition Causes Nearly Half (45%) of Deaths in Children under Five – 3.1 Million Children Each Year." Online: https://www.foodaidfoundation.org/world-hunger-statistics.html.

Freed, E. D. "Who or What Was Before Abraham in John 8:53." *Journal for the Study of the New Testament* 17 (1983): 52–59.

Friedmann, R. E., ed. *The Poet and the Historian: Essays in Literary and Historical Biblical Criticism*. Chico: Scholars Press, 1983.

Frymer-Kensky, T. "Deborah: Bible." In *Jewish Women's Archive's Encyclopaedia*. Online: https://jwa.org/encyclopedia/article/deborah-bible.

Furnish, V. P. *The Moral Teaching of Paul*. Nashville: Abingdon, 1979.

Gaston, L. *Paul and the Torah*. Vancouver: University of British Columbia, 1987.

Georgi, D. *Remembering the Poor: The History of Paul's Collection for Jerusalem*. Nashville: Abingdon, 1992.

Giddens, A. *The Consequences of Modernity*. Stanford: Stanford University Press, 1990.

Gill, D. W. J., and C. Gempf. *The Book of Acts in Its Graeco-Roman Setting*. Grand Rapids; Carlisle: Eerdmans; Paternoster, 1994.

Gladwell, M. *The Tipping Point: How Little Things Can Make a Big Difference*. Lebanon: Back Bay Books, 2002.

Gooding, D., and J. Lennox. *Questioning Our Knowledge: Can We Know What We Need to Know?* Belfast: Myrtlefield, 2019.

Gow, M. D. "Fall." In *Dictionary of the Old Testament: Pentateuch*, edited by T. D. Alexander and D. W. Baker. Downers Grove: InterVarsity Press, 2003.

Greenberg, M. *Ezekiel 1–20: A New Translation with Introduction and Commentary*. Garden City, NY: Doubleday, 1983.

Grenz, S., and D. Muir Kjesbo. *Women in the Church: A Biblical Theology of Women in Ministry*. Downers Grove: InterVarsity Press, 1995.

Grudem, W. "Does Kefalē ('Head') Mean 'Source' or 'Authority Over' in Greek Literature? A Survey of 2,336 Examples." *Trinity Journal* 6, no. 1 (1985): 38–59.

———. *Systematic Theology*. Downers Grove: InterVarsity Press, 1994.

Gunderson, S. R. "Your Father the Devil: A New Approach to John and the Jews." *Journal for the Study of the New Testament* 84 (2001): 122.

Gundry, J. "Male and Female in Creation and New Creation: Interpretation of Galatians 3:28c in 1 Corinthians 7." In *To Tell the Mystery: Essays on New Testament Eschatology in Honor of Robert H. Gundry*, edited by T. E. Schmidt and M. Silva, 95–121. Sheffield: JSOT Press, 1994.

——— "Spirit, Mercy and the Other." *Theology Today* (Jan 1986): 97–110.

Gunner, G., P. Slotte, and E. Kitanović. *Human Rights, Religious Freedom, and Faces of Faith*. Geneva: Globethics.net, 2019.

Gushee, D. P. *The Sacredness of Human Life: Why an Ancient Biblical Vision Is Key to the World's Future*. Grand Rapids: Eerdmans, 2013.

Guthrie, D. "1 Timothy." In *New Bible Commentary*, edited by D. A. Carson et al. Downers Grove: InterVarsity Press, 1953; repr. 1994.

Haaker, K. "'Ende des Gesetzes' und kein Ende." In *Ja und Nein: Christiliche Theologie im Angesicht Israels*. FS Wolfgang Schrage. Neukirchen: Neukirchner Verlag, 1998.

Hacola, R. *Identity Matters: John, the Jews and Jewishness*. Leiden: Brill, 2005.

Haenchen, E. *Acts*. Oxford: Blackwell, 1972.

Hagen, K. T. "The Nature and Psychosocial Consequences of War Rape for Individuals and Communities." *International Journal of Psychological Studies* 2, no. 2 (2010): 14–25.

Halévy, Elie. *The Birth of Methodism*. Chicago: Chicago University Press, 1971.

———. *England in 1815*. New York: Barnes & Noble, 1961.

———. *The Liberal Awakening 1815–1830*. New York: Barnes & Noble, 1961.

Ham, K. "Is There Hope for This Planet." *Answers in Genesis*. Online: https://answersingenesis.org/racism/is-there-hope-for-this-planet/.

Hamerton-Kelly, R. *Jews, Greeks and Christians*. Leiden: Brill, 1976.

Hansen, G. W. "The Letter to the Galatians." In *The Dictionary of Paul and His Letters*, edited by G. Hawthorne, 323–334. Downers Grove: InterVarsity Press, 1993.

Harari, Y. N. *Homo Deus: A History of Tomorrow*. New York: Harper, 2017.

Hardin, G. "The Tragedy of the Common." *Science* 162 (1968): 1243–1248.

Harpur, J. *The Atlas of the Sacred Places: Meeting Points of Heaven and Earth*. London: Cassell, 1994.

Haslam, S. A., and M. K. Ryan. "The Road to the Glass Cliff: Differences in Perceived Sustainability of Men and Women for Leadership Positions in Succeeding and Failing Organisations." *The Leadership Quarterly* 19 (2008): 530–543. Also online: https://web.archive.org/web/20131225013107/http://blog.aelios.com/mbawg/wp-content/uploads/2010/05/The-glass-cliff.pdf.

Hawthorne, G., R. P. Martin, and D. G. Reid. *Dictionary of Paul and His Letters (DPL)*. Downers Grove: InterVarsity Press, 1993.

Hays, R. *Echoes of Scripture in the Letters of Paul*. London: Yale University Press, 1989.

———. *The Moral Vision of the New Testament*. Edinburgh: T & T Clark, 1996.

Hengel, M. "Einleitung." In *Die Heiden: Juden, Christen und das Problem des Fremden*, edited by R. Feldmeier and U. Heckel. Tübingen: Mohr Siebeck, 1994.

———. *The Pre-Christian Paul*. London: SCM, 1991.

———. *Zur urchristlichen Geschichtsschreibung*. Stuttgart: Calwer Verlag, 1979.

Hengel, M., and A. M. Schwemer. *Paul between Damascus and Antioch*. Translated by J. Bowden from the unpublished text. Louisville: Westminster John Knox, 1997.

———. *Paulus zwischen Damaskus und Aniochien*. Tübingen: Mohr Siebeck, 1998.

Hengel, M., and R. Deines. *The Septuagint as Christian Scripture: Its Prehistory and the Problem of Its Canon*. Edinburgh & New York: Baker Academic, 2002.

Herman, J., and L. Hirschman. "Families at Risk for Father-Daughter Incest." In *The Gender Gap in Psychotherapy*, edited by P. P. Rieker and E. Carmen, 237–258. New York: Plenum Press, 1984.

Hermann, T. "Barbar und Skythe: Ein Erklärungsversuch zu Kol 3,11." *ThBl* 19 (1930): 106.

Hildebrandt, T. "Genre of Proverbs." In *Dictionary of the Old Testament: Wisdom, Poetry and Writings*, edited by Longman and Enns, 528–539. Downers Grove: IVP Academic, 2008.

Hodge, C. *Romans*. Wheaton: Crossway, 1994.

Hoeckema, A. *The Bible and the Future*. Grand Rapids; Carlisle: Eerdmans; Paternoster, 1994.

Hoehner, H. W. *Ephesians*. Grand Rapids: Baker, 2002.

Holt-Gimenez, Eric. "We Already Grow Enough Food for 10 Billion People – And Still Can't End Hunger." *HuffPost*, 5 Feb 2012. Online: https://www.huffpost.com/entry/world-hunger_b_1463429?guccounter=1&guce_referrer=aHR0cHM6Ly93d3cuZ29vZ2xlLmNvbS8&guce_referrer_sig=AQAAAKC4XP2emPOO0UfeQxjz9KCTO0cpAU_0y-cU_J2etLe8H9fM2Qhrk6B6fukok-Hc1qzbjeVr7xoYgGXtqbhqtlE-Jhpiswelf2ONSIwbiJJ_ZdjizrGA3C2neuLi4-ijKlEhUCMaLsnNjK8e2BRV9ZLNQ9sniNjGJUW5qq9uUcQA.

Hooker, M. D. "Adam in Romans I." *NTS* 6 (1960): 297–306.

———. "A Further Note on Romans I." *NTS* 13 (1966–7): 181–183.

International Labour Office. *Profits and Poverty: The Economics of Forced Labour*. Online: https://www.ilo.org/wcmsp5/groups/public/---ed_norm/---declaration/documents/publication/wcms_243391.pdf.

Iowa State University News Release. "Gender Roles: Men and Women Are Not So Different After All." Posted on 29 Jan 2015. Online: https://www.news.iastate.edu/news/2015/01/29/genderdifferences.

Jackson, S. M., ed. *The New Schaff-Herzog Encyclopaedia of Religious Knowledge*, vol. 2. New York: Funk & Wagnalls, 1908–1912.

Jaspers, K. *The Great Philosophers*. London: Rupert Hart-Davis, 1962.

———. *Kant*. New York: Harcourt, Brace & World, 1962.

———. *The Origin and Goal of History*. London: Routledge Revivals, 2010.

Jones, S. *Feminist Theory and Christian Theology: Cartographies of Grace*. Minneapolis: Augsburg Fortress, 2000.

Jülicher, A. "Die Jungfrauen im ersten Korintherbrief." *Protestantische Monatshefte* 22 (1918): 97–119.

Jüngel, E. "Römer 13,1–7." In *Dokumentation EPD*. Frankfurt: Evangelischer Pressedienst, 1985.

Kant, I. *Immanuel Kant's Critique of Pure Reason*. London: Macmillan, 1987.

Käsemann, E. *Commentary on Romans*. Grand Rapids: Eerdmans, 1980.

Katz, S. T., ed. *The Cambridge History of Judaism: The Late Roman-Rabbinic Period*, vol. 4. Cambridge: Cambridge University Press, 2006.

Keienburg, F. *Geschichte der Auslegung von Römer 13, 1–7*. Gelsenkirchen: Kommissionsverlag, 1956.

Key, W. K. "God in Creation: A Reflection on Jürgen Moltmann's Theology." *Rural Theology* 2 (2005): 75–84.

Khan, M. "Global: Shift to the Right." In *San Francisco Examiner*, 23 Dec 2002. Online: http://www.glocaleye.org/shift.htm.
Kittel, G. *Christus und Imperator: Das Urteil der ersten Christenheit über den Staat*. Stuttgart; Berlin: Kohlhammer, 1939.
Klein, G. "Paul's Purpose in Writing the Epistle to the Romans." In *The Romans Debate*, edited by K. Donfried, 29–43. Edinburgh: T & T Clark, 1991.
Knox, J. "Romans 15:14–33 and Paul's Conception of His Mission." *JBL* 83 (1964): 1–11.
Kochhar, R. "Are You in the Global Middle Class?" In *Pew Research Centre*. Online: https://www.pewresearch.org/fact-tank/2015/07/16/are-you-in-the-global-middle-class-find-out-with-our-income-calculator/.
Kraemer, R. "Women in the Religions of the Graeco-Roman World." *Religious Studies Review* 9 (1983): 127–139.
Krasny, R. "Men Who Buy Sex Tend to Commit More Crimes." *Boston Reuters*, 19 July 2011. Online: https://www.reuters.com/article/us-prostitution-survey/men-who-buy-sex-tend-to-commit-more-crimes-study-says-idUSTRE76I73F20110719.
Kümmel, W. G. *Römer 7 und die Bekehrung des Paulus*. Leipzig: Hinrichs, 1929.
Kutsko, J. F. *Between Heaven and Earth: Divine Presence and Absence in the Book of Ezekiel*. Winona Lake: Eisenbrauns, 2000.
Kvam, K. E., L. S. Schearing, and V. H. Ziegler. *Eve and Adam*. Bloomington: Indiana University Press, 1999.
Kvanvig, H. S. *Roots of Apocalyptic: The Mesopotamian Background of the Enoch Figure and of the Son of Man*. Neukirchen: Vuyln, 1988.
Lampe, P. "Junia/Junias: Sklavenherkunft im Kreise der vorpaulinischen Apostel (Röm 16,7)." *ZNW* 76 (1985): 132–134.
———. *From Paul to Valentinus: Christians at Rome in the First Two Centuries*. Minneapolis: Fortress, 2003; German: *Die stadtrömischen Christen in den ersten beiden Jahrhunderten*. Tübingen: Mohr Siebeck, 1987.
———. "The Roman Christians of Rom 16." In *The Romans Debate*, edited by K. Donfried, 216–230. Edinburgh: T & T Clark, 1991.
Leibig, Janis E. "John and the 'Jews': Theological Antisemitism in the Fourth Gospel." *Journal of Ecumenical Studies* 20, no. 2 (1983): 209–234.
Leithart, P. *Defending Constantine: The Twilight of an Empire and the Dawn of Christendom*. Downers Grove: InterVarsity Press, 2010.
Ler Sofronič, Nada. "Fragmenti ženskih sjećanja, 1978. i danas." Ed. u Dugandžić Živanović D. *ProFemina 2*. Online: http://pro-femina.eu/ProFeminasadrzaj_specijalni_broj_2_leto-jesen_2011.html.
Lietzmann, H. D. *An die Römer*. Tübingen: Mohr Siebeck, 1971.
Lincoln, A. T. *Paradise Now and Not Yet: Studies in the Role of the Heavenly Dimension in Paul's Thought with Special Reference to Eschatology*. Cambridge: Cambridge University Press, 1981.
Loades, A. *Feminist Theology: A Reader*. London: SPCK, 1996.

Longenecker, R. N. "A Realized Hope, a New Commitment, and a Developed Proclamation: Paul and Jesus." In *The Road from Damascus: The Impact of Paul's Conversion on His Life, Thought, and Ministry*, edited by R. N. Longenecker, 18–42. Grand Rapids: Eerdmans, 1997.

———, ed. *The Road from Damascus: The Impact of Paul's Conversion on his Life, Thought, and Ministry*. Grand Rapids: Eerdmans, 1997.

Longman III, T. "Book of Proverbs I." In *Dictionary of the Old Testament: Wisdom, Poetry, and Writings*, 539–552. Downers Grove: IVP Academic, 2008.

Luimes, W. "Love and Power – or Powerful Love: Submission, Headship and Abuse." *Mutuality* (Summer 2016): 18–20.

Lujić, B. *Božja vladavina kao svijet novoga čovjeka. Biblijska teologija Novoga zavjeta*. Zagreb: KS, 2010.

Lumpkin, W. L. *Baptist Confessions of Faith*. Valley Forge: Judson Press, 1969.

Luther, M. *Commentary on the Epistle to the Romans*. Grand Rapids: Kregel, 1979.

———. *Kommentar zum Galaterbrief*. Göttingen: Vandenhoeck & Ruprecht, 1989.

Lyons, K. "Generation Y, Curling or Maybe: What the World Calls Millennials." In *The Guardian* (8 March 2016). Online: https://www.theguardian.com/world/2016/mar/08/generation-y-curling-or-maybe-what-the-world-calls-millennials.

MacArthur, J. *Ephesians*. Chicago: Moody Press, 1986.

MacDonald, M. Y. "The Ideal of the Christian Couple: Ign. Pol. 5.1–2 Looking Back on Paul." *NTS* 40, no. 1 (1994): 105–125.

———. "Women Holy in Body and Spirit: The Social Setting of 1 Corinthians 7." *NTS* 36 (1990): 161–181.

MacGrath, A. *Christian Theology: An Introduction*. Chichester: Wiley-Blackwell, 1997; repr. 2011.

Magda, K. *Paul's Territoriality and Mission Strategy*. Tübingen: Mohr Siebeck, 2009.

———. "Unity as a Prerequisite for a Christian Mission: A Missional Reading of Romans 15:1–12." *Kairos* 1 (2008): 39–52.

Magda, K., and M. Wachsmuth. "'Discerning the Body' in Cross-Cultural Relationships: A Critical Analysis of Missional Partnership in Southeastern Europe." *Kairos* 1 (2014): 25–43.

Malina, B. *On the Genre and Message of Revelation: Star Visions and Sky Journeys*. Peabody: Hendrickson, 1995.

———. *The Social Gospel of Jesus: The Kingdom of God in Mediterranean Perspective*. Minneapolis: Fortress, 2001.

Malina, B. J., and J. H. Neyrey. *Portraits of Paul: An Archaeology of Ancient Personality*. Louisville: Westminster John Knox, 1996.

Marshall, H. "Luke's Portrait of the Pauline Mission." In *The Gospel to the Nations: Perspectives on Paul's Mission*, edited by P. Bolt and M. Thompson, 99–114. Downers Grove: InterVarsity Press, 2000.

Mayer, G. "Aspekte des Abrahambildes in der hellenistisch-jüdischen Literatur." *ET* 32 (1972): 118–127.

McGiffert, A. C. *The Church History of Eusebius*. Cincinnati: Lane Theological Seminary, 1890.
McGrath, A. *The Re-Enchantment of Nature: Science, Religion, and the Human Sense of Wonder*. London: Hodder & Stoughton, 2002.
McVean, A. "The History of Hysteria." *McGill's Office for Science and Society*, 31 July 2017. Online: https://www.mcgill.ca/oss/article/history-quackery/history-hysteria.
Medin, J. *Welcome to Sin City: Swedish Male Sex Tourists in Prostitution Abroad, a Report from Sweden's Fair Travel Network* (October 2018). Online: https://schystresande.se/media/filer/087ab2/welcome-sin-city.pdf.
Meeks, W. A. *The First Urban Christians: The Social World of the Apostle Paul*. New Haven: Yale University Press, 1983; repr. 2003.
———. "Image of Androgyne: Some Uses of a Symbol in Earliest Christianity." *HR* 10 (1973/4): 165–208.
Melanchton, P. *The Loci Communes of Philip Melanchton: With a Critical Introduction by the Translator*, translated by C. L. Hill. Eugene: Wipf & Stock, 2007.
Michel, O. *Der Brief an die Römer*. Göttingen: Vandenhoeck & Ruprecht, 1966.
Milne, S. "Women Are Now to the Left of Men: It's a Historic Shift." *The Guardian* (5 March 2013). Online: https://www.theguardian.com/commentisfree/2013/mar/05/women-left-of-men-historic-shift.
Minear, P. S. *The Obedience of Faith: The Purposes of Paul in the Epistle of Romans*. London: SCM, 1971.
Modola, S. "In Rural Kenya, Traditions Run Deeper than Law on Cutting Girls." *Reuters* (12 Nov 2014). Online: https://www.reuters.com/article/us-kenya-circumcision-widerimage/in-rural-kenya-traditions-run-deeper-than-law-on-cutting-girls-idUSKCN0IW1BK20141112.
Moessner, D. P. "The 'Leaven of the Pharisees' and 'This Generation': Israel's Rejection of Jesus according to Luke." *JSNT* 34 (1988): 21–46.
Moghe, S. "3 US Women Share the Horrors of Female Genital Mutilation." *CNN* (11 May 2017). Online: https://edition.cnn.com/2017/05/11/health/fgm-us-survivor-stories-trnd/index.html.
Moltmann, J. *The Coming of God in Christian Eschatology*. London: SCM, 1996.
———. *God in Creation*. Minneapolis: Fortress, 1993.
Moo, D. J. *The Epistle to the Romans*. Eerdmans: Grand Rapids, 1996.
Mosher, S. *God's Power, Jesus' Faith and World Mission*. Scottdale: Harold Press, 1996.
Motyer, S. *Antisemitism and the New Testament*. Cambridge: Grove, 2002.
———. *Israel in the Plan of God: Light on Today's Debate*. Eugene: Wipf & Stock, 2004.
———. "Paul and Pilgrimage." In *Explorations in a Christian Theology of Pilgrimage*, edited by C. Bartholomew and F. Hughes, 50–72. Aldershot: Ashgate, 2004.
Munck, J. *Salvation of Mankind*. London: SCM, 1951.
Myers, C. *Binding the Strong Man: A Political Reading of Mark's Story of Jesus*. Maryknoll: Orbis, 2000.
Nagel, T. *The View from Nowhere*. New York; Oxford: Oxford University Press, 1986.

———. "What Is It Like to Be a Bat?" *The Philosophical Review* 83, no. 4 (1974): 435–50.
Nason-Clark, N. *The Battered Wife*. Louisville: John Knox Press, 1997.
Nason-Clark, N., and B. Fisher-Townsend. *Men Who Batter*. Oxford: Oxford University Press, 2015.
Newton, C. T., and R. P. Pullan. *A History of Discoveries at Halicarnassus, Cnidus, and Branchida*, Vol II. 2. London: Day & Son, 1863. No. 6 Plate LXXXVII.
Nickle, K. *The Collection: A Study in Paul's Strategy*. London: SCM, 1966.
Niebuhr, K.-W. *Heidenapostel aus Israel*. Dissertation vol. 1. Halle: Mohr Siebeck, 1991.
Nolan, Michael. "Do Women Have Souls?" In *Church History Information Centre*. Online: http://www.churchinhistory.org/pages/booklets/women-souls-1.htm.
O'Brien, P. T. *The Letter to the Ephesians*. Grand Rapids: Eerdmans, 1999.
Oakes, P., ed. *Rome in the Bible and the Early Church*. Carlisle: Paternoster, 2002.
Open Doors. *World Watch List for 2018*. Online: https://www.opendoorsusa.org/christian-persecution/.
Origen. *Homilies on Genesis and Exodus*. Washington: Catholic University of America Press. Online: https://www.bc.edu/content/dam/files/research_sites/cjl/sites/partners/cbaa_seminar/CBA_members_only/Origen.pdf.
Parker, C. "Lottie Moon." In *New Georgia Encyclopaedia: Religion*. Online: https://www.georgiaencyclopedia.org/articles/arts-culture/lottie-moon-1840-1912.
Patnaik, P. "The Global Shift to the Right." In *People's Democracy* 22 (2019). Online: https://peoplesdemocracy.in/2019/0602_pd/global-shift-right.
Pauček Šljivak, M. "Bojite se migranata?" In *Index.hr* (1 Nov 2018). Online: https://www.index.hr/vijesti/clanak/bojite-se-migranata-evo-koliko-ih-je-u-zadnjih-12-godina-ostalo-u-hrvatskoj/2036314.aspx.
Paxman, J. "Why We Can't Trust Politicians." Online: https://www.youtube.com/watch?v=uUlv6r8c_hI.
Payner, P. B. *Man and Woman One in Christ: An Exegetical and Theological Study of Paul's Letters*. Grand Rapids: Zondervan, 2009.
———. "Ms. 88 as Evidence for a Text without 1 Cor 14:34–5." *NTS* 44 (1998): 154.
———. "Sigla for Variants in Vaticanus, and 1 Cor 14:34–5." *NTS* 41, no. 2 (1995): 240–262.
Pegles, E. *The Gnostic Paul: Gnostic Exegesis of the Pauline Letters*. Philadelphia: Trinity Press, 1975.
Perica, V. "Religion in the Balkan Wars." In *Oxford Handbooks Online* (October 2014). Online: https://www.oxfordhandbooks.com/view/10.1093/oxfordhb/9780199935420.001.0001/oxfordhb-9780199935420-e-37.
Peterlin, D. "'Tabitha': The First Baptist Women's Association in Zagreb." *Kairos* 2 (2007): 247–272. Online: file:///C:/Users/Korisnik/Downloads/6_Peterlin_Tabitha%20(1).pdf.

Petrović, I., and K. Magda. "Globalna kršćanska misija i povratak Efrajima: Neke egzegetske mogućnosti za tumačenje Rimljanima 11, 25–26." *Nova prisutnost* 2 (2018): 297–312.

Pohl, A. *Offenbarung des Johannes, Teil 1*. Wuppertal: Brockhaus, 1973.

Pomeroy, S. B. *Goddesses, Whores, Wives, and Slaves: Women in Classical Antiquity*. New York: Schocken Books, 1975.

Post, C., I. M. Latu, and L. Y. Belkin. "A Female Leadership Trust Advantage in Times of Crisis: Under What Conditions?" *Psychology of Women Quarterly* 43, no. 2 (2019): 215–231.

Probst, J. "Seven Reasons Why the World Is Improving." *BBC Future* (11 Jan 2019). Online: https://www.bbc.com/future/article/20190111-seven-reasons-why-the-world-is-improving.

Pröpper, T. *Erlösungsglaube und Freiheitsgeschichte: Eine Skizze zur Soteriologie*. München: Kösel-Verlag, 1988.

Rabbinowitz, N. "Matthew 23:2–4: Does Jesus Recognize the Authority of the Pharisees and Does He Endorse Their Halakhah?" *JETS* 46, no. 3 (2003): 423–447.

Rahner, K. "Autorität." In *Christlicher Glaube in moderner Gesellschaft*. Freiburg: Herder, 1981.

Ramsay, W. M. *The Cities of St. Paul*. London: Hodder & Stoughton, 1907.

———. *The Letters to the Seven Churches*. Whitefish: Kessinger, 2004.

———. *Paul the Traveller and Roman Citizen*. London: Hodder & Stoughton, 1895.

Randall, I. M. *Baptist Beginnings in Europe*. Schwarzenfeld: Neufeld Verlag, 2009.

Rapske, B. M. "Acts, Travel and Shipwreck." In *The Book of Acts in Its Greco Roman Setting*, edited by Gill et al., 1–47. Grand Rapids: Eerdmans, 1994.

———. *The Book of Acts and Paul in Roman Custody*. Grand Rapids; Carlisle: Eerdmans; Paternoster, 1994.

Reasoner, P. M. *The Strong and the Weak: Romans 14.1–15.13 in Context*. Cambridge: Cambridge University Press, 1999.

Regalado, A. "Is It Time to Worry about Human Cloning Again?" *The Guardian* (20 April 2018). Online: https://www.theguardian.com/lifeandstyle/2018/apr/20/pet-cloning-is-already-here-is-human-cloning-next.

Reimarus, H. S. *Apologie für die Vernünftigen Verehrer Gottes*. Leipzig: Brockhaus, 1986.

Reizenstein, R. *Die hellenistischen Mysterienreligionen, ihre Grundgedanken und Wirkungen*. Leipzig: Treubner, 1910.

Resurrección, B. P. "Gender and Environment from 'Women, Environment and Development.'" In *Routledge Handbook of Gender and Environment*, edited by S. MacGregor, 71–85. Oxon: Routledge, 2017.

Ridderbos, H. *Paul: An Outline of His Theology*. Grand Rapids: Eerdmans, 1975.

Riechers, M. "How Women's Voices Get Silenced and How You Can Learn to Speak Up." In *The Best of Our Knowledge* (27 July 2019). Online: https://www.ttbook.org/interview/how-womens-voices-get-silenced-and-how-you-can-learn-speak.

Riesner, R. *Die Frühzeit des Apostels Paulus*. Tübingen: Mohr Siebeck, 1994.

Rinnelt, J. "Bottom-up Approach." In *Human Business* (8 December 2016). Online: http://www.humanbusiness.eu/bottom-up-approach/.

Roberts, J. J. M. "The Davidic Origin of the Zion Tradition." *JBL* 92 (1973): 329–344.

Rohland, E. *Die Bedeutung der Erwählungstraditionen Israels für die Eschatologie der alttestamentlichen Propheten*. Dissertation. Heidelberg, 1956.

Rosenhäger, U., and S. Stephens, eds. *Walk My Sister: The Ordination of Women; Reformed Perspectives*. Geneva: WRAC, 1993.

Roth, J. D. *Constantine Revisited*. Eugene: Wipf & Stock, 2013.

Rowley, H. *The Book of Ezekiel in Modern Study*. Manchester: Manchester University Press, 1953.

Rueckert, V. *Outspoken: Why Women's Voices Get Silenced and How to Set Them Free*. New York: HarperCollins, 2019.

Sack, R. *Homo Geographicus*. Baltimore; London: Johns Hopkins, 1997.

———. *Human Territoriality: Its Theory and History*. Cambridge: Cambridge University Press, 1986.

Sanday, W., and A. C. Headlam. *A Critical Exegetical Commentary on the Epistle to the Romans*. Edinburgh: T & T Clark, 1964.

Sanders, E. P. *Paul and Palestinian Judaism*. London: SCM, 1977.

———. *Paul, the Law, and the Jewish People*. Minneapolis: Fortress, 1983.

Sayoon, K. *Paul and the New Perspective: Second Thoughts on the Origin of Paul's Gospel*. Tübingen; Grand Rapids: Mohr Siebeck; Eerdmans, 2002.

Schlier, H. *Der Römerbrief*. Freiburg: Herder, 1977.

Schnabel, E. *Early Christian Mission*. Downers Grove; Leicester: InterVarsity Press; Apollos, 2004.

Schonberg, M. W. "Huiothesia: Adoptive Sonship of the Israelites." *American Ecclesiastical Review* 143 (1960): 261–273.

———. "St Paul's Notion on the Adoptive Sonship of Christians." *Thomist* 28 (1960): 51–75.

Schöpflin, K. *Theologie als Biographie im Ezechielbuch: Ein Beitrag zur Konzeption alttestamentlicher Prophetie*. Tübingen: Mohr Siebeck, 2002.

Schrage, W. *Erste Brief an die Korinther*. EKK. Zürich: Benzinger, 1991.

———. "Zur Ethik der neutestamentlichen Haustafeln." *NTS* 21 (1974–1975): 1–22.

Schürer, E. *The History of the Jewish People in the Age of Jesus Christ*. Vol 2. Edinburgh: T & T Clark, 1979.

Schüssler Fiorenza, E. *The Book of Revelation: Justice and Judgment*. Minneapolis: Fortress, 1998.

———. *But She Said: Feminist Practices of Biblical Interpretation*. Boston: Beacon, 1992.

———. *In Memory of Her: A Feminist Theological Reconstruction of Christian Origins*. London: SCM, 1996.

———. *Zu ihrem Gedächnis*. München: Kaiser, 1988.

Scott, J. *Adoption as Sons of God*. Tübingen: Mohr Siebeck, 1992.

———. *Paul and the Nations: The Old Testament and the Jewish Background of Paul's Mission to the Nations with Special Reference to the Destination of Galatians*. Tübingen: Mohr Siebeck, 1995.

———. "Restoration of Israel." In *Dictionary of Paul and His Letters*, edited by G. F. Hawthorne and R. P. Martin, 796–805. Downers Grove: InterVarsity Press, 1993.

Scroggs, R. "Paul and the Eschatological Woman." *JAAR* 22 (1972): 283–303.

Shaw, I. J. *Christianity: The Biography – Two Thousand Years of the Global Church*. Leicester: Inter-Varsity Press, 2016.

Shulam, J. A. *Commentary on the Jewish Roots of Romans*. Baltimore: Messianic Jewish Publishers, 1997.

Silva, M. "Galatians." In *New Bible Commentary*, edited by D. A. Carson et al. Downers Grove: InterVarsity Press, 1994.

———. "Old Testament in Paul." In *Dictionary of Paul and His Letters*, edited by G. F. Hawthorne and R. P. Martin, 630–642. Downers Grove: InterVarsity Press, 1993.

Smallwood, E. M. *The Jews under the Roman Rule from Pompey to Diocletian*. Leiden: Brill, 1976.

Smith, C. "Here's How Much Plastic You Eat Every Year." *Huffpost* (7 June 2019). Online: https://www.huffpost.com/entry/microplastic-food-bottled-water_n_5cf93154e4b0e3e3df16ab9d.

Smith, M. B. *Gender or Giftedness*. Manila: World Evangelical Fellowship Commission on Women's Concerns, 2000.

Snow, D. L. "A Review of Research on Women's Use of Violence with Male Intimate Partners." Online: https://www.ncbi.nlm.nih.gov/pmc/articles/PMC2968709/.

Stegemann, W. "War der Apostel Paulus ein römischer Bürger?" *ZNW* 78 (1987): 200–229.

Stendahl, K. *Final Account: Paul's Letter to the Romans*. Minneapolis: Fortress, 1996.

———. *Paul among the Jews and Gentiles*. Philadelphia: Fortress, 1976.

Stern, D. H. *Jewish New Testament: A Translation of the New Testament That Expresses Its Jewishness*. Translated by David H. Stern. Clarksville: Jewish New Testament Publications, 1996.

Stiefel, J. H. "Women Deacons in 1 Tim: A Linguistic and Literary Look at 'Women Likewise . . .' in 1 Tim 3.11." *NTS* 41, no. 3 (1995): 442–457.

Storkey, E. *Scars across Humanity: Understanding and Overcoming Violence against Women*. London: SPCK, 2015.

———. *The Search for Intimacy*. Grand Rapids: Eerdmans, 1995.

Stott, J. *The Message of the Sermon on the Mount*. Downers Grove: InterVarsity Press, 1978.

Strabo. *Geography*. Online: B. Theyer's *Locus Curtius* http://penelope.uchicago.edu/Thayer/E/Roman/Texts/Strabo/home.html.

Strack, H. L., and P. Billerbeck. *Die Briefe des Neuen Testaments und die Offenbarung Johannis erläutert aus Talmud und Midrasch*. München: C. H. Beck'sche Verlagsbuchhandlung, 1926.

Stuhlmacher, P. *Biblische Theologie des Neuen Testaments: Grundlegung – Von Jesus zu Paulus*, vol. 1. Göttingen: Vandenhoeck & Ruprecht, 1992.

———. *Das paulinische Evangelium I*. Göttingen: Vandenhoeck & Ruprecht, 1968.

———. *Paul's Letter to the Romans*. Westminster: John Knox, 1994.

———. *Revisiting Paul's Doctrine of Justification: A Challenge to the New Perspective*. Downers Grove: InterVarsity Press, 2001.

Tacitus. *Annals*, Book XV. Online: B. Theyer's *Locus Curtius* http://penelope.uchicago.edu/Thayer/E/Roman/Texts/Tacitus/Annals/15B*.html.

———. *Histories*, Book V. Online: B. Theyer's *Locus Curtius* https://penelope.uchicago.edu/Thayer/E/Roman/Texts/Tacitus/home.html.

Tajra, H. W. *The Martyrdom of St. Paul: Historical and Judicial Context, Traditions, and Legends*. Tübingen: Mohr Siebeck, 1994.

———. *The Trials of St. Paul*. Tübingen: Mohr Siebeck, 1989.

Taylor, V., and K. Lahad, eds. *Feeling Academic in Neoliberal University: Feminist Flights, Fights, and Failures*. London: Palgrave Macmillan, 2018.

Tertullian. *Contra Marcione*. Ante-Nicene Christian Library. Vol 7. Edinburgh: T & T Clark, 1868.

———. *On the Apparel of Women*. Online: *New Advent* https://www.newadvent.org/fathers/0402.htm.

The Rave Project. "Family Violence." Online: https://www.theraveproject.org/resources-categories/looking-at-the-data/.

The Vatican. *Dogmatic Constitution on the Church: Lumen Gentium*. Online: https://www.vatican.va/archive/hist_councils/ii_vatican_council/documents/vat-ii_const_19641121_lumen-gentium_en.html.

Theißen, G. *Der historische Jesus. Ein Lehrbuch*. Göttingen: Vandenhoeck & Ruprecht, 2001.

———. *Die Soziologie der Jesusbewegung: Ein Beitrag zur Entstehungsgeschichte des Urchristentums*. Tübingen: Mohr Siebeck, 1989.

———. *The Social Setting of Pauline Christianity: Essays on Corinth*. Edinburgh: T & T Clark, 1990.

Theißen, G., and A. Mertz. *The Historical Jesus: A Comprehensive Guide*. Minneapolis: Augsburg, 1998.

Theobald, M. *Studien zum Römerbrief*. Tübingen: Mohr Siebeck, 2001.

Thorsteinsson, R. M. *Paul's Interlocutor in Romans 2: Function and Identity in the Context of Ancient Epistolography*. Stockholm: Almqvist & Wiksell, 2003.

Titkemyer, S. "Male Headship and the Problem of Power." *Pantheos* (27 May 2014). Online: https://www.patheos.com/blogs/nolongerquivering/2014/05/male-headship-and-the-problem-of-power/.

Tollefson, J. "The Hard Truths of Climate Change by the Numbers." In *Covering Climate Now* (18 September 2019). Online: https://www.nature.com/immersive/d41586-019-02711-4/index.html.

Topić, T., et al. *Akademija političkog osnaživanja žena: Učešće žena u politici*. Canada Fund for Local Initiative and Transparency International Bosnia and Hercegovina. Banja Luka: Grafix, 2017.

Tuan, Y.-F. *Cosmos and Hearth: A Cosmopolitan's Viewpoint*. Minneapolis: University of Minnesota Press, 1996.

Turčin, K. "Razvodi u Hrvatskoj: Prva analiza takve vrste ikad napravljena u Hrvtaskoj." *Jutarnji Life* (18 Nov 2017). Online: https://www.jutarnji.hr/life/obitelj-i-djeca/prva-analiza-takve-vrste-ikad-napravljena-u-hrvatskoj-evo-zasto-kako-i-kada-krahiraju-brakovi-gradana/6757746/.

United Nations. "Sustainable Goal Number 5 on Gender Equality." Online: https://www.un.org/sustainabledevelopment/sustainable-development-goals/.

United Nations Women. "Facts and Figures: Ending Violence against Women." Online: https://www.unwomen.org/en/what-we-do/ending-violence-against-women/facts-and-figures.

———. "Global Platform on Gender Equality and Religion in 2017." Online: https://www.unwomen.org/en/news/stories/2017/3/news-global-platform-on-gender-equality-and-religion-launched.

Unnk, W. C. van. "Lob und Strafe durch die Obrigkeit. Hellenistisches zu Röm 13,3–4." In *Jesus und Paulus, Festschrift für Georg Kümmel zum 70. Geburtstag*, edited by E. E. Ellis, 336–340. Göttingen: Vandenhoeck & Ruprecht, 1975.

Valerio, Adriana. "Women in Church History." In *Women: Invisible in Church and Theology*, edited by E. Schüssler Fiorenza and Mary Collins. Edinburgh: T & T Clark, 1985.

Vlačić Ilirik, Matija. *O načinu razumijevanja Svetoga Pisma*. Translated by Ž. Puratić. Zagreb: Hrvatska Sveučilišna naklada, 1993.

Volf, M. *Exclusion and Embrace: A Theological Exploration of Identity, Otherness, and Reconciliation*. Nashville: Abingdon, 1996.

Volf, M., C. Krieg, and T. Kucharz, eds. *The Future of Theology: Essays in Honour of Jürgen Moltmann*. Grand Rapids: Eerdmans, 1996.

Vollmer, J. "Jedermann sei untertan der Obrigkeit." In *Arbeitshefte des Bundes für freies Christentum*. Stuttgart: Tempelgesellschaft, 1997.

Von Dautzenberg, G. "Zur Stellung der Frauen in den Paulinischen Gemineden." In *Die Frau im Urchristentum*, edited by G. Dautzenberg, H. Merklein and K. Müller. Freiburg: Herder, 1983.

Von Rad, G. *Genesis: A Commentary*. Revised edition. Philadelphia: Westminster Press, 1972.

Voysey, C. *Fragments from Reimarus*. London; Edinburgh: Williams & Norgate, 1879. Online: https://archive.org/details/fragmentsfromrei00reim/page/n3.

Wagner, J. R. "The Christ, Servant of Jew and Gentile: A Fresh Approach to Rom 15:8–9." *JBL* 116, no. 3 (1997): 473–485.

Walker, P. *Studie zu Römer 13,1–7*. München: Kaiser, 1966.

Wallace, R., and W. Williams. *The Three Worlds of Paul of Tarsus*. London; New York: Routledge, 1998.

Ward, J. W. "Pentecostal Theology." In *New Dictionary of Theology*, edited by S. G. Ferguson and D. F. Wright, 502–505. Downers Grove: InterVarsity Press, 1988.

Watson, F. *Paul, Judaism and the Gentiles: A Sociological Approach*. Cambridge: Cambridge University Press, 1986.

———. "The Two Roman Congregations: Romans 14:15–15:13." In *The Romans Debate*, edited by K. Donfried, 203–215. Edinburgh: T & T Clark, 1991.

Wedderburn, A. J. M. "Adam and Christ: An Investigation into the Background of 1 Corinthians XV and Romans V, 12–21." PhD Thesis. Cambridge: University of Cambridge, 1971.

———. *Baptism and Resurrection: Studies in Pauline Theology against Its Graeco-Roman Background*. Tübingen: Mohr Siebeck, 1987.

Weinfeld, M. "Zion and Jerusalem as Religious and Political Capital: Ideology and Utopia." In *The Poet and the Historian: Essays in Literary and Historical Biblical Criticism*, edited by R. E. Friedmann, 75–116. Chico: Scholars Press, 1983.

Wenham, G. J. "Genesis." In *New Bible Commentary*, edited by D. A. Carson et al. Leicester: Inter-Varsity Press, 1994.

Westerholm, S. "The New Perspective at Twenty-Five." In *Justification and Variegated Nomism*, vol. 2 – The Paradoxes of Paul, 1–38. Tübingen; Grand Rapids: Mohr Siebeck; Baker, 2004.

———. *Preface to the Study of Paul*. Grand Rapids; Cambridge: Eerdmans, 1997.

Wilkens, U. *Weisheit und Torheit: Eine exegetische Untersuchung zu 1. Kor. 1 und 2*. Tübingen: Mohr Siebeck, 1959.

Windisch, E. *Imperium und Evangelium im Neuen Testament*. Kiel: Lipsius & Tischer, 1931.

Wink, W. *The Powers That Be: Theology for a New Millennium*. New York: Doubleday, 1998.

Winninge, M. *Sinners and the Righteous: A Comparative Study of the Psalms of Solomon and Paul's Letters*. Stockholm: Almqvist & Wiksell International, 1995.

Winter, B. D. "The Public Honouring of Christian Benefactors in Romans 13.3–4 and 1 Pet 2.14–15." *JSNT* 34 (1988): 87–103.

———. *Roman Wives, Roman Widows: The Appearance of New Women in the Pauline Communities*. Grand Rapids: Eerdmans, 2003.

———. *Seek the Welfare of the City*. Carlisle: Paternoster, 1994.

Winter, B. D., and A. D. Clarke. *The Book of Acts in Its First Century Setting*. Vol 1. Carlisle: Paternoster, 1993.

Wire, A. *Corinthian Women Prophets: A Reconstruction Through Paul's Rhetoric*. Minneapolis: Fortress, 1990.

———. "The Social Functions of Women's Ascetism in the Roman East." In *Images of the Feminine in Gnosticism*, edited by K. L. King, 308–323. Philadelphia: Fortress, 1988.

Witherington III, B. *Conflict and Community in Corinth: A Socio-Rhetorical Commentary on 1 and 2 Corinthians*. Grand Rapids; Carlisle: Eerdmans; Paternoster, 1995.

———. *Paul's Letter to the Romans: A Socio-Rhetorical Commentary*. Grand Rapids: Eerdmans, 2004.

———. *The Paul Quest: The Renewed Search for the Jew of Tarsus*. Leicester: InterVarsity Press, 1998.

Witte Jr., J., and F. Alexander. *Christianity and Law: An Introduction*. Cambridge: Cambridge University Press, 2008.

Witte, W. "Medical Consequences of Antibiotic Use in Agriculture." *Science* (1998): 996–997.

Wolff, R. P., Barrington Moore Jr, and Herbert Markuse. *A Critique of Pure Tolerance*. Boston: Beacon, 1969.

Wood, S. J. "Rape as a Practice of War: Toward a Typology of Political Violence." *Politics and Society* 46, no. 4 (2018): 513–537.

Woodhead, L., ed. *Feminism and Christian Ethics: Studies in Christian Ethics*. Edinburgh: T & T Clark, 1992.

World Data Lab. *World Poverty Clock*. Online: https://worldpoverty.io/headline.

World Health Organization. *Female Genital Mutilation: A Student's Manual*. Geneva: WHO, 2001. Online: https://www.who.int/gender/other_health/Studentsmanual.pdf.

———. "Global and Regional Estimates of Violence against Women: Prevalence and Health Effects of Intimate Partner Violence and Non-Partner Sexual Violence." WHO, 2013. Online: https://apps.who.int/iris/bitstream/handle/10665/85239/9789241564625_eng.pdf;jsessionid=203523B7248B9108F17D6CB5CCED756B?sequence=1.

Wright, C. J. H. *The Mission of God: Unlocking The Bible's Great Narrative*. Downers Grove: IVP Academic, 2006.

Wright, N. G. *A Theology of the Dark Side: Putting the Power of Evil in Its Place*. Carlisle: Paternoster, 2003.

Wright, N. T. *The Climax of the Covenant: Christ and the Law in Pauline Theology*. Edinburgh: T & T Clark, 1991.

———. "The Law in Rom 2." In *Paul and the Mosaic Law*, edited by J. Dunn. Tübingen: Mohr Siebeck, 1996.

———. *The Letter to the Romans*. Nashville: Abingdon, 2002.

———. "Paul and Caesar: A New Reading of Romans." In *A Royal Priesthood*, edited by C. Bartholomew. Carlisle: Paternoster, 2002.

———. *Paul and the Faithfulness of God: Christian Origins and the Question of God*. London: SPCK, 2013.

———. *What St Paul Really Said*. Oxford: Lion, 1997.

Yoder, J. H. "Is There Such a Thing as Being Ready for Another Millennium." In *The Future of Theology: Essays in Honour of Jürgen Moltmann*, edited by M. Volf, C. Krieg, and T. Kucharz, 63–69. Grand Rapids: Eerdmans, 1996.

Zell, E., Z. Krizan, and S. R. Teeter. "Evaluating Gender Similarities and Differences Using Metasynthesis." *American Psychologist* 70, no. 1 (2015): 10–20. https://doi.org/10.1037/a0038208.

Zhu, A. "The Woman Who Wants to Legalize Female Genital Cutting." In *Bright* (8 Mar 2018). Online: https://brightthemag.com/legalize-female-genital-cutting-fgm-kenya-health-f5335243b4e2.

Zimmerli, W. *Ezekiel 2: A Commentary on the Book of the Prophet Ezekiel Chapters 25–48*. Philadelphia: Fortress, 1983.

Zovkić, M. "Različite teologije, a jedna vjera u Novom zavjetu." In *Bogoslovska smotra* 3–4, no. 61 (1991).

Index of Names

B
Barnes, Albert 64
Bauckham, R. 90, 210
Bernstein, A. 76
Briscoe, Jill 200

C
Caldwell, Chris 34
Charcot, J. M. 128

D
Duchrow, Ulrich 5, 66

F
Fee, Gordon D. 176
Feuerbach, Ludwig 49
Freud, S. 128
Frymer-Kensky, Tikva 165

G
Gladwell, Malcolm 45

H
Harari, Yuval Noah 66
Hays, Richard 211
Hinkelammert, Franz 66
Holt-Gimenez, Eric 33

J
Jaspers, Karl 66
Jones, K. M. 76

K
Kroeger, Catherine 3, 51, 176
Kroeger, Richard 176

L
Lessing, Gotthold 60

M
Meeks, W. A. 130
Moltmann, Jürgen 15, 94

N
Nason-Clark, Nancy 3, 51, 71, 148

P
Paxman, Jeremy 35
Probst, Julius 33

R
Raber, Mary 164
Reimarus, H. S. 49, 60
Roth, Michael 5

S
Sack, Robert 42
Schüssler Fiorenza, Elisabeth 3, 40, 102, 171
Silva, Moses 108
Smith, M. B. (Lynn) 3, 135
Storkey, Elaine 49, 69
Stott, John R. W. 89

T
Theißen, Gerd 40, 89

V
Volf, Miroslav 38, 71
Von Rad, Gerhard 78

W
Weaver, A. 148
Wink, Walter 104
Winter, Bruce 145
Wire, Antoinette 3, 175
Wright, N. T. 4

Index of Scriptures

OLD TESTAMENT

Genesis
1:26 .... 64, 66
1:26–28 65
1:31 .... 15, 18
2:9 15
2:13–15 186
2:15 .... 18, 66
2:17 .... 74, 217
2:18 .... 18, 70, 78
2:20 18
2:24 151
3:5–6 79
3:11 19
3:12 .... 19, 28
3:13 19
3:14 19
3:14–15 19
3:14–24 76
3:16 .... 19, 26, 77
3:17 19
3:17–19 19
3:17b 31

4:25 217
4:26 217
5:4 217
11:1–9 83

Numbers
11:5 115

Judges
4:4 165
4:4–5:31 137
4–5 101
4:8 166
4:8–10 166
4:9 166

1 Samuel
13:14 167

Psalms
24:1 .... 43, 68, 209
25:2 207

Proverbs
31:10–31 200

Isaiah
42:8 .... 68, 150
61 195
61:1–4 39
61:3 195
61:3b–4 120
61:4 196

Ezekiel
2:9–3:14 122

Joel
3:1–3 137

Habakkuk
2:4 94

NEW TESTAMENT

Matthew
5–7 93
5:21 116
5:27 116
5:31 116
5:31–32 215
5:33 116
5:39 104
12:43 110
18:7 165

Mark
8:31–10:27 67
8:31–32 157
8:32 157
8:34–38 157
9:31 157
9:33–35 67
9:34 157
9:36–37 157
10:1–12 167
10:5 167
10:6 167

10:7–8 167
10:13–16 157
10:14 157
10:17 157
10:17–22 106
10:21 157
10:22 157
10:28 157
10:33–34 157
10:34–43 46
10:34–44 203
10:35–37 157

10:37 157
10:41 157
10:42–43 18
10:43 .... 68, 138, 157, 168, 205
10:44–45 .... 18, 144, 158

Luke
4:14–21 48
4:18 39
4:19 89
8:2–3 168
8:9 39
10:38–42 137
10:42 168
11:27 .... 168, 199
11:27–28 .... 128, 198
11:28 169

John
3 168
3:16 68
4 168
4:1–42 193
4:4 102
4:34 102
5:6 111
5:8 111
5:14 111
5:19–20 68
13:12–16 18
15 134
15–17 95

Acts
9:15–16 62
11:19–26 91
13:22 167
14:1–7 92
15:4–35 94
16:6–8 174
16:13 174
17:1–9 92
18:1 175
18:18–20 173

18:24 173
21:27 94
22:3 ....61, 62
22:4 93
26:5 61

Romans
1:16 ....72, 94
1:16–17 74
1:18 73
1:18–32 ....75, 82
1:21 ....73, 79
1:24 ....73, 75
1:26 ....73, 75
1:28 ....73, 75
1:29 73
3:9 13
3:12 93
3:19–20 93
3:21–23 93
3:28 94
4:3 93
5:4 107
5:12 ....12, 93
5:14 ....13, 75
7:5 12
7–8 111
7:12 93
7:14–24 82
7:14–25 12
8 100
8:2–4 ....94, 96
8:4 96
8:4–9 119
8:5 108
8:9 .... 107, 114
8:9–11 107
8:11 .... 39, 72, 109, 110, 115
8:12–13 107
8:18 .... 4, 112, 114, 115, 120, 122, 211, 225
8:19 72
8:19–21 112
8:19–22 35

8:22 74
10:11 122
12:1 ....94, 144
12:1–13 137
12:19 167
13:1 145
15:8 92
15:18–19 .... 103, 216
15:20 174
15:22–29 174
16:1 .... 102, 171
16:1–16 .... 137, 171
16:3 173
16:4 102
16:6 102
16:7 .... 102, 173
16:12 102
16:13 173

1 Corinthians
1:12 175
3:4 175
3:5 171
3:5–6 175
3:19 175
3:20 175
3:22 175
4:6 175
7:7–8 177
7:10 177
7:21 145
10:23 178
11 ....4, 177
11:10 177
11:11 178
11:13 178
11:17–34 ....92, 130
11:21–22 .... 130, 131
11:22 .... 131, 133
11:28 133
11:29 133
11:34 133
12:4–31 137
13 .... 148, 182
14:32–33 143

14:33 178
14:34 141
14:34–35 176
15:54 114
16:12 175

2 Corinthians
1:21–22 107
3:18 111
4:16–17 111
5:4 122
5:5 .... 107, 109
5:6 109
6:7 103
6:16b–18 154
8:14 224
12:14 125

Galatians
1:13 93
1:14 61
2:1–10 94
2:11–14 94
2:16 97
3:1 100
3:1–5 103
3:11 94
3:13 .... 94, 96
3:27–29 101
3:28 100
3:28–29 .... 96, 176, 178
4:1–10 99
4:21–31 99
5:1 99
5:16–21 108
5:19–21 119
5:19–22 143
5:20 122
5:21 .... 108, 119, 142
6:7 56

Ephesians
1:17–23 143
2:10 .... 72, 187, 194
4:16 135

4:18 143
5:8 143
5:15 .... 143, 181
5:16 181
5:18 .... 143, 181
5:19–20 181
5:21 .... 138, 143, 146,
                    180, 182
5:21–6:9 179
5:21–33 .... 144, 151
5:22 .... 142, 146, 180
5:23 147
5:25 182
5:25–33 149
5:27 151
5:32 151
6:4 156
6:5 146

Philippians
2:5–11 .... 46, 138
2:7 .... 68, 94
3:6 93

Colossians
3:18–4:1 179
4:5 180

1 Thessalonians
4:16 105
5:20 124

1 Timothy
2:2 .... 135, 146
2:5 185
2:7 185
2:8 186
2:12 .... 185, 186
2:15 .... 98, 141,
                    169, 196
6:1 182

Hebrews
2:14 130

1 Peter
2:18–3:7 179
2:24 96
3:1 182
3:6 145

Revelation
2:9 213
7:17 226
9:20–21 122
10:10 122
11:3–11 121
11:13 122
16:21 122
18 .... 90, 210
18:4 224
18:4–5 .... 213, 225
18:7 213
18:9 211
18:9–10 213
18:11–17 213
18:12–13 214
18:17 213
21:9 226
21:15–16 226
21:22 226
21:26 226
21:27 225
22:2 226

Langham Literature and its imprints are a ministry of Langham Partnership.

Langham Partnership is a global fellowship working in pursuit of the vision God entrusted to its founder John Stott –

> ***to facilitate the growth of the church in maturity and Christ-likeness through raising the standards of biblical preaching and teaching.***

Our vision is to see churches in the Majority World equipped for mission and growing to maturity in Christ through the ministry of pastors and leaders who believe, teach and live by the word of God.

Our mission is to strengthen the ministry of the word of God through:
- nurturing national movements for biblical preaching
- fostering the creation and distribution of evangelical literature
- enhancing evangelical theological education

especially in countries where churches are under-resourced.

Our ministry

Langham Preaching partners with national leaders to nurture indigenous biblical preaching movements for pastors and lay preachers all around the world. With the support of a team of trainers from many countries, a multi-level programme of seminars provides practical training, and is followed by a programme for training local facilitators. Local preachers' groups and national and regional networks ensure continuity and ongoing development, seeking to build vigorous movements committed to Bible exposition.

Langham Literature provides Majority World preachers, scholars and seminary libraries with evangelical books and electronic resources through publishing and distribution, grants and discounts. The programme also fosters the creation of indigenous evangelical books in many languages, through writer's grants, strengthening local evangelical publishing houses, and investment in major regional literature projects, such as one volume Bible commentaries like *The Africa Bible Commentary* and *The South Asia Bible Commentary*.

Langham Scholars provides financial support for evangelical doctoral students from the Majority World so that, when they return home, they may train pastors and other Christian leaders with sound, biblical and theological teaching. This programme equips those who equip others. Langham Scholars also works in partnership with Majority World seminaries in strengthening evangelical theological education. A growing number of Langham Scholars study in high quality doctoral programmes in the Majority World itself. As well as teaching the next generation of pastors, graduated Langham Scholars exercise significant influence through their writing and leadership.

To learn more about Langham Partnership and the work we do visit **langham.org**

www.ingramcontent.com/pod-product-compliance
Lightning Source LLC
Chambersburg PA
CBHW070729160426
43192CB00009B/1370